# Working Toward Enlightenment

Master Nan Huai-Chin

# Working Toward Enlightenment

## The Cultivation of Practice

## Master Nan Huai-Chin

SAMUEL WEISER, INC.

York Beach, Maine

First published in 1993 by
Samuel Weiser, Inc.
Box 612
York Beach, Maine 03910

Library of Congress Cataloging-in-Publication Data
Nan, Huai-chin
    Working toward enlightenment : the cultivation of
practice / Huai - Chin Nan.
        p.      cm.
    Includes index.
    1. Spiritual life--Buddhism.   2. Buddhism--Doctrines.
    I. Title.
    BQ4302.N36   1993
    294.3'444--dc20                                      93-13536
                                                             CIP

ISBN 0-87728-776-7
EB

Translated by J. C. Cleary

Cover art is titled "Seeking the Tao in the Autumn
Mountains," attributed to Chu-jan, Five Dynasties. Used by
kind permission of the National Palace Museum, Taipei,
Taiwan, Republic of China.

Typeset in 10 point Palatino

Printed in the United States of America

99 98 97 96 95 94 93
1 2 3 4 5 6 7 8 9 10

The paper used in this publication meets the minimum
requirements of the American National Standard
for Permanence of Paper for Printed Library Materials
Z39.48-1984.

# TABLE OF CONTENTS

# INTRODUCTION

Over the past few years, many books have appeared on Zen, Taoism, yoga, Buddhism and the Tantric teachings from Tibet. While many are written by authentic practitioners, most have been written by dabblers, theoreticians, or simply reporters who know little of the great matter of mind-body transformation.

For instance, many of the materials presently available on the Zen school treat Zen as if it were a collection of psychological puzzles that need to be solved. While most authors on Zen greatly appreciate the legacy of artistic refinement that has resulted from the influence of Zen, they remain oblivious to the road of practice that constitutes the heart of Zen, as well as the fundamental principles that form the bedrock of Zen cultivation. You can hardly pick up a modern day work on Zen without being led astray.

Quite a few English translations of Taoist and Esoteric Buddhist classics have recently appeared as well, but many of these give one the feeling that cultivating the physical body and its esoteric energy structures is the path to enlightenment when this is only a means of laying the foundation for approaching realization through investigating the world of form. Unfortunately, the New Age movement prevalent today has greatly misinterpreted these works. This has resulted in many people being led down false cultivation paths that go nowhere.

As to the classics left to us by Confucius and Mencius, even scholars have trouble recognizing that these spend a great deal of time disclosing the spiritual cultivation path to enlightenment, and were not simply philosophical works or manuals for moral behavior. They go into the actual details on methods of self-cultivation and the stages of practice involved in attaining realization. In these cases, most Westerners have false pre-biases of these works and are antagonistic to the idea of even investigating these oriental classics. Just hearing the name of Confucius is enough; to go beyond this is a daunting task.

In this first series of lectures originally presented to students, Master Nan Huai-Chin corrects many of these mistaken notions and actually explains how to follow these schools to cultivate toward enlightenment. In a step-by-step fashion, he moves from topic to topic, pulling together a wide variety of seemingly unrelated material to expose the road of self-cultivation. Clearly delineated are the three stages of preparatory study, practice and realization that are essential for anyone treading the path to self-realization. Furthermore, in welding together the information from a wide variety of cultivation schools, Master Nan separates fact from fiction and corrects many of the mistaken notions in fashion today—especially the idea that cultivation is simply a psychological phenomenon. He discusses the proper method of cultivating the breath, cultivating the energy channels of the physical body, surmounting sexual desire, contemplating mind, surmounting the barriers to realization, studying the ancient records, matching one's experiences with modern science, examining one's behavior, understanding the Zen school, and so on. The material within is tremendous in its scope and application—much of it has never been seen before. Because of its breadth and clarity, no work of this kind has ever appeared before in the Chinese or English language. However new or strange it may seem to the seasoned reader of Zen material, they must recognize that this is Zen!

Master Nan offers a priceless guide to anyone who really wants to understand Zen and Buddhism, and begin the task of mind-body transformation. The journey toward realization is the undertaking of a great task which entails more than just sitting in a room learning how to meditate silently or solve some ancient meditation koan. Master Nan points out that this pathway of study, effort and achievement is never apart from accumulating merit and striving to recover one's inherent wisdom. Although what is revealed may at first startle one like thunder, the pathways he exposes are like arrows in flight sure to hit their mark.

Nan Huai-Chin is a well-known teacher in Taiwan and in mainland China, and some people consider him to be a modern Manjusri or Tsong-kapa. Master Nan is still relatively unknown in the West because his many published works have not been translated into English. He was first introduced in *Tao and Longevity*, a book translated by Dr. Wen Kuan Chu. This book was well-received by serious students of the subject, and is now available in German, Spanish, Italian and Portuguese. The present volume, *Working Toward Enlightenment*, was first presented in Chinese as a series of lectures and was so enthusiastically received that students asked that this material be made available to a wider audience. The more advanced lectures are soon to be published as *To Realize Enlightenment* and will take students on to the next stages of cultivation.

Master Nan Huai-Chin has studied the Chinese classics, modern science, military strategy, and medicine. Some consider him to be China's only remaining Zen master, as well as a recognized master of Taoism and Esoteric Buddhism. He is an individual whose first principle has always been to test and prove all that dare speak about cultivation, including the claims of Buddhism, Taoism, Confucianism, yoga, or the Tibetan schools, and so his words carry the weight of personal experience. The information presented here constitutes the result of his lifelong search for verification of cultivation claims.

Thanks go out to the many individuals who participated in the arduous task of recording and editing Master Nan's original lectures in such a way that they could be produced in book form. In this regard, special thanks must go to the Lee family who supported this project and to J. C. Cleary, who had the task of translating this work. Producing translations of this type of material is always difficult at best and we are grateful for his wonderful efforts.

Bill Bodri
Hong Kong, 1993

# Working Toward Enlightenment

# 1

# THE PATH OF
# CULTIVATING ENLIGHTENMENT

There is a story behind this book. An old friend, Mr. Xiao, came to see me. As he was about to leave, he asked me a question: "Shakyamuni Buddha left home when he was 18, and finally—much later, after years of effort—lifted his head, saw a bright star, and was enlightened. What was it that he was enlightened to?"

If it had been someone else who had asked this question, it would not have had any great importance. But Mr. Xiao has been studying Buddhism for many years, so when he raised this question, it was no ordinary matter.

According to what is recorded in the scriptures and the traditional accounts, as soon as Shakyamuni Buddha was born, he was already equipped with an extraordinary natural endowment. Because he had cultivated enlightenment practices through past lifetimes over many eons, as soon as he was born in this life, various kinds of auspicious things happened. He renounced his princely position and left home, and for twelve years he sought enlightenment. Everyone should pay attention to these twelve years, because it is very easy to pass over them lightly.

At the moment, we will emphasize the twelve years when Shakyamuni Buddha cultivated various religious practices. At that time there were many Indian religious sects that had been in existence for quite a while, each with its own methods of cultivating practice. Shakyamuni Buddha fully studied the various kinds of ascetic practices and used various methods to cultivate and refine himself. He was not like present-day students who study Buddhism and who vacillate back and forth, paying homage to one teacher after another, going from one conventional formulation to the next. Every time Shakyamuni took up a method of practice, he would study with complete sincerity and dedication, and do the necessary work.[1]

---

[1] The Chinese word *kung-fu*, translated here as "work," is a general term for many methods of self-cultivation and religious effort. It will often be translated here as "meditation work."

After Shakyamuni worked his way through all of them, he recognized that none of these methods was the true, ultimate way to enlightenment.[2] At this point, he went into the freezing snow-covered mountains and practiced austerities. After six years, he also recognized that austerities were not the path to enlightenment, and that it would be best to leave them behind. After this, he sat in meditation under the bodhi tree on the banks of the Ganges River and made a vow he would not arise unless he achieved supreme perfect enlightenment; if not, he would stay there until he died. After all these efforts, he one day looked up to see a bright star and awakened to enlightenment.

Certainly everyone knows this story. I have told it again because I want to focus everyone's attention on it: I want everyone to know what Shakyamuni Buddha did during those twelve years, and how he cultivated practice. When we read his biography, we read only that he studied *avrha-samadhi*, "concentration without thought," for three years, and in the end, "realized it was wrong and abandoned it." We always overlook the fact that during these twelve years he earnestly cultivated practice.

Let us first talk about what "concentration without thought" is. This is an ancient Indian method, which also existed in China and in every part of the world where people cultivated realization. It is the stage of "having no false thoughts." People who cultivate the path of enlightenment strive to master this particular state of attainment.

For example, when all of us sit in meditation, can we or can we not reach the stage where we draw up our legs and we have no thoughts? We absolutely cannot do this. In fact, we often joke that there are only two kinds of people who can do this—people who have not yet been born, and people who have already died. Apart from these two kinds of people, there is almost no one who can accomplish this.

Recently a fellow student from Belgium discussed this question of thinking and not thinking with me. We spoke of how Shakyamuni Buddha, after studying *avrha-samadhi* for three years, discovered that it was not the path to enlightenment and gave it up. It was not that he

---

[2] The Chinese term *Tao* literally means "Path" or "Way," and is used with different connotations in Taoism and Confucianism. In Chinese Buddhism, the word *Tao* can mean the path to enlightenment, or enlightenment itself, according to the context.

had cultivated it without success, but that after he had successfully cultivated it, he abandoned it. Why? Because it is not the path to enlightenment. Because the text of the sutra is so simple, it is very easy for us to read past this and overlook it.

In Buddhism there is a meditative state called the *samadhi* that is neither thinking nor not thinking. This term is very beautiful. "Not thinking" means that it is not our common customary world of thought. But "nor not thinking" does not mean that it is thinking. If we must describe it, we might say that it is a kind of spiritual feeling that transcends thinking. At present there is something called "transcendental meditation" but in reality this is by no means the same as this "nor not thinking."

The word *samadhi* has two entirely different meanings; "the *samadhi* that is neither thinking nor not thinking," and "the *samadhi* without thinking." The latter means totally obliterating thinking. The term, "neither thinking nor not thinking" means "absolutely without thoughts," but it is not like not knowing anything at all, as in *samadhi* without thinking. It is not a kind of meditation work that is without awareness and without spiritual feeling. "The *samadhi* that is neither thinking nor not thinking" was advertised at the time of Shakyamuni as the highest method of cultivation. In three years' time, Shakyamuni Buddha reached this realm, but he discovered that it was not the true path to enlightenment, so he abandoned it. On the whole, these are two very important points in the account given in the scriptural biographies of the course of Buddha's cultivation.

Why don't the scriptures mention any other forms of cultivation? The reason is that the effort and the effects involved in these two kinds of cultivation already include many of the methods of cultivating practice in the world, and these are very important methods. That's why it was not necessary to relate in detail any of the other studies cultivated by Shakyamuni Buddha. For example, before Buddha studied the path to enlightenment, he had attained the loftiest levels in his studies of mathematics, martial arts, and literature. After he left home, he perfected his study of these two most lofty methods (the *samadhi* without thought, and the *samadhi* that is neither thinking nor not thinking), but he recognized that these were not the true path to enlightenment.

In reality, if you are really able to accomplish these two forms of concentration and remain in them day after day without moving, then even if you are not enlightened, other people will still think that you are, and all kinds of disciples will gather around you.

Readers should note that Shakyamuni Buddha recognized that these are not the path to enlightenment, and at the time he could not find an enlightened teacher, so all he could do was go by himself into the mountains to practice austerities. Every day he ate only a piece of dried fruit, so naturally he became emaciated, to the point that he barely looked human any more. By practicing like this, Shakyamuni wanted to find the real truth. But after six years he realized that austerities are not the path to enlightenment either, so he came down out of the mountains.

When Shakyamuni Buddha reached the banks of the Ganges River, a shepherd girl offered him some fine milk curds. Because he accepted them, the five attendants sent by his father abandoned him. They left because they thought that Buddha had abandoned his will to cultivate practice. Later on, these five men were the first to be delivered by Buddha at the Deer Park,[3] and became his first great disciples.

When Shakyamuni accepted the milk curds from the shepherd girl, everyone thought he had retreated from the path—that he had backed out. The men following him withdrew, because at that time in India everyone thought that one who left home to cultivate the path must practice austerities.

There is one point that we must pay attention to! Buddha saw the bright star and awakened to enlightenment only after he had accepted nourishment and recovered his physical strength. This is why I always alert the people around me to pay particular attention to their physical health and nourishment. Without a healthy body, there is no way to cultivate the path and realize enlightenment—this is a fact. We must investigate, step-by-step, the relationship between physical health, nourishment, and the cultivation of the path to enlightenment.

Only after Buddha accepted nourishment and recovered his physical abilities did he cross Ganges River and arrive under the bodhi tree. At that time, he had no way to find an enlightened teacher able to guide him: all he could do was rely on himself, sit in meditation under the bodhi tree, and make his vow.

The few simple words of Shakyamuni's vow are easy to ignore. When we read them, it seems we have understood their meaning, but we have not entered into them deeply or comprehended them

---

[3] The Deer Park was the site of Shakyamuni Buddha's first public exposition of his teaching.

fully. The vow that Buddha made at that time dispensed with religion, and dispensed with grand phraseology. It was like making an oath or making a bet: "If I do not achieve enlightenment this time, then I will die right here, and that's all there is to it. I will not get up from this seat." With these sentences, he expressed how intent he was on seeking enlightenment.

According to the record in *The History of the Manifestations of the Tathagata Shakyamuni*, within six days Buddha first attained the four dhyanas and the eight samadhis, then gained an embodiment generated by will,[4] and after that went on in one night to attain the six supernatural powers.[5]

At dawn on the seventh day, he raised his head and looked up—pay attention now! When Shakyamuni Buddha sat in meditation, he was not as lifeless as we are, not daring to raise his head. He probably wanted to take a rest, and when he raised his head and looked up, he saw in the sky a bright star, and awakened to supreme perfect enlightenment.

I have just gone on at such length explaining the course of Shakyamuni Buddha's enlightenment because I wanted to explain the question asked by my old friend Mr. Xiao: "When Shakyamuni Buddha saw the bright star and was enlightened, what was he enlightened to?"

Shakyamuni raised his head at that moment and was enlightened. Tell me, after he was enlightened, was all the cultivation he had done before wasted, were those twelve years of effort all in vain? In other words, when he awakened to enlightenment, he was about 30 years old, and when he began to spread the Dharma, he was no more than 32. His disciples were all much older. All the instruction he received from childhood on, and all the various forms of cultivation and austerities he practiced after he left home—were these all done in vain or not?

---

[4] The *bodhisattvas*, or enlightened beings, can take on embodiments at will in order to accomplish their work of delivering sentient beings. The Sanskrit term for the "body generated by will" is *manomaya*, the Chinese term is *yi-sheng-shen*.

[5] The six supernormal powers are: the ability to know previous lives, the unimpeded ability to hear all things, the ability to know the minds of other sentient beings, the unimpeded ability to know all things, inconceivable powers to teach sentient beings, and the ability to appear in any form.

At the time I answered my old friend Mr. Xiao by saying, "What he was enlightened to was interdependent causation and inherent emptiness." Mr. Xiao said, "Oh . . . right," pushed the door open, and left.

I don't know whether everyone has taken note of this or not. This is a very serious question. After he left, a thought came to me: Mr. Xiao has studied Buddhism for many years. If someone else asked this question, it wouldn't matter much, but since he was asking this question, it was very serious. In other words, when he asked this question, it had extraordinary depth.

In truth, Shakyamuni Buddha awakened to inherently empty interdependent origination.[6] Interdependent origination is inherently empty: this truth is very simple, so at the time, why was it so difficult for Shakyamuni to awaken to it? What was the difficulty? Buddha left home and cultivated practice for many years, and only then was able to understand this truth. But now all of us understand it, everyone who reads a Buddhist scripture understands it, right? What is so special about this? If he was enlightened to the inherent emptiness of interdependent origination, then he penetrated everything with this one principle, he comprehended everything. So what truth is this? Assuming that he awakened to this truth correctly, then what do we say about his previous efforts? How can we account for them?

The second question is this. Right now we are studying Buddhism. Having read the Buddha Dharma, we then understand that inherent identity is fundamentally empty, we understand inherent emptiness and interdependent causation. Though we understand these truths clearly, why then do we still have to cultivate practice for such a long time? Moreover, we ourselves have been unable to become even first stage arhats of the lesser vehicle,[7] let

---

[6] Buddhist ontology points out that all relative phenomena arise and disappear through processes of cause and effect: this is called "interdependent origination" (in Sankrit *pratityasamutpada*; in Chinese *yuan-ch'i*). Accordingly, all such phenomena are dependent on the (temporary) linking of casual factors that bring them into existence and maintain them, and thus they have no stable, absolute identities independent of the web of causation. Lacking absolute, independent identities, they are said to be "inherently empty."

[7] An arhat is a person who has destroyed the delusion that stands in the way of enlightenment, but has only achieved small realization because unlike the bodhisattva, this person is not concerned with devoting efforts to save all sentient beings. He or she wishes to avoid vexation.

alone bodhisattvas. How it makes us lament, that in this present age, we have not seen anyone who has been able to realize even half of the fruit of enlightenment.

Thus, after Mr. Xiao had left me, a certain thought made my mind uneasy. I lamented that in the civilization of the present-day world, where religious activities and spiritual studies of various kinds and styles are all so extraordinarily well-developed both at home and abroad, society is getting more and more chaotic, cultured thinking is getting more and more confused, and the general mood is getting worse and worse. Everywhere there is confusion and chaos. Alas! It is true that everything and everyone is in chaos: this is what is called a world in chaos.

This question of Mr. Xiao's—where does the question lie? Take note! All of us who study Buddhism are to some extent inverting cause and effect. What do I mean by this? "Inverting cause and effect" means that we are reversing cause and effect, basis and results, and taking the cause for the effect.

We all understand that inherent nature is fundamentally empty; we all understand that everything is a product of interdependent causation, and so on. But these principles, these truths, are not truths that we have discovered on our own. They are the answers that Shakyamuni Buddha gave to his disciples after he spent so many years practicing austerities. After other people took these answers and recorded them, and we read them, we understand them. In fact, it is not that we have understood them ourselves. It is only that, with the aid of the Buddhist scriptures, we have accepted the results achieved by the Buddha and appropriated them for ourselves.

So what should we do? The answer is that we ourselves must travel the road of cultivating practice. We must imitate Shakyamuni Buddha and travel the road of meditative concentration. We must seek realization on the road of true, correct practice. We ourselves must realize and witness interdependent origination and inherent emptiness.

After we have understood these truths, we often mistakenly assume that they are results we ourselves have achieved. In recent years, those who lecture on sitting meditation all understand Taoism, and understand Esoteric Buddhism, and are full of things to say. But when we take a look to see how they really are, it doesn't seem that way at all. As for whether they have achieved anything or not, whether they have found realization or not, one glance and it is obvious that they have not. As the Sung dynasty Zen master Ta-hui Tsung-kao said, "I know whether or not you are enlightened when you just stand there: what need is there to wait for you to speak?"

But people nowadays have many theories, especially theories of the special meridians and eight *ch'i* channels.[8] They open this one and that one and they get very excited. I say to them, "You shouldn't get your bodies into total chaos."

All of this happens because we have learned a bit of knowledge from the Buddhist scriptures and have appropriated the results achieved through the practice of the people before us. We have reversed cause and effect, taking the effect as the cause and the cause as the effect.

This great canon of teaching by Shakyamuni Buddha is truth, sure enough, and it is also experience. He had doubts about the question of birth and death, and about the question of life. What Shakyamuni pursued was how to completely comprehend human life.

It is very easy to use the experience of people who have gone before, adopt the insights that they have accumulated, appropriate these insights for ourselves—thus inverting cause and effect—and make this the study of Buddhism. The result is that we remain ourselves, and the study of Buddhism remains the study of Buddhism: the two are placed in opposition, and it is useless for cultivating practice. Therefore I always say that the Buddha Dharma—which is one method of cultivating practice—and the merely conceptual study of Buddhism, have totally different implications. Right now we follow the road of preparing to learn to be buddhas. This is the reason for this book.

The sutras we will draw from are as follows: *The Great Perfection of Wisdom Sutra, The Nirvana Sutra, The Avatamsaka Sutra, The Diamond Sutra, The Heart Sutra, The Vimalakirti Sutra, The Lankavatara Sutra, The Sandhinirmocana Sutra, The Sutra of Queen Shrimala, The Ratnakuta Sutra, The Lotus Sutra, The Surangama Sutra,* and *The Complete Enlightenment Sutra.* From the Vinaya, the Buddhist codes of discipline: *The Four-Part Vinaya* (of the Hinayana) and *The Bodhisattva Vinaya* (of the Mahayana). From the shastras, the Buddhist philosophical treatises: *The Treatise on the Adornments of Direct Contemplation,* and the greater

---

[8] For a discussion of this, see Master Nan's *Tao and Longevity*, translated by D. Wen Kuan Chu (York Beach, ME: Samuel Weiser, 1984).

and lesser treatises: *The Great Cessation and Contemplation*, *The Source Mirror*, *The Record of Pointing at the Moon*, *The Continuation of the Record of Pointing at the Moon*, *The Great Perfection of Wisdom Treatise*, *The Treatise on the Progression of the Esoteric Path*, *The Treatise on the Stages of Yogacara*, and *The Extended Treatise on the Progression of the Bodhi Path*.

Suppose people want to learn to become buddhas—want to study the Buddha Dharma. If they were to take these works listed above, and spend three to five years of effort reading and studying to enter deeply into them and put their contents into practice, this would definitely be enough. It would be best if everyone could awaken without departing from these scriptures and treatises. Some think that all that is necessary is to cultivate practice and do meditation work; they think that it is not necessary to read the scriptures and treatises. This is absolutely wrong. We must recognize that in doing meditation work, if we do not clearly understand the principles, if our views are not correct, then our meditation work will not be able to get on the right track. In other words, if our meditation work is not done well, it is just because we have not mastered the principles involved.

For example, one of our fellow students said, "For two days it seems there is something in my mind." He asked me what this was. He felt that there was a problem and was working very hard at his meditation to reach it. Everyone can have things like this happen. The student said, "I observe this thing, and I search for it, but when I search for it, I don't know whether or not I can find it." I told him, "Of course you cannot find it. This is your physical state influencing your psychological state. The last few days the weather hasn't been right and you have caught a cold."

This sort of phenomenon is exactly the kind of affliction spoken of by Buddha. The more this student searched for the source of his affliction, the more he felt he could not find it; the more he searched, the more afflicted he became. I told him, "When you go to search for it, it has already run away. It is like a thief. By the time you cry out 'Thief!' the thief has already fled. Sometimes afflictions are in the mind, and you do not try to manage them because you cannot find their original cause." When he heard this, the student changed his thinking and his point of view changed.

This example only illustrates the way ordinary people engage in cultivation. More informed people would know that if there is something in the mind, they would not be able to find it. Hasn't *The*

*Diamond Sutra* told us: "[With mental states] there is nowhere they come from and nowhere they go to?" They come without a shadow and vanish without a trace. As soon as you recognize them, they already no longer exist. The best thing to do is not try to manage them. But you tell me: right now, when our afflictions come on, if we insistently arouse our minds to control them, doesn't this effort to take control in itself also become a real affliction? This kind of uncontrolled thought is, in itself, already a real affliction, and we have added something else to it.

The point that we are discussing right now is that we must pay attention to the relationship between physical states and psychological states. For example, a pious Buddhist laywoman suddenly had a stroke that affected her face. She still had her faith, and she asked me whether or not there was a blockage of the flow of her *ch'i*, her vital energy.[9] There was another pious layman, who had kept the precepts of discipline for many years, whose eyes suddenly lost their sight. He had developed cataracts, and later, with acupuncture, he recovered. He also asked me whether or not the cataracts had formed because his *ch'i*, his vital energy, could not pass through that place. These examples illustrate that when we study Buddhism, there is a closely connected double relationship between meditation work and our bodies and minds. We must discuss questions about this double relationship in detail, for if we do not, the problems can get more serious.

When you are cultivating practice, what is subject to the influence of your physical state? What is subject to the influence of your psychological state? How can you get free of problems of the body and mind? You must be clear about these questions before you can proceed.

Let us consider another example. Last year a friend passed away. He had studied Buddhism for many years, but liberation was still difficult. He wanted to leave his body, to say, "I'm going," and simply pass away, but he could not do it. What was the reason for this? If you could really do this, if you could separate your body and mind,

---

[9] "Vital energy" is a translation of the Chinese term *ch'i*, a concept that has played a crucial role in Chinese religion, philosophy, and medicine. For a discussion of this in its relation to meditation, see Master Nan's *Tao and Longevity*.

that would almost be it. But this does not count as enlightenment—it can only be called liberation. The Zen records speak of "[the ability] to die sitting or die standing up," that is, to sit cross-legged and just depart, and it is not only monks and nuns who have left home who can accomplish this. Buddhist lay people living as householders can also do it and even those who have reached a high level of cultivation by reading books can do it.

By cultivating practice and doing meditation work, it is certainly possible to separate body and mind. But when we have managed to separate body and mind, this is no more than being capable of liberation. Do we arrive at enlightenment by doing this or not? The answer is: not necessarily. To get to the level in our meditation work where we can "die sitting or die standing up" is not easy, but it is much easier than awakening to enlightenment.

In the past I was unwilling to talk about this kind of technique, but in fact, it is clearly mentioned in all the Buddhist scriptures. The Buddha Dharma has eighty-four thousand methods, but if we were to speak of them too clearly in public lectures, it might leave a legacy of sicknesses. People might attempt these methods if they knew about them, and such ill-informed attempts would produce sicknesses. There are also people who, if they knew these techniques, could use them to kill themselves, or use them as a form of escapism. For these reasons, certain techniques are prohibited by the code of conduct of the Mahayana and the Vajrayana.[10]

But if we speak from the point of view of doing scientific research, it is possible to know how to separate the physical body and the spirit. The question remains: if we rely only on our own cultivation of practice, and go on polishing and refining it, after several decades, will we be able to find our way to achieving this or not?

There are three important points we have to discuss now—seeing the truth of Buddhism, cultivating realization, and carrying out vows.

What is the stage of seeing truth? If we use the technical language of the Chinese Zen School, the stage of seeing truth means seeing the Tao, seeing the path to enlightenment. After we have seen

---

[10] Vajrayana, the "Diamond Vehicle" means esoteric Buddhism, Tantric Buddhism. Dealing in powerful techniques that can easily be abused, Vajrayana adepts have traditionally kept their methods secret, divulging them only to qualified practitioners who have undergone the long preparatory work of purification and dedication.

the path to enlightenment, how do we go about cultivating the realization of it? Everybody knows that interdependent origination is inherently empty, that inherent emptiness involves interdependent origination. But after we know this, how should we go about actually experiencing it?

Many decades ago, when I began to study Buddhism, I had an old-fashioned psychology professor, and he said, "I respect the theories of Buddhism very much, but I recognize that there is no way to prove the theories of Buddhism. Buddhism says that all things are only mind. But suppose right now that I want to create a golden chicken in my mind, and I want it to be able to produce a golden egg. According to the theory that all things are only mind, I should be able to create it, but in reality, this is impossible."

Seeing the truth of Buddhism means understanding its theoretical principles. Carrying out vows and cultivating realization are the concrete facts. In the Buddhist phrase, they are "phenomenal appearances." In Zen parlance, they constitute "effort," commonly called meditation work or *kung-fu*.

Whenever people study Buddhism, the first thing they mention is *samadhi*. They want to know: can you achieve *samadhi* or not? This is all they care about. The first thing they ask is whether or not you can sit cross-legged. But sitting cross-legged is not *samadhi*: it is only the most basic technique for learning *samadhi*. If you cannot sit cross-legged, what else is there to talk about? If the theoretical principle is there, but you cannot do the actual thing, it won't work. If you can manage the phenomenal appearance of sitting meditation, but you cannot manage to carry out vows, it will not work either.

Now we will discuss these three things; we must discuss them very accurately—very frankly. As for cultivation and realization, all the scriptures and codes of discipline and philosophical treatises are included within cultivating realization. Cultivating realization is not apart from meditative concentration—this point is very important.

Regarding concentration, at first it was translated into Chinese with a transliteration of the Sanskrit word *dhyana* giving the Chinese form *ch'an-na* [from which, via Japanese, we get the English term Zen]. Later, using concepts from Chinese culture—the phrase in the Confucian classic *The Great Learning*, "He knows where to stop and then has stability"—it was called *ch'an-ting*, "meditative stability" [*ting* means stability]. In the scriptures translated in a later period, with the recognition that the term *ch'an-na* could not fully express the meaning contained in the concept, it was retranslated as *ssu-wei hsiu* "contemplative cultivation." Later it appeared that this term was easily misinterpreted to mean psychological thoughts, and therefore the Dharma master Hsuan-tsang retranslated it as *ching-lu* "stilling thoughts." It is fine to use "stilling thoughts" or "stable concentration"—both come from *The Great Learning*. In fact, the definition of this term is hard to pin down. The school of the Bodhisattva Maitreya, one of the founders of Yogacara Buddhism, simply would not speak in these terms, and called it yoga. Later on, this Chinese transliteration of the word yoga came to designate those people who cultivate this set of religious techniques, and so another Chinese transliteration of yoga became the general term for this set of religious techniques.

In India, these two terms were originally two definitions of the same thing. For example, in the title of the *Yogacarabhumi Shastra*, *yogacara* designates people who have cultivated and perfected practice; *bhumi* refers to a progression of stages; and *shastra* means a discursive philosophical treatise. Thus, the meaning of the title of this book is "a discussion of the step-by-step progression of cultivating practice."

The scriptures, codes of discipline, and philosophical treatises of the Buddha Dharma all tell us methods of cultivating realization. But nowadays we do not apply them to our own lives. We cannot bring the Buddhist teachings and our own lives together at all, and we cannot match theoretical truths with actual facts. In particular, we cannot unify our bodies and our minds. Our brains know these theoretical truths, but when it comes to aligning them with our real situation, we are unable to do it. This is the main issue of the work of cultivating realization.

Usually when we lecture on realization and practice there are three parts to it: seeing, cultivation, and conduct. To see the path to enlightenment, we must have *prajna*, great transcendent wisdom. Seeing the path is great wisdom, and the reward of great merit. True great merit is also great wisdom; a person with great wisdom is a person of great merit. When wisdom has not yet developed, it is because merit is insufficient. Where do great wisdom and merit come from? From our conduct. Therefore, seeing, cultivation, and conduct are three aspects of a single whole, and none of them can be lacking.

Now there is one major issue. When we discuss cultivation, then we are raising the issue of *samadhi*. No matter whether here or abroad, people in general are very familiar with religious cultivation and meditation work: they know that cultivation means cultivating *samadhi*.

What is the biggest misconception in everyone's idea of cultivating *samadhi*? It is the idea that what is called *samadhi* means not being aware of anything at all. This flatly contradicts the meaning of the scriptural admonition that we "must activate our minds without abiding anywhere." This idea that *samadhi* means not being aware of anything at all is one of people's biggest misconceptions.

The next most serious misconception is that people in general are all going after esoteric spiritual secrets—spiritual feelings, supernormal spiritual powers, the sixth sense, transcendent intuitions and so on. All sorts of terms for spiritual secrets are added on. This is a very serious mistake. Everyone must realize that insanity and supernormal spiritual powers are twins. This is really a very grave problem, because in the quest for supernormal powers, if you go wrong by the slightest little bit, you end up thousands of miles away.

Let me say it again: what is meditative concentration? We must certainly recognize it clearly. The four *dhyanas* and the eight *samadhis* are the central foundation of Buddhist methods of cultivating realization. However, the Buddha Dharma does not have a monopoly on meditative concentration; meditative concentration is a common technique. But the Buddha Dharma does not depart from meditative concentration. In the biographies of eminent monks down through the generations, the monks and nuns who worked at cultivating realization until they arrived at *samadhi* are very numerous. Various Chinese emperors in the Northern and Southern Dynasties period [A.D. fourth-sixth centuries] also had connections with Buddhism: for example, Liu Yu, the founder of the Liu Sung dynasty, Emperor Wu of the Liang dynasty, and Emperor Wen of the Sui dynasty all had deep ties to Buddhism.

Buddha showed us the road of cultivating realization, but we ourselves have not traveled it. Instead, we have taken what we have heard from Shakyamuni Buddha as if it were something we ourselves had realized. This is what I have been calling inverting cause and effect, taking the cause as the effect and the effect as the cause.

Instead of genuinely cultivating realization, people pursue all sorts of misguided practices such as "the special channels and eight meridians," "three meridians and seven chakras," passing through this barrier and that barrier, working with *ch'i* channels, working at sitting meditation, and so on. None of these lead to true correct *samadhi*. What is the reason for this? Those who work with *ch'i* channels all undergo some manipulations of the condition of their physi-

cal sensations. If they cannot get beyond the condition of their physical sensations and they assume that this is the path to enlightenment,
they are wrong. In other words, a path such as this rests on a philosophical basis that is materialistic; it is not oriented toward mind.
This is because these transformations in the *ch'i* channels can only be
generated while the body exists, while the body is healthy. Without
the body, would there be transformations in the *ch'i* channels? From
this it is evident that the transformation of *ch'i* channels proceeds
from the body and belongs to the realm of the physical, the material. Thus, in their philosophy, aren't such physically-based practices
materialistic? This is a very serious issue.

If you say that they are not materialistic, but mentalistic, well
then, what else besides physical effects can you show us? Don't say
that you can show people that you can enter *samadhi* and that this is
something marvelous. As soon as you enter *samadhi*, does this physical body separate off from you?

This is why I have just discussed the three aspects of seeing the
truth of Buddhism, cultivating realization, and carrying out vows.
These three encompass everything. They are three aspects of the same
whole, all equally important.

If you want to cultivate realization correctly, works like *The
Lankavatara Sutra, The Yogacarabhumi Shastra,* and *The Abhisamayalamkara
Shastra* are very important. If you cannot achieve a "body generated
by will," then you will not be able to succeed in cultivating practice.
All the efforts that you cultivate will only belong to the elementary
stage of the four intensified practices.

The four intensified practices, *prayoga*, are called "warming,"
"the peak," "forbearance," and "the supreme worldly dharma."

When we discuss Buddhism, we all understand the four intensified practices. The intensified practices are like working in a factory
to finish goods that still need to be finished with extra work. The
four fruits of the arhats, the ten stages of the bodhisattvas, the ten
levels of meditation work—at no stage can we depart from the four
intensified practices. In other words, the first *dhyana* has the four
intensified practices of the first *dhyana*, the second *dhyana* has the
four intensified practices of the second *dhyana*, and so on. In *The
Abhisamayalamkara Shastra* the Bodhisattva Maitreya mentions them,
and they are also mentioned in *The Yogacarabhumi Shastra*. Both works
emphasize the four intensified practices very much. In other words,
when we research Buddhism properly, if we are totally incapable of

truly realizing even a little bit of meditation work, it is because we have not carried out the work of the four intensified practices.

In the theory of the teaching, the four intensified practices are "warming," "the peak," "forbearance," and "the supreme worldly dharma." Naturally they have their explanations, and they are very reasonable. If we discuss them by strict inference from the theory of the teaching, each step of the four intensified practices requires its own type of cultivation work. For example, when we study Buddhism and study Taoism, we immediately talk of questions of physical transformations and *ch'i* channels. I have never seen a person who, by the standards of Taoism, has opened up the special meridians and the eight channels. Even if they were opened up, basically it still wouldn't count as consummating the path and achieving enlightenment. As for the first step in the four intensified practices—the phenomenon of "warming"—this also doesn't involve opening the *ch'i* channels.

After the *ch'i* channels are truly and correctly opened, what kind of a realm is it? The person is sitting cross-legged with both legs drawn up: not only doesn't he think of putting his legs down, but on the contrary his whole body has become supple, he is merged with emptiness, his spirit is very light, and he is incomparably comfortable and at ease. Only after the *ch'i* channels are truly and correctly opened up can light within the body be generated. Even if there is no light, inside the person there still is an expanse of light. Normally, when the average person closes his eyes, what is before him is all black: this is called the mass of unenlightened ignorance.

But we must not assume that this expanse of light is the realm of the great light. This would be very wrong! This is still a light that has form. I tell you, only at this time, after this light is generated, can the *kundalini* rise. (In Chinese, *kundalini* is also called spiritual power, or the spiritual capability.) The relationship of this fundamental capability of our inherent nature to our bodies is like "the taste of salt in water, or the pigment in something colored." If we put some salt into a cup of pure water, after we mix it in, the water is salty. Can you take the salt out? If we add pigment to water, we cannot take it out either. In the same way, this inherent spiritual capability in our lives cannot be separated from these bodies of ours. Even someone who could separate it still would not awaken to the path. This is the work of cultivating realization. Only when this spiritual capability comes forth, have we reached the phenomenon of "warming" in the four intensified practices.

No matter how old they may be, people whose work of cultivating realization has arrived at "warming" are like babies—their whole bodies are soft and supple. But this is not enlightenment, there's nothing rare about it! This ability to reach the level of "warming" is inherent from the beginning in the basic capacity of our lives. The question is, how will you be able to cultivate practice to the point that you reach this phenomenon of "warming"? In the scriptural teachings, many different explanations are given regarding this issue. We will explain it in terms of phenomenal appearances.

When we speak of the phenomenon of "the peak," this definitely does not mean "opening the flower at the peak of the head." Rather, it means forming one body with the void, as in the saying of Chuang Tzu: "The spirit coming and going together with heaven and earth." Only this is reaching the phenomenon of "the peak." Having first reached the phenomenon of "warming," only then do we reach the phenomenon of "the peak."

When we have cultivated practice to the point where we have reached "the peak," this is the first *dhyana*. As I said before, the first *dhyana* has the four intensified practices of the first *dhyana*, the second *dhyana* has the four intensified practices of the second *dhyana*, and so on. Only after this can we arrive at the phenomenon of "forbearance."

What is this thing called forbearance? It means cutting everything off. At this point, false thoughts are cut off, you escape from the worldly, and you stand alone, transcendent. In the phrase "forbearance [based upon the realization that all things are] unborn," forbearance is a descriptive word. We have cut off everything, but we have still not yet realized emptiness. It's just that everything has been cut off, that's all.

When we have cut off all worldly thoughts and afflictions and have reached this stage, this is still no more than the highest achievement of worldly cultivation of practice. It still does not leap beyond the world. Therefore, only when we take another step, do we reach "the supreme worldly dharma."

At the stage when a person has cultivated practice to the point of reaching the "supreme worldly dharma," only then can he or she be reckoned as a true person. When the person has reached the highest pinnacle of being human, he or she equals what Chuang Tzu called "a real person." In other words, in the eyes of Chuang Tzu, someone who has not attained the path is a false person.

Even if we reach this level in our meditation work, this is still no more than the "supreme worldly dharma." We still have not transcended the world. So then, how can we walk upon the road that transcends the world? Whatever steps we take on the road of the work of cultivation and realization, we can never leave behind the four intensified practices. Every step of the way, we cannot depart from them. This includes the study of Pure Land Buddhism, the study of T'ien-t'ai Buddhism's cessation and contemplation, the study of Esoteric Buddhism, etc. It's the same for them all. All of them depend on success in the four intensified practices. Only after we have succeeded in meditative concentration can we speak of cultivating world-transcending dharmas. This is the sequence and the order of cultivation and realization.

In what I have just said, I have proceeded in my exposition by raising the issue of three procedures: seeing truth, cultivating realization, and practicing vows. First is the stage of seeing truth. After we have seen the truth of the Buddhist path, then the question is how to cultivate the path, and how to practice our vows.

Now let us turn back to the issues we have settled, to the real truths we have discussed and defined. This is still the first step. In the future we will go step-by-step and discuss them in great detail. In the process of cultivation and realization, everyone must pay attention to the principles of the four intensified practices.

# 2

# MIND AND
# EXTERNAL FORM

We discussed the phenomenal aspects of methods of cultivation and realization, and described the situation of the four intensified practices. There were a number of students, however, who did not understand me; they could not follow the conversation because we went from topic to topic. They felt that there was no general outline, so we will now use *The Surangama Sutra* in our discussion. The work of cultivating realization is laid out in order in *The Surangama Sutra*, so you can get right to work understanding it directly.

Our friends in the scholarly world, especially those scholars who do research in Buddhist studies, must especially take note. There are people who view *The Surangama Sutra, The Sutra of Complete Enlightenment, The Treatise on Awakening of Faith in the Mahayana, The Sutra in Forty-Two Sections,* and other such scriptures as false scriptures, as counterfeits. This misconception is derived from textual research and because of this, some people in Buddhist studies think it fundamentally beneath them to take a look at these scriptures. Nevertheless, if I may dare to be so presumptuous, let me say that I find this exhibition of mere book learning meaningless.

When Chinese culture came to the Ch'ing Dynasty, the so-called "Han Learning" flourished, which emphasized the analysis of meanings, the analysis of poetry and prose, and research into textual sources and historical narratives. From the standpoint of Chinese culture, Western philosophy is included in what we call "the study of meanings." From the standpoint of Western culture, what we call the study of meanings is included in philosophy. Since each takes a different standpoint, their concepts are also different. T'ang poetry and Sung lyrics are covered by the study of poetry and prose. The culture of each era[1] has its own representative type: for example, literary essays from the Han Dynasty, calligraphy from the Wei-Chin Period, poems from the T'ang Dynasty, lyrics from the Sung Dynasty, drama from the Yuan Dynasty, vernacular novels from the Ming Dynasty, linked verse from the Ch'ing Dynasty, and so on.

We will not speak of the study of poetry and prose. The Ch'ing Dynasty Confucians put special emphasis on the study of meanings. This was because since the rise of Neo-Confucianism in the Sung Dynasty, most Confucians only talked about the learning of the nature of mind and essence and life. By the Ch'ing Dynasty, there was a very great reaction among Confucians against this metaphysically oriented learning of essence and life, and so they moved toward learning that was based on the factual study of evidence. This they called "Han Learning" because they sought to rediscover the original meaning of the Confucian texts as understood in the Han Dynasty, before the Buddhist-influenced reinterpretations advanced by the Sung Dynasty Neo-Confucians.

Foreigners today call all of our learning "Han Learning," but fundamentally this terminology is wrong. If we ourselves follow them and call our own learning "Han Learning," this is even more ridiculous.

The Ch'ing Dynasty scholarly movement called *k'ao-chu* "evidentiary studies" was just one style of research. The claim that all the Buddhist scriptures mentioned above are forgeries comes from this "evidentiary studies" approach, whose authoritative figure was Liang

---

[1] The usual periodization of Chinese history by dynasties is approximately as follows:

Han: 206 B.C.-219 A.D.
Wei-Chin: 220-420
North-South Period: 420-589
Sui: 589-618
T'ang: 618-906
Sung: 968-1279
Chin (Jurchen): 1126-1235
Yuan (Mongol): 1235-1368
Ming: 1368-1644
Ch'ing (Manchu): 1644-1911

Ch'i ch'ao. However, Liang Ch'i ch'ao only understood Buddhism very superficially, and he must be counted as an outsider, or non-specialist. He thought that the literary style of these scriptures was too good, and that they didn't seem to be Indian texts, so his opinion was that they were forged by people in China. But I think that from the point of view of their contents, these scriptures are definitely not forgeries or fakes, and therefore this "evidentiary research" approach is problematic.

Now let us speak of a second question concerning *The Surangama Sutra*. The beginning of this scripture contains within it a great secret about the work of cultivating practice. It reads: "The Great Buddha Crown Tathagata's ultimate truth of cultivating realization of the secret basis, *The Surangama Sutra* of the myriad practices of the bodhisattvas." Apart from this, there is no other secret basis for true correct cultivation of realization.

Nevertheless, in the course of several decades, I have never met anyone who has done genuine research on this scripture or who has been truly able to find *The Surangama Sutra's* method of cultivating realization. In reality, in this scripture the whole process of going from an ordinary person to achieving buddhahood through cultivating realization is explained. Anyone who understands the written language reads it and understands, but most people have been tricked by the very beautiful language of this scripture and have not understood its contents.

In *The Surangama Sutra* there is an important point, a great secret: this is a method of cultivating realization. In reality, among the three aspects of seeing truth, cultivating realization, and carrying out vows, not one can be lacking. If you really have seen truth, then you will surely be able to accomplish the cultivation of realization. If you have truly accomplished the cultivation of realization, then you will surely be able to carry out your vows. If any point is deficient, then everything is incorrect.

*The Surangama Sutra* begins with "controlling the mind in seven places, and discerning the eight returns." In a dialogue between Buddha and Ananda, they ask the question: Where is mind? They discuss the matter back and forth in seven points, called "the seven places." Mind is not inside, and it is not outside, and it is not in between. Finally Buddha tells Ananda where mind is. The discussion goes as follows.

Buddha told Ananda: "Since time without beginning, all sentient beings have suffered from various kinds of errors. The seeds of karma have arisen spontaneously, like evils gathering around. The fact that people who cultivate practice have not been able to attain supreme enlightenment, and have instead become literalist disciples (*shravakas*) and solitary illuminates (*pratyekas*) and people following outside paths, and celestial deities (*devas*), and demon kings and members of the retinue of the demons of delusion: this is entirely due to their not knowing the two roots. To cultivate practice wrongly and in a confused way is like cooking sand to make a cake. Though you do it for countless eons, you will never be able to succeed.

"What are the two roots? The first, Ananda, is the root of beginningless birth and death. This is the way you right now, along with all sentient beings, take the mind that clings to objects as your own inherent nature. The second is beginningless *bodhi-nirvana*, the perfect peace of enlightenment, the original pure essence. This is the original illumination of your conscious essence, which can give birth to objects, and which is there when objects have been cast away. Due to the fact that sentient beings lose this fundamental illumination, even though they practice throughout their lives, they cannot awaken themselves, and they wrongly enter into the various planes of existence."

Buddha asks: Why can't we ourselves illuminate mind and see our true nature? Because since time without beginning, there has been something operating in our lives: it is the mind that clings to objects, continuing from thought to thought. Because our thoughts can never stop, because even when we are asleep and dreaming, we are still thinking, this is called the mind that clings to objects.

The average person mistakenly accepts this mind that clings to objects as [fundamental, true] mind. This is the same as what the Western philosopher Descartes said, "I think, therefore I am." I think, therefore I am: this is the how the common person thinks. Nevertheless, this is wrong, this is not the fundamental mind. But what is right?

"Beginningless *bodhi-nirvana*, the perfect peace of enlightenment, the original pure essence." Buddha said that this mind is the [real] phenomenon, this is the function aroused by the fundamental essence. Life's basic mind, its basic capability, is called *bodhi*, enlightenment. It is also called the fundamental essence. The phenomena which it sends forth are parts of it, which leap forth like lightning, or waves. You should not try to grab hold of these kinds of phenomena. You should turn back and recognize that fundamental essence.

"This is the original illumination of your conscious essence, which can engender objects, and is there when objects have been cast away." "The original illumination of your conscious essence" encompasses [the sense of the term] consciousness in Vijnanavada.[2] "Essence" is the true essential spirit, this original spiritual illumination: this is the thing in you that is capable of knowing and sensing and is spiritually aware and illuminated. What is this thing? [The sutra says:] "It can give birth to objects." Once this thing moves inside us, once our thoughts move, once we become aware in our minds, then it starts to function outside.

What are objects? The words I speak are objects. I emit sounds and you hear them—these are objects. As I write sentence after sentence like this, and you read and your thoughts follow, this is clinging to objects. When we sit in a group our bodies may feel warm. This is the "original illumination of the conscious essence" within us responding to the heat outside us. In our minds we may feel that it is hot and oppressive: this is us generating feeling toward the object heat, this is "being able to give birth to objects."

[The sutra calls the original illumination] "Something that is there when objects are cast away." As the Zen school says, "Abandon the myriad objects." When all external objects are cast aside, there is something left over, something that cannot be gotten rid of. For

---

[2] Vijnanavada, or Yogacara, is the Indian name of a school of Buddhist philosophy known as the "Consciousness Only" school in Chinese. It teaches that ordinary unenlightened sentient beings do not ordinarily perceive the world as it is; instead, what they perceive is a system of mental representations, *vijnapti*, which are products of their conditioning and acculturation, and which they project upon the world of phenomena. Vijnanavada distinguishes three levels of identity: the imaginary identity (which is the system of representations the unenlightened project on phenomena, giving them a dualistic self vs. others perception of the world); the interdependent identity (which is the phenomenal world in its real state as a ceaseless flux of cause and effect, with no independently existing entities); and the absolute identity (which is the identitylessness of relative phenomena, their underlying ontological oneness).

The term "consciousness only" or "mind only" expresses the double perspective of Vijnanavada ontology. For the unenlightened, the world is "mind only" because all they see are the projections of their own consciousness. For the enlightened, the world is "mind only" because they see that the Buddha-Mind is the ontological basis of all phenomena, that all phenomena are emanations of the Buddha-Mind.

example, if you sit for a long time and you feel discomfort in your legs and arms—these are objects. What objects? The objects that make up the physical body, the responsive functions of the body, which have nothing to do with the real you. *That* one knows that your body is uncomfortable and your legs are uncomfortable. Since *that* one is not in your legs, and not in your arms either, it is something that is left after you have gotten rid of objects, "that is there when objects are cast away." These words refer to that thing that has been there all along, that thing that is left after external objects have all been cast away.

"Due to the fact that sentient beings lose this fundamental illumination, even though they practice throughout their lives, they cannot awaken themselves, and they wrongly enter into the various planes of existence." Everything comes forth from the changes in that thing, that fundamental illumination. Therefore sentient beings are deluded, they consistently run off after the myriad objects, they cycle around in the six planes of existence as celestial beings, human beings, demigods, animals, hungry ghosts, and hell-beings, and they revolve within birth and death. This is the apparent side, not the esoteric phenomena: here we are still not discussing the reverse side.

I always try to make everyone mindful of this: right when you are sitting down, and you are drawing up your legs into the cross-legged posture, at that very instant, is it or is it not very good? But after you have sat down properly, it is not so good. Why is this? Because after you have seated yourself properly, you become aware "I am sitting in meditation." You notice your breath is not right, your body is not right. But at that moment when you just sat down, there seemed to be a bit of a feeling of abandoning the myriad objects, of not being concerned with anything at all. After you have crossed your legs properly, everything comes into your thoughts: you think of achieving enlightenment, you think of having your posture upright and correct, you think of not engaging in false thoughts. False thoughts arrive, and you want to chase them away. After you've chased them away, you start thinking again. Alas! Why must you chase them away? After you chase them away, again there are false thoughts. No matter what you do, you are always sitting there playing with ghosts.

In fact, you simply must let external objects fall away spontaneously so that the thing which is left does not move. This is what the sutra calls the one that remains "when objects are cast away."

These are the instructions that Buddha gave to us so directly. It is because we confuse them that we "falsely enter into the various planes of existence," that we revolve around in the six planes of existence.

Now let us discuss "discerning the eight returns." What is seeing? When we ordinary people sit in mediation and when we get up, what phenomena appear? This is just what is discussed in *The Surangama Sutra*: "False thoughts defiled by form consider form as the body. Gathering together objects, we disturb ourselves within, running off in disarray toward externals, benighted and confused by forms, considering this as the true nature of mind."

Buddha said that all sentient beings are unable to find this mind. Why? Because of "false thoughts defiled by form," because our physical reactions follow false thoughts in our minds, creating a reciprocal interaction. Then, within us, we "consider form as the body." In fact, within our body there is a physical body, which is just the self that has been assembled by our own thoughts. For example, a student recently said that originally his body was not very good, but when he ran around outside, it changed for the better. One can see the psychological function is just this principle.

In this mind there is a physical body that has been formed by false thoughts. These thoughts themselves are the internal embryo of this body of form. This thinking gathers together outside objects, and transforms them into a physical body within your body.

Therefore the sutra says: "Gathering together objects, we disturb ourselves within." This means taking thoughts of external objects, sentiments, etc., and gathering them all together. When you are meditating, as you are sitting there, what is often happening is described by these words: "Gathering together objects, we disturb ourselves within." Thoughts proliferate like cotton candy spun out of a tube. The more it spins, the more there are. The mind gets very confused: it's like a crowd milling around at a mass demonstration.

"Running off in disarray toward externals" means that thoughts run off in confusion toward externals. After this, our eyes close and we are "benighted and confused by forms." With our brains dim and dark, rumbling along, we sit for an hour or so. We call this Zen meditation and we think being like this is the true nature of mind. How can we fail to realize that this is not true mind? If we commit this kind of major error, we are still "totally deluded about mind and certain to be confused by considering it to be within our physical bodies."

Thus, we have no clear recognition: we still think that we are culti-vating the path and we still think that the mind is in the body. If the mind were really in the body, then when you die, wouldn't the mind be impossible to find?

Buddha explained this very clearly. "[Deluded sentient beings] do not know that their physical bodies, along with the mountains and rivers and space and the whole world outside them, are all things within the wondrously illuminated true mind." Buddha was saying, "Ananda, you don't realize it, but when you are sitting in medita-tion, it doesn't matter if you open your eyes or close your eyes: you must not hold onto your body. You do not know it, but everything, from your body out to the whole of space, the whole of the sky, is all within your mind." So what is this physical body? It is no more than us "thinking of form as the body." Realizing this is seeing truth.

When you are sitting in meditation, do you hold onto your phys-ical bodies as they are turning or not? If you do not, have you reached the stage of seeing truth, the realm where "the mountains and rivers and space and the whole world outside are all things within the won-drously illuminated true mind"?

The sutra says that true mind "is like a hundred thousand pure oceans. You abandon it, and just accept this one floating bubble of your body. [True mind] is called the golden tide; it exhausts the oceans and the seas."

Buddha says the fundamental essence of us sentient beings is like a great ocean, who knows how much vaster than the Pacific Ocean, while your body is no more than a little speck. But we take this great one and throw it away, and just hold onto that little speck, and think that this physical body is our life. Everyone grabs hold of this lit-tle speck and is busy "gathering together objects, disturbing ourselves within." It's like spinning cotton candy—the more we spin, the bigger it gets.

The Zen school's ancestral teacher Yun-men said, "Within heaven and earth, inside space and time, there is a jewel, hidden in the moun-tain of form." In fact, this wondrously illuminated true mind of "mountains and rivers and space and the whole world" is right in your body. It's just that it is covered over by the physical body and other karmic forces, "false thoughts defiled by forms." We must search out this jewel, this true mind.

Right now I am discussing *The Surangama Sutra*. Have you under-stood everything? Have you directly comprehended it all? "Outside

it is like empty space." Have you studied this deeply? Have you realized this? It will only work when you do the meditation work and
manage to realize it. How can you cultivate practice to the point that
you can use your six senses at the same time, while the One Mind is
pure and clear? Only this is the study of Zen. The Zen schools in
America and Japan specialize in studying *koans* and meditation sayings such as the wild duck flies back and forth,[3] but what has this got
to do with Zen? Those are no more than chance devices in didactic
method. Hui-ming asked the Sixth Patriarch, "Master, what secret
did the Fifth Patriarch tell you?" The Sixth Patriarch said, "How could
there be any secret? The secret is not in me, it's in you." This saying is
itself a great secret!

In *The Surangama Sutra*, Buddha explains that none of these seven
places, internal or external, is the mind. Buddha says that if you take
yourself as the basic center, and extend out till you reach the whole of
space, all of these are things within your mind. In other words, the
seven internal and external places are all mind. Do you understand?
This is the Tathagata's esoteric basis, but you will not find out about
it in your studies.

But what mind are the seven internal and external places? They
are the functioning of mind, not the basic essence of mind. When
functioning, it is the functioning of Buddha's form body (*nirmanakaya*)
and response body (*sambhogakaya*). When it goes back to its essence,
it is the purity of the body of reality (*dharmakaya*).[4]

---

[3] Once when Master Ma-tsu and Pai-chang were walking together, they saw
some wild ducks fly by. Ma-tsu asked, "What is that?" Pai-chang said, "Wild
ducks." Ma-tsu said, "Where have they gone?" Pai-chang said, "They've
flown away." Ma-tsu then twisted Pai-chang's nose, and Pai-chang cried out
in pain. Ma-tsu said, "When have they ever flown away?" *The Blue Cliff Record*
(case #53), translated by Thomas Cleary and J. C. Cleary (Shambhala, Boston,
1992).

[4] The three bodies of Buddha are distinguished as follows: *Dharmakaya*, the
body of reality, the truth-body, is the ontological essence, the absolute, the one
reality, omnipresent, everywhere equal, the true essence of all things.
*Sambhogakaya*, the body of reward, the body of enjoyment, is Buddha as
experienced by bodhisattvas, for whom nirvana and birth-and-death are
equal. *Nirmanakaya*, the form body, the emanation body, encompasses the
many diverse forms in which Buddha appears to ordinary sentient beings,
according to their levels of understanding.

Yun-men said: "Within heaven and earth, inside space and time, there is a jewel, hidden in the mountain of form. Pick up the lamp and take it into the buddha-shrine, take the monastery gate onto the lamp: what is it?" To take the external lamp into the buddha-shrine—this can be done. But is it possible to take the monastery gate onto the lamp? This is a Zen master's way of talking. Here he talks in a confusing way of this and that, as if he's acting on television. The result was when Yun-men looked around at the audience, among everyone present there, there was no one who understood. All he could do was say himself: "Pursuing objects, the intellect moves." He also said, "Clouds arise and thunder rolls."

In Chinese culture, lecturing is a literary form, so monks must pay attention to this, and do a good job on their literary rough drafts. Yun-men's meaning is: Ah! Too bad. As soon as I say a sentence, your minds immediately run outside. This is what is meant in *The Surangama Sutra* by "Running off in disarray toward externals." After our ancestral teacher Yun-men had made that statement, he looked around at everyone, and there was no one who understood, so he said, "Clouds arise and thunder rolls." He saw that his students could not answer him, so all he could do was answer on their behalf.

Let me also quote a saying by Zen teacher Hsueh-tou: "I have a jewel within. I cannot get hold of it and bring it out, I cannot separate myself from it." Hsueh-tou wrote a verse:

> Look! Look! Look!
> Who is that on the ancient bank
>     holding a fishing pole?
> The clouds are slowing moving by
> The waters are overflowing
> The bright moon over the reed flowers:
>     Look for yourself.

Look! This is not looking outside, this is looking within at yourself. Someone is standing on an ancient river bank; he wants to help you across up onto the bank, but you will not take the hook so there is nothing he can do. The realm of Zen is what's there after you have abandoned the myriad objects, after you have taken your body and mind and cast them aside. Under the bright moon, you see the reed flowers. Reed flowers are white, and so is the moon. With white facing white, what is it? The whole expanse is white, empty all the way through—he wants you to go try and find it.

Again, it's like what Zen teacher Lin-chi said up in the teaching hall:

"In this lump of red flesh, there is a true person without position constantly going in and out through your faces. Those who have not verified this yet, look, look!" That is to say, for those of you who have not been able to find this true person without position, those of you who still don't understand, I bring it out so you can see.

At the time there was a monk who stood up and said, "What is the true person without position?" As soon as Zen teacher Lin-chi heard him speak he got down from the teacher's seat and grabbed him tight and said, "Speak! Speak!" That is, you tell me! The story continues: "The monk hesitated thinking what to say." As the monk was thinking of something to say, Zen teacher Lin-chi released him and exclaimed, "The true person without position—what a dry piece of shit it is!" When he had finished speaking, he turned around and returned to his quarters.

Stories like this are called "Dharma words in the teaching hall." When you read the public cases of the Zen school, you must act as if you are watching a show on television. You must read them by throwing your whole body and mind into them: you cannot read them in a lifeless way.

When it came to "discerning the eight returns" Buddha explained about seeing the truth of his teaching, and only at the end did he speak about the road of practical work for cultivating realization of his teaching. In this scripture Buddha explained all the highest secrets. Therefore we carry *The Surangama Sutra* with us everyday. If we do not read and understand it, then we will not get on the right road in terms of cultivating practice. This would be very lamentable, and we would also be spurning the benevolence of the Buddha.

Now I will cite one example of "discerning the eight returns," a dialogue between Buddha and King Prasenajit, from *The Surangama Sutra*, Volume 2.

Buddha said, "Now I will teach you about the true nature which is neither born nor destroyed.

"Great King, how old were you when you saw the Ganges River?"

The King said, "When I was three years old, my compassionate mother took me along on a visit to Jivadeva, and we passed by a stream, and at the time I knew it was the water of the Ganges River."

Buddha said, "Great King, according to what you said, from the time you were twenty, you got weaker with every passing decade, until you have now reached the age of sixty. During all this time, your thoughts kept moving and changing. From the time you saw this river at the age of three, until you saw it again at thirteen, how was the river?"

The King said, "It was the same as when I was three: there was no difference. Up until today, when I am sixty-two, there is still no difference in the river."

Buddha said, "Now your hair is white and your face is wrinkled. Surely your face is more wrinkled now than it was when you were young. But now when you view the river, is there any difference due to age from your vision when you viewed the river in your youth?"

The King said, "There is no difference, O World Honored One."

Buddha said, "Great King, though your face has become wrinkled, your vision in its real nature has never become wrinkled. The wrinkled one has changed; the one that does not become wrinkled does not change. What changes is subject to destruction. What does not change is fundamentally without birth or destruction."

To paraphrase the story in the sutra: One day, King Prasenajit came to question Buddha. He said, "The way you teach is very easy to understand, but I have doubts about your teaching that the true nature of mind is neither born nor destroyed."

Buddha said, "How old were you when you saw the Ganges River?"

The King said, "I saw it when I was little on a trip with my mother."

Buddha asked, "How old were you then?" "Three." "How old are you now?" "Sixty-two."

Buddha asked, "Now your vision has become blurred, but when you pass by the river, can you see it?"

The King said, "Certainly I can see it."

Buddha said, "At your age there is weakness and old age, birth and destruction, and death, but this nature of yours that is able to see has not changed along with your age, it has not moved."

When you are sleeping, even though your eyes are closed, this visual consciousness is still seeing things, and in this seeing, the true nature of vision has not changed. I have written a verse on this passage from the sutra:

> Do not bear a deep grudge against birth
>     and death for no reason

The wave-borne flowers flow through past,
    present, and future
A white haired man in the mist, looking
    at the river
It is still the mind of youth long past.

Human beings—again and again they are born and die. To the human race, birth and death are very fearful. We are born, we die, we enter the womb again: each passage of birth and death is like a section of a flowing stream. We follow the waves forever, arising and disappearing, without stopping.

The poem above draws on the story of King Prasenajit. "A white haired man in the mist, looking at the river." He is old, and when he looks at things his vision is blurred, but this true nature that can see, is still the same as it ever was, it is still the same as when he was young. "It is still the mind of youth long past."

The sutra says: "Everything that can be returned [i.e. attributed back to something else], is naturally not you. As for that which does not return to you, if it is not you, then who is it?" Vision is attributed to the spirit of the eye, light is attributed to the sun. After everything which can be returned has been returned, there is left something that cannot be gotten rid of, which has nowhere it can be returned to: if this is not you, then who is it?

Of course you may say, "Didn't Buddha say there is no self?" This is correct, but when Buddha said there is no self, he meant that the physical self, the false self, does not exist [in the ultimate sense]. He did not throw away the self of inherent nature.

There was a Zen teacher named T'ien-mu, who made up this poem when he was enlightened:

If it doesn't return to you, who is it then?
Remnants of sunset red descend on the fisherman
    and the pebbles along the water's edge
The sun is slanting low, the wind stirs, but
    no one sweeps
The swallow flies over the water carrying
    something in its beak.

When falling flowers drop on the ground, they are returning to their original position. It is like sitting meditation: false thoughts come and come, but when you recognize them, they immediately run away. You don't have to try to control them.

That is the scene in the poem. "Remnants of sunset red descend on the fisherman and the pebbles along the water's edge." T'ien-mu took a scene from the natural world at that moment, and very spontaneously pulled it into his verse—it was ready-made. This is likened to your mental state, very spontaneous and natural, as it slowly quiets down. The sun going down behind the mountains, the wind slightly stirring: this is a metaphor for still having a slight bit of false thinking. "No one sweeps" means you should not try to control these false thoughts: you cannot sweep them away, you shouldn't concern yourself with them. "The swallow flies over the water carrying something in his beak"—this slight bit of false thinking doesn't matter at all.

I myself will add two lines to the end of the verse:

> "Caw! Caw! [The bird's cries are] a supreme mantra
> A matchless spell."

This is to tell you that this piece by T'ien-mu is not a poem: if you have understood this verse, then you have awakened to a little bit of enlightenment.

Now we have explained "discerning the eight returns" and we have understood this aspect of illuminating mind and seeing true nature. The thing that is still not lost, this is our vision, right? But I want to raise a question. If Shakyamuni Buddha were to come, I would certainly want to ask him: "Master, you have been explaining for quite a while that what is not lost is [the real] self. But I need to have this physical body of mine existing. After my physical body is dead and gone, where can that thing go to? I still cannot find it."

So even if you try hard and do meditation work, you still cannot find where it comes from and where it goes. Even if you witness the true emptiness of mind, and are absorbed in meditative concentration for three-hundred-and-sixty-five days, it still is useless, it still won't work. This is the secret.

Now those of you who have done your meditation work properly may think: Very well then! You have made a lot of progress that has depended on your physical body, this lump of red flesh. When your flesh decays, where will you go? How will you run away? "I have a jewel, hidden in the mountain of form." How will you run from it?

How will you run to it? How will you search it out? Thus *The Surangama Sutra* first tells of seeing the truth, and later continues on to tell you all about the secret of cultivation and realization.

This secret of how to do meditation work is all in the last one or two volumes, a place in the sutra to which everyone customarily pays the least attention, especially the sutra's account of the fifty kinds of delusions caused by the *skandhas*[5] of form, sensation, conception, synthesis and consciousness, and liberation from the five skandhas.

In *The Heart Sutra* it says, "See the five skandhas as all empty." How can the five skandhas be empty? We must do meditation work to empty them! I have discussed "inverting cause and effect," taking the results achieved by the Buddha and appropriating them as your own without doing the work necessary to realize them for yourself. Now I will return to this issue of "inverting cause and effect" for you must indeed go seek realization for yourself.

When I talk about the fifty forms of delusion caused by the *skandhas*, everyone has to read the text. If you do not read the text it is arrogance, it is a violation of the precepts. The buddhas and bodhisattvas have bestowed teachings and methods on you: this is the basis of the Dharma.

In Volume 9 of *The Surangama Sutra* in the section called "The Domain of the Skandha of Form," Buddha says:

"You should sit in the place where you work toward enlightenment and dissolve away all thoughts. When thoughts are exhausted, then you are detached from thought, and everything is pure illumination that does not stir whether you are moving or still, that is the same whether you remember it or forget it. You must abide in this place, and enter into *samadhi*.

"It is like a clear-eyed man who is put in total darkness. His essential nature is wondrous and pure, but his mind does not yet emit light. This is called 'the domain of the skandha of form.'"

At such a time, thoughts are absent and everything is pure and clear; movement and stillness are one, and no miscellaneous thoughts

---

[5] The word *skandha* literally means "aggregate," "heap," "cluster." Buddhist seers analyzed the life-world of sentient beings into the five clusters of form, sensation, conception (by which we categorize sensation to create perception), synthesis (by which we evaluate perceptions and motivate our actions), and consciousness.

arise. Your meditation has reached the point that "it is the same whether you remember it or forget it." You must enter *samadhi* at this point. This is just like "a clear-eyed man put in total darkness"—in the darkness, there is a subtle light. "His essential nature is wondrous and pure, but his mind does not yet emit light." At such a time the realm of life's fundamental true nature is very pure, very subtle.

But the average person's mind is restless, chaotic, messy: when he shuts his eyes, everything goes black. If right now someone managed to "dissolve away all thoughts" and reach the realm where "it does not stir whether moving or still and is the same whether he remembers it or forgets it," this would not be understood as something to brag about. In fact, it is just one kind of realm, that's all.

What realm is it? The sutra says: "Essential nature is wondrous and pure, but that mind does not yet emit light: this is called the domain of the skandha of form." This is a kind of psychological change that occurs when the mind is about to be transformed—there's nothing so special about it! In other words, when you are sitting in meditation, with your mind empty clear through, perhaps for some years or months or days or hours, this is because your physical body has been tempered and tamed. The blind cat has bumped into the dead rat: it's like being plugged into an electrical outlet. By no means is this true meditation work. After a moment passes, you lose it. This all belongs to the domain of the skandha of form.

When we speak of the domain of the skandha of form, there are several books you must read: the biographies of spiritual monks and nuns, and the records of the buddhas and patriarchs down through the ages. When you read these biographies and stories, you will be able to develop an attitude of truly and sincerely turning toward the path of enlightenment.

There is a book called *A Year-by-Year Account of the Life of Master Han-shan*.[6] When Master Han-shan was 28, he went various places to study. He came to the peak of Mt. Pan-shan. There was a thatched hut there, and inside it a Buddhist monk meditating. This monk paid no attention to Master Han-shan. When the monk ate, Master Han-shan ate along with him, and when the monk drank tea, Master Han-shan, too, drank tea. Later on, when it was time to eat, Master Han-shan cooked for the monk and when it was time for tea, he

---

[6] This story can be found in *Practical Buddhism* by Charles Luk (London: Rider, 1971).

brewed tea for the monk. After they had eaten, Master Han-shan went for a walk by himself. Things went on like this for several days. Only on the seventh day did the monk talk to Master Han-shan. The monk said, "I have lived on this cliff for over thirty years, and only now have I met a kindred spirit."

One evening, after eating some gruel, Han-shan was walking with some incense on the mountain peak as usual. Suddenly he stopped and stood still: he felt that the whole world of heaven and earth was within a single light. This was precisely the realm described in the sutra of "dissolving away all thoughts." When Han-shan came back to the thatched hut, as soon as the monk saw him, he said, "Let me tell you, this is the domain of the skandha of form. The point you have reached in your meditation work is no more than this. I have been taking walks here every night for thirty years, always within this realm. What's so special about it?"

Cultivating practice is this hard, and it is also this easy. That monk went walking every night for thirty years, and he always forgot about his body and mind. Take note, you people who are cultivating practice! You are still only halfway there in the domain of the skandha of form. When you close your eyes it is all black. Wherever you are, you are groping blindly, sitting blindly.

The sutra says: "If your eyes are bright, and the light shines through in all directions, and there is no more darkness, this is called the end of the skandha of form." A single expanse of light penetrates through everything—walls and mountains and rivers and the whole world. But by no means should you think that at this point you have attained supernatural powers. If at this point you would like to be a Buddhist teacher, you are playing around inside the domain of the skandha of form.

In this domain of the skandha of form, there are still ten kinds of realms that are all realms of delusion. Go read the sutra for yourself and find out about them. You will be completely deluded again and again if in that domain you fool around with the *ch'i* channels, the three channels and the seven chakras, or the upper and lower fields of elixir.[7] What are you doing there? All of this is in the domain of the skandha of form. You want to get to the point where the skandha of form is exhausted, and empty out your physical existence. Do you

---

[7] For the fields of elixir (in Chinese: *tan-t'ien*), see Master Nan's *Tao and Longevity*, pp. 10-11, 25-28, 57-58.

think you will achieve enlightenment when you have opened your *ch'i* channels? You can do this to the full extent possible, and you will have done no more than reached the end of the skandha of form. If you can reach the point where the skandha of form is exhausted, and your body is truly emptied out, it is not a matter of talking about energy channels or no energy channels: this is still something that belongs to the most elementary step.

Buddha said that at this time you at last can "transcend the eons of defilement." You have only leaped to a stage above the five defilements [the defilement of the era, the defilement of afflictions, the defilement of views, the defilement of sentient beings, and the defilement of life], that's all. But have you achieved enlightenment? No!

Further on, Buddha continued and said: "If we observe what this comes from, solidified false thoughts are its basis." These are false thoughts, and they are major false thoughts, not minor ones. When we are sitting there right now, these are minor false thoughts. In that realm, body and mind are both forgotten. It is a major false thought, a big solidified false thought, to think that we ourselves do not have false thoughts.

In this section, Buddha tells you that in the domain of the skandha of form, there are ten forks in the road. The ten are important principles: if I were to discuss them thoroughly, I would have to lecture for at least three months. You should go investigate them yourselves. These are all in the realm of the skandha of form and its solidified false thoughts.

The sutra says: "Good people, as you cultivate *samadhi* and *shamata*,[8] the skandha of form will be exhausted, and you will see the mind of all the buddhas, just as images appear in a clear mirror. If you have attainment, but cannot use it, you are still like a person in a nightmare. Your hands and feet are the same, and your vision and hearing are not deluded, but when your mind comes in contact with alien evils, you cannot move. This is called the domain of the skandha of sensation."

There are some people, who have made the effort and have managed to empty their minds, and have emptied them out for a long time, whose bodies become stiff and rigid. The Zen school calls this "dead tree Zen." A Zen verse says:

---

[8] *Shamata* is one form of meditation: it means becoming still, and curbing the scattering of thoughts.

> There are many forks in the road
>   in front of dead tree cliff
> When travelers get here they all slip.

You think you must empty your thoughts, and you think that when you just empty these thoughts, you will be all right. But this is far from it! After you have done it for a long time, your body and mind can both become rigid. A hundred out of a hundred take the wrong road. This is the teaching of the ancients. You should all go take a look at it.

Now you understand. There is nothing at all you should fear: this is something you must pass through. At this point you have arrived in the range of sensation. When you advance another step, it seems that your body is being pressed down by something, that you are being tied down, and you cannot overturn it. When you make the effort to struggle free of it, you will overturn it. Some people then feel that there seem to be ghosts! In fact, this is the functioning of the imaginary imagery of your own consciousness: how could there be ghosts? These are all physical discomforts, things concocted by the mind: there are no such things as ghosts here.

When you have overturned these discomforts, "It is like the end of a nightmare. Your mind detaches from your body. When you look back at your face, you are free to go or stay: there are no more hindrances. This is called exhausting the skandha of sensation." The Taoists speak of the feeling that you have left your body behind as "sending forth the *yin* spirit." What is so wonderful about sending forth the *yin* spirit? You still have not detached from the seventh and eighth consciousnesses.[9] Warmth, life, consciousness are still there, and so you can see yourself breathing.

---

[9] Vijnanavada theory distinguishes eight forms of consciousness. The first five consciousnesses are associated with the senses of sight, hearing, smell, taste, and touch. The sixth consciousness is the conceptual faculty, the intellectual mind that categorizes experiences. The seventh consciousness (*manas*) evaluates experiences and produces motivations accordingly. The eighth consciousness, called the storehouse consciousness (*alaya*), acts in each person as the repository of all the impressions or seeds that build up through experience, and are used as templates for perceiving further experiences. The eight consciousnesses are analytic categories: in life, they all act simultaneously, and are intertwined. These explanatory divisions of consciousness are much superior to the simple division of consciousness, subconsciousness and supraconsciousness used by psychologists, or the division of consciousness into sleeping, dreaming and waking states, etc.

The sutra says: "Such a person can transcend the defilement of views." At this time it is not a matter of different views, or very learned people, or great thinkers. In reality, so-called learning and thinking are no more than collections of false thoughts.

The sutra says: "When we observe where this comes from, vain understanding and false thinking are its basis." These are still false thoughts, but these are not the solidified false thoughts of the skandha of form. This time the body and mind can get away from them, and false thoughts become like bubbles, and empty out.

"Vain understanding and false thoughts" are still a major form of false thinking. In fact, all the five skandhas are large false thoughts. If you are in the domain of the skandha of sensation, and you cannot be clear, you are still in the realm of the ten major delusions. But spiritual powers and insanity are twins. When these realms come to you, do not interpret them as holy. Hold fast to what *The Diamond Sutra* says: "Whatever has form is all false. If you see that all forms are not forms, this is seeing the Tathagata."[10] Don't pay any attention to your mystical experiences, and don't think you have attained enlightenment. This will help you make progress. "If you understand them as holy," if you think your accomplishments in your meditation work are wonderful, and that this is enlightenment, "then you are subject to a multitude of evils," and you will fall into the planes of the angry demigods and demons.

Thus, between enlightenment and delusion, between hell and heaven, between sentient beings and buddhas, there is just a momentary gap, and then, too, there is no gap; there is just a fine line separating them, and then, too, there is no line. To go from an ordinary person to achieve buddhahood, all along the way you rely on the principle of *prajna*, of wisdom. If this idea is not clear, we must rely on the Buddha's experience. In *The Surangama Sutra* account of the fifty forms of delusion caused by the skandhas, Buddha has taken almost all the realms of meditation work, almost all the secrets, and revealed them to you. In fact, if you can employ this account of the fifty forms of delusion caused by the skandhas properly, then you

---

[10] "Tathagata" is an epithet of the Buddha, meaning "the one who has come from Thusness." Buddha as the teacher of the path of enlightenment is an emananation of Reality-As-It-Is, or Thusness (*tathata*).

will not be deluded. If you cannot use them properly, then you're finished, then down you go. It is like climbing up a staircase of ten or more flights: if you cannot climb up two flights, then down you go. This is an area you must pay attention to in the work of cultivating practice.

Therefore, the statement in the title of *The Surangama Sutra* about "the ultimate meaning of cultivating and realizing the secret basis of Great Buddha Crown Tathagata" truly enunciates clearly a secret meaning. Thus in *The Diamond Sutra* Buddha says: "Subhuti, the Tathagata is one who speaks truthfully, one who speaks factually, one who speaks about things as they are, one who does not lie, one who does not speak words that diverge from the truth." Shakyamuni Buddha has not cheated us, and he has not deceived us. It's just that when we read the sutras, we ourselves have not comprehended his secret basis or comprehended the methods of cultivation and realization he has told us about.

The foregoing has been our second outline, an outline about cultivation and realization.

# 3

# THE FIVE SKANDHAS

When you read this book, it is like going to the market to buy vegetables. Once you have bought the vegetables, you have the basic
ingredients to do your cooking. I hope that when you read the material, after you have understood my ideas, you yourselves will go seek
realization and cultivate practice. The essential framework for the
previous two chapters was threefold: seeing the truth of the Buddhist
teaching, cultivating realization, and carrying out vows. These are
the keys to self-cultivation.

Cultivating *samadhi* is no more than one item in the process of
cultivating realization. *Samadhi*, or meditative concentration, is a common method in the world that the Buddha Dharma and the non-
Buddhist paths have in common. Meditative concentration is not a
method peculiar to the Buddha Dharma. Therefore, do not equate
meditative concentration with the Buddha Dharma. You must clearly
recognize that the method that the Buddha Dharma does not share
with other paths is *prajna*, or wisdom.

*Samadhi* is one form of cultivating practice, but cultivating wisdom is not apart from *samadhi*. In other words, people following non-
Buddhist paths can all achieve meditative concentration. How could
it be that those of you who are studying Buddhism could not manage
to do this? Shakyamuni Buddha said, "The buddhas can master all
forms of knowledge, and penetrate to the source of the myriad dharmas." The buddhas can master all the myriad teachings, and be teachers to devas and humans. Since you want to study Buddhism,
naturally you must all learn *samadhi* and develop *prajna*.

In your *prajna* is not sufficient, then the Buddha Dharma becomes
a realm of delusion, which we cling to and make into a "self." For
example, the realms of the five skandhas—the skandha of form, the
skandha of sensation, the skandha of perception, the skandha of synthesis, the skandha of consciousness—become equal to the fifty kinds
of delusion involving the skandhas that they can generate. When
some people sit in meditation, as soon as they hear of "running into

the fire and going among the demons of delusion," they are terrified. Thus they go among the demons of delusion on the spot, and cannot keep sitting.

In reality, where does the fire come from? Where do the demons of delusion come from? The Chinese character for "demon of delusion" is a transformation of another character, which was devised in order to transliterate the Sanskrit word *mara*; originally there was no such character. Just as the people of the whole world speak of ghosts, this concept of demons cannot be separated from the pattern of thinking of the human race. When it comes to "heaven" and "spirits," the ideas of West and East are all the same. When there are ghosts in your consciousness, then ghosts come. As the saying goes, "You open your mouth and the spirit breath scatters, your mind moves and the fire work goes cold." Running into the fire and going among the demons of delusion is your mental activity going wrong, something you make for yourself. It is yourself deluding yourself, that's all. There are fundamentally no such things as demons in the world: it is just a case of ordinary people making trouble for themselves.

The saying, "Running into the fire and going among the demons" is something written at random in a novel about wandering warriors. Why do I mention it? Because we have cited the realms of the five skandhas. Each of the skandhas has ten realms of delusive demons. In fact, there are not only ten: Buddha was just speaking of the basic principle when he used the figure ten. Everything in present-day society, and human psychology, and the development of civilization, is the realm of the demons of delusion, but no one has seen this clearly. One reason is that the Buddhist scriptures are already too ancient, and people are perplexed by them. The other reason is that people are too modernized, and do not see clearly. Combining these two factors, we know that our Buddha, the Tathagata, with his great compassion, has already explained everything.

If I were to give a complete explanation of the fifty kinds of delusion associated with the skandhas, it would take several months, so for now I'll be brief.

When I first introduced the realm of the skandha of form, I mentioned the scriptural statement that "solidified false thoughts are its basis." Buddha has analyzed false thinking very clearly. Some people do not understand what the phrase "solidified false thoughts" means. You have all paid a visit to a hospital for the mentally ill, haven't you? That unbreakable pathological psychology which creates mental illness is one form of solidified false thoughts. Strictly speaking, if we enlarge our scope of discussion, the whole of the realm of the skandha of form is all in the province of solidified false thoughts. We must exhaust the skandha of form: only then can we break out of the boundaries of false thought.

Let us now take another look at what the situation is after we have exhausted the skandha of sensation. The sutra says: "When a person has cultivated *samadhi* to the point that the skandha of sensation is exhausted, even though defilements are not totally ended, the mind separates from the physical form like a bird escaping from a cage. This the person can already accomplish. From this body of an ordinary person, he mounts through the sixty holy stations of the bodhisattvas, and attains an embodiment generated by will, so that he is unobstructed wherever he goes."

When we feel comfortable as we sit in meditation, when after a little while our legs get numb, these feelings are all within the scope of the skandha of sensation. The skandha of sensation is exhausted only when we escape from these configurations of feeling. When the skandha of sensation is exhausted, by no means is it like being a dead man. It is a feeling of joy, of comfort, of merging with the universe, of merging with space. It is indescribable, and I don't want to describe it, because if you have not reached this realm, there is no way for you to understand.

After the skandha of sensation is exhausted, even though we have still not reached the end of defilement, still the mind is already capable of leaving the physical body, like a bird escaping from a cage, and we attain the bodhisattva's body generated by will.

When you read this, do not falsely imagine that if you can reach this level you can go to America without having to buy an airline ticket, that you can say "I'm going" and just go, that other people will not be able to see you, but you will be able to see them!

[The sutra says:] "It is like a man sound asleep who talks in his sleep. Though this man knows nothing about it, his words are clearly enunciated and in order. Those who are not asleep understand everything he says. This is called the domain of the skandha of conception."

When you arrive in this realm, you are like a man talking in his sleep while dreaming. In his dream, he talks very clearly and in an organized way, but after he has spoken he forgets it. He must ask a bystander, and the bystander will tell him exactly what went on.

Buddha uses this metaphor to explain that while people can detach from mind, but cannot be their own masters, it is like talking in a dream. The person talking in his dream seems to understand, and also seems not to understand. When you reach this realm, you are still within the scope of the abilities of thinking, you still have not left the realm of consciousness. This still is within the scope of the skandha of conception. In other words, your false thoughts are still moving.

But Buddha did not stop when he had said this. He went on to add: "If moving thoughts are ended, and floating conceptions are dissolved away, toward the mind of enlightenment it is like getting rid of dust and dirt, so that birth and death are equalized, and there is perfect awareness from beginning to end. This is called exhausting the skandha of conception. The person who does this then can transcend the defilements of affliction. If we observe what this comes from, dissolving through false thoughts is its basis."

When you have transcended the realm of conception, then it is as if there is no more dust and dirt on the illuminated true nature of mind. If no thoughts are moving in the mind, and floating ideas and miscellaneous concepts are all gone, then it is as if there is no more dust and dirt on the mind of illumination. Only at this point can you begin to talk of birth and death. The biggest problem for people is the fear of death: they do not know where they come from when they're born, or understand where they go when they die. Hence the saying, "On the road ahead, birth and death are both very vague." If a person in the dark is afraid of ghosts, it isn't really ghosts that he fears, it's mainly fear of the unknown. When you find out what sort of thing ghosts are, then you no longer fear them.

If at this very moment the skandha of conception were ended, then you would know how you come to be born and where you go when you die. Arhats of the lesser vehicle can end the portioning out of birth and death to themselves. What is the birth and death portioned out to us? It is the retributive reward of the three realms [the realm of desire, the realm of form, and the formless realm] and the six planes of existence [as celestial beings, as human beings, as angry demigods, as animals, as hungry ghosts, as hell-beings] that we attain in response to all our defilements, our good and evil karma, the barriers of affliction, and the factors which help us toward enlightenment. These retributive rewards have differences in the way they are portioned out, and so they are called "portioned out birth and death."

All ordinary people with deluded perceptions and thoughts are all in the midst of portioned out birth and death.

Cycling in the six planes of existence is the birth and death portioned out to us. Arhats can stop the portioning out of birth and death to them, but this is not the ultimate stage, because they have not finished with the birth and death of transformation: they have only asked for some time off. (The so-called "birth and death of transformation" refers to the rewards of pure lands beyond the world, brought about by the karma of stainless virtue and the factors aiding enlightenment, but which still rely on the barriers of knowledge. This is the birth and death experienced by the sages, from the level of arhats who have cut off deluded perceptions and thoughts, on up.) Only when they reach the realm of bodhisattvas can they finish with the birth and death of transformation. Therefore, if you don't want to come back next time, it won't be that easy! Even arhats can do no more than request a long vacation.

At this point, after you have managed to achieve the state where thoughts do not stir, you have to pay attention to the next sentence in the sutra's teaching: "Floating conceptions are dissolved away." Many people who study Zen fall into this realm where thoughts do not stir, and think that this is the ultimate. Thus it is very easy for those in the Zen school to fall into the realm of the lesser vehicles, hold onto that emptiness, and think that it is enlightenment. Though this lecture is on the Mahayana, in fact the goals of Mahayana are very difficult to accomplish. Mahayana takes carrying out the bodhisattvas' vows as the principle thing, with seeing truth and cultivating realization as auxiliaries. How could it be to carry out the vows of bodhisattvas? It is very difficult!

When your meditation work reaches this level, this is still only dissolving false thoughts. You must reach another realm before you can be free of afflictions. At this point you have only dissolved away superficial false thoughts—"Floating conceptions are dissolved away"—this cannot be separated from the functioning of false thoughts. Buddha has given a very clear account: at this point, you are still within the scope of the capabilities of thought.

The sutra says: "When a person has cultivated *samadhi* and the skandha of conception is ended, this person's ordinary dreamlike thoughts are dissolved away, and he is always the same whether awake or asleep. Illumination is empty and pure, like a clear sky, without any more reflections of the coarse sensory objects before him.

He views the world's lands and mountains and rivers as images in a clear mirror, which come without sticking, and depart without a trace. He perceives and responds with empty receptivity, without any of his old habits. All there is is a single pure essential reality. From this point, the root source of birth and death is revealed. He sees all classes of sentient beings in all the worlds of the ten directions in all their varieties. Though he has not yet fully comprehended the particular originating points of each of their lives, he sees the basis for the life they have in common. It is like a wavering haze, glittering, pure but whirling about. This is the ultimate pivot point of floating sense faculties and sense objects, so this is called the domain of the skandha of synthesis."

Form, sensation, conception, synthesis, and consciousness—the five skandhas—are equivalent to fifty realms. According to the principles in the Buddhist scriptures, there are more than several tens of millions of kinds of realms. Thus, the average person's mental state is never correct nor everlasting. Saying they are not correct nor everlasting doesn't sound too good, so the average person is termed an upside-down deluded sentient being.

The spiritual powers that go with ending the skandha of conception are great indeed! First of the supernormal spiritual powers is the power of remembering past lives. In the past when I was in Mainland China, there was an old monk whose mindfulness was unified and purified, whose practice was always consistent, and who was able to influence the material world using his spiritual powers. He asked me to become his disciple, but I did not. Indulging in spiritual powers is forbidden by the disciplinary precepts of monks: they cannot be trifled with. Those who violate the precepts are usually punished. Later on this monk lost both his arms, and he was driven out of the monastery.

What then does it mean, to exhaust the skandha of conception? *The Heart Sutra* tells you: "There is no ignorance, and no ending of ignorance." Where does ignorance go? It is transformed. Doesn't Vijnanavada philosophy tell you that we transform consciousness into wisdom? In reality, this explains it completely, but this explanation is useless, and has harmed people. But if it did not explain completely, this would also harm people. Thus Buddha said, "Don't speak! Don't speak!" It's best to keep our mouths shut about such matters, because they are too difficult to go into.

The foregoing discussion is all in the area of the skandha of conception. I'll tell you a secret, the Tathagata's secret basis: the center of the five skandhas is conception. In Vijnanavada, they categorize conception and thinking among the "five omnipresent actions" as the most important.[1]

Thus, you take the Buddhist scriptures and try to reach a synthesized understanding of them; you search through the whole Buddhist canon section by section; you bore into it until you cannot crawl out of it. Anyone who is able to crawl out of it then will be able to say, "It's no more than this." However, the people who can bore their way out of it are not the same: this is idle talk. Now I'm telling you: it is this realm when the skandha of conception is exhausted.

If we move along another step, it is the realm of the skandha of synthesis. After the skandha of conception is exhausted, ordinary dreamlike thoughts are obliterated. In *The Heart Sutra* it says: "Far removed from delusions and dreamlike thoughts is final nirvana." The phraseology is similar to *The Surangama Sutra's* "dreamlike thoughts are dissolved away," but what is being described metaphorically in the two texts is not the same. *The Heart Sutra* is talking about reality itself, while *The Surangama Sutra* is talking about cultivation and realization. The main themes are not the same, and so we should not confuse them.

What does it mean to say "dreamlike thoughts are dissolved away"? There's the saying, "Sages have no dreams, ignorant people have no dreams." For now it doesn't matter whether or not you have dreams while you sleep, because many people forget them when they wake up.

But if we are talking about having no false thoughts and still being able to speak and do things, "to respond when things come, and not try to hold onto them when they pass away," so that this mind is even and still—can people who study Zen manage to be like

---

[1] The five omnipresent actions are: intentionality, contact, sensation, conception, thinking. *The Ch'eng Wei-shih Lun*, a Vijnanavada treatise, says: "This [*alaya*] consciousness interacts with several mental states. It is always interacting with contact, intentionality, sensation, conception, and thinking. The *alaya* consciousness, from time without beginning, as long as it is not yet transformed, revolves through all stations, always interacting with these five states of mind. Thus it is controlled by these five omnipresent mental states."

this? They cannot! Opinions are very numerous. Only if you can genuinely reach the end of the skandha of conception can you reach the
level where "dreamlike thoughts are dissolved away, and you are
always the same whether asleep or awake."

Have you gotten to the level where you are the same whether
asleep or awake? We can say there's no such thing as getting halfway
there. If you can really get to this stage, you will sleep very com-
fortably there, you will be able to hear yourself snoring, and you
will only have to sleep for an hour to get the equivalent of seven
hours' sleep. There is also another interesting thing. You will know
clearly that while you are asleep, there are no crudities in your mind:
how nice this is! Compared to this, the great treasury of light that
Zen master Han-shan experienced that time on the summit of Mt.
T'ai-shan falls far short.

The sutra says: "He views the world's lands and mountains and
rivers as images in a clear mirror, coming without sticking, and going
without a trace. He perceives and responds with empty receptivity,
without any of his old habits. All there is is a single pure reality. From
this point, the root source of birth and death is revealed."

When the person cultivating practice reaches this realm, he looks
upon all the things and events in the world, and it is very good, it is
just like looking at all this in a mirror. At this point, as the Zen saying
goes, "The people of the time see the flower before their eyes as if in
a dream."

Thus, when people who only read books read this kind of sutra,
how can they possibly understand? This text explains a realm of meditation work, like the light of a lamp illuminating myriad forms.
"When things come he responds, and when they go he does not try to
hold them back." There is mutual influence and response: after he
has responded, that's it, they are not there any more. "Without any of
his old habits," he looks upon everything in the world as empty illusions: they come to him and he deals with them, they depart and
they're not there. He still gets angry, but after he is finished, he har-
bors no leftover feelings at all. If you are wrong, he rebukes you,
because you should be rebuked; but after the incident is over, it
doesn't exist any more. He is not like the average person, who is concerned in his mind with every little thing.

By this time, all the habits of the past have been transformed,
and all he sees is that there is one thing in his life. What thing? "In
heaven and earth, in the midst of space and time, there is a jewel

within, hidden in the mountain of form." This thing is really there. If I speak at the level of phenomenal appearances, when your meditation work reaches this point, you will truly become aware that there is something in life that has come back to your personal existence. It is not a soul, and it is not a material substance. It is absolute mind only, and it can give birth to the myriad things and events. It is precisely what Mahasattva Fu was talking about in this verse:

> There is a heaven and earth before things
> Formless, fundamentally quiet and still
> It can act as the master of the myriad forms
> It does not wither along with the four seasons.

When this comes, it will be however you want it to be, and you are absolutely able to control mental objects. There is no way for *The Surangama Sutra* to describe this thing, so it called it "pure essential reality." The word *jing* "pure essence" also can mean "semen" in Chinese, but what is meant here is not physical semen. In other words, physical sperm and ova are things that come from transformations of that thing, that pure essential reality: every cell and every nerve and all the rest are all produced by transformations of it.

Therefore, if you have not reached this realm, you shouldn't even be talking about cultivating *samadhi*. Nevertheless, to reach this realm is only a start. When you have just begun to cultivate its practice, you cannot figure that you have succeeded. Thus, to study Buddhism is scientific: one plus one equals two. If you haven't reached this "one," you shouldn't brag! At the moment, you may not be able to understand this portion of the Buddhist scriptures. You will only be able to understand it when your meditation work gets there.

"Pure essential reality" was also what Zen teacher Pai-chang was talking about when he said: "The light of spiritual awareness, shining alone, far removed from sense faculties and sense objects, revealing in its essential body true eternity, not confined to words, detached from false objects: this is the Buddha of Thusness." This is the same thing.

But when people investigate the Zen school, in general when they say they have found this, or they have seen this—that stage is certainly not Buddha: it is just that they have been able to recognize the road to go toward buddhahood. Even if, as *The Surangama Sutra* says in this passage, you "perceive and respond with empty receptivity, without any of your old habits, and all there is is a single pure essential reality," it is still the case that after this, "from this point, the root source of birth and death is revealed." That is, you have still not become enlightened. In fact, after the skandha of conception has been exhausted, it is still false thought.

When the skandha of conception has been exhausted, you enter into the phenomena of the realm of the skandha of synthesis.

"He sees all classes of sentient beings in all the worlds of the ten directions in all their varieties. Though he has not yet fully comprehended the particular originating points of each of their lives, he sees the basis for the life they have in common. It is like a wavering haze, glittering, transparent but swirling about. This is the ultimate pivot point of floating sense faculties and sense objects, so this is called the domain of the skandha of synthesis."

At this stage, you see the many different species of living beings. Altogether there are twelve classes of sentient beings distinguished in the sutras. (These are also abbreviated to ten kinds of different forms of birth: born from wombs, born from moisture, born from eggs, born from transformations, with form, without form, with thought, without thought, not with thought, not without thought, etc., twelve classes of living things.) When you reach this realm, you can see all the various species of living beings in the worlds of the ten directions, and see them very clearly. At the same time, you "see the basis for the life they have in common." You see the original motive force of this life of ours. That is, you see the basis in the force of karma for every form of life, you see that there is something moving there.

To shift to a materialist analogy, it is like seeing atoms in science: there are atoms in motion, and although the forms of things are not the same, and each has its own configuration, their basic structure is all composed of atoms. The "basis for life" in the formation of these mental objects is like electric power in motion.

Recently journalists have been writing about reproduction without sex. People have asked me whether this is possible or not. I say it is possible: in theory it is possible, but whether it can be accomplished in science or not, I don't know. There was a fellow student of ours who just returned from overseas, and he said we must not be deceived, that this is just a counterfeit, and he himself was not sure whether or not this could in fact be accomplished.

Talking from the Buddhist perspective, natural life in the realm of desire depends on two sexes, depends on desire. No matter whether in the realm of desire, the realm of form, or the formless realm, all life has something in motion. This thing is "like a wavering heat haze." In Chuang Tzu's ancient colloquial Chinese, the word for "wavering heat haze" *yeh-ma* literally means "wild horse," but this is not a horse. Chuang Tzu says: "A wavering heat haze, blowing dust and dirt, living things blown back and forth by its breath." This thing in motion, the life-force, is like flames, like reflections of light. These bodies that we receive as our karmic reward, our lives, come from a common basis of life. When the sutra says "shimmering," it does not mean emitting light with physical form; rather, it is describing this flash of movement when it stirs and enters the womb. This is also the inner *yin* body, a phenomenon of the skandha of synthesis.

Sometimes those of you who have power from meditative concentration suddenly see a shadow flashing by right in front of you—it is this inner *yin* body headed into a womb. Naturally it is not looking for you and it just passes by, and is gone very quickly.

"Pure but whirling about" refers to the chaotic motive force in the midst of a pure and still realm. The sutra speaks of "floating sense faculties and sense objects." When you rub your eyes, immediately there are points of light. These are a kind of illusory phenomenon, the light produced by physical stimulation. Investigate this phenomenon: if you do not investigate it and believe in it, you will be confused.

The sutra speaks of "the ultimate pivot point." When the meditation work of a person cultivating practice within the realm of the skandha of synthesis reaches this point, it is precisely the skandha of synthesis, the process of putting together the life-worlds of sentient beings. For *samadhi*, you do not have to rely on sitting meditation: in the midst of *samadhi*, you know the source of every form of life very clearly. You even clearly comprehend the motive force for your own life and the motive force in the formation of mental objects.

This realm is called the "domain of the skandha of synthesis." Synthesis [in Sanskrit, *samskara* "putting together"] is motion. *The Book of Changes* says: "Heaven moves with strength, and the superior person uses this to strengthen himself ceaselessly." Synthesis, the process of putting together the life-worlds of sentient beings, is the perpetual motion of the universe. In Chinese culture this is called, "leaping with life, with everything in motion." If it were not moving, the universe would crumble. Some people say that sitting meditation is stillness. In fact, entering *samadhi* is a great movement, reaching this domain of the skandha of synthesis, and then clearly seeing the motive force of birth and destruction.

The sutra says: "This pure but chaotic shining original nature enters into its original clarity. Once it clarifies its original habits, it is like the change to clear water when the waves die down. This is called exhausting the skandha of synthesis. Then the person can transcend the defilements of sentient beings."

When the waves are not functioning, the universe returns to a state of great stillness and transcends this state of great stillness. It is described as clear water: the waves of change do not arise. A Zen verse says:

> The night is still:
>     thirty thousand miles of ocean waves
> The moon is bright in the sky:
>     under the staff the heavenly wind.

Buddhist monks must make special efforts toward Chinese culture to preserve the records it contains of times of pure cultivation, as in this verse. These records should be contemplated often. The time described in this verse is this realm of the end of the skandha of synthesis. Another Zen verse says:

> Lake T'ai-hu stretches thirty-six thousand acres
> Whom can I tell about the moon in the wave-mind?

This verse also describes this realm, that is, the realm where the skandha of synthesis is exhausted.

Buddha has given you a step-by-step, sequence-by-sequence explanation, and there is no way to skip stages. *The Surangama Sutra* says: "With inner truth, there is sudden enlightenment. Through this awakening, everything is dissolved. But phenomena cannot be suddenly cleared away. They are exhausted through a step-by-step process." There is no way to let you skip stages. When you cultivate practice and reach this point, then you can transcend the defilements of sentient beings and you can be liberated from the basis of birth and death.

The sutra says: "Observing what it comes from, hidden false thinking is its basis." This is still major false thinking. Buddha is not wrong when he talks about this major false thinking. Take note! This is how to cultivate realization of the secret basis. You must get a firm grasp of the title of this scripture: the secret is in this. Buddha was not speaking incorrectly about this false thinking.

Buddha lets you recognize clearly the following points. False thinking is transformed into solidified false thinking: this is the realm of the skandha of form. It is transformed into the false thinking of empty awareness: this is the realm of the skandha of sensation. It is transformed into comprehensive false thinking: this is the skandha of conception. It is transformed into hidden false thinking: this is the skandha of synthesis. But where is the one that is not transformed?

Shakyamuni Buddha's Buddhism is really a big dictionary: each and every word in it is extremely good. Hidden false thinking raises false thinking to another form. It is hidden and deep, at a limitless depth, so deep it becomes hidden and generates the functioning of unknowable thoughts.

Look at it! False thought can make formless true mind function as solidified thought, as empty awareness, as comprehensive processing, and as hidden false thought. So when you investigate the Buddhist scriptures, you must pay special attention to this.

The sutra says: "When through the cultivation of *samadhi*, the skandha of synthesis is exhausted, then all worldly identities moving in confusion in the dark purity and sharing alike in the workings of life, suddenly crumble away. In the hidden fine net, in the various planes of rebirth, in the deep channels of karmic retribution, deluded responses are cut off. There will be great awakening to the sky of nirvana. It is like looking up in the east after the cock crows, and seeing the pure color of the sun already there. The six sense faculties are empty and still, and no longer run off in disarray. Inside and outside the person is profoundly clear and illuminated, entering without entry. The person profoundly comprehends the original source from which all classes of sentient beings in all the worlds of the ten direction receive life. Observing the source, holding to the origin, he does not beckon all the various kinds of beings. He has already found what is common to all the beings in all the worlds of the ten directions. The pure color of the sun does not sink down: it reveals all the hidden secrets. This is called the realm of the skandha of consciousness."

This is the realm of consciousness only. In reality, the five skandhas are all transformations of consciousness, they are all born from consciousness only. The explanation of the functioning of the five skandhas in *The Surangama Sutra* is not the same as the way they are explained in the Vijnanavada philosophy. Everyone should match them up and study them: only then will you be able to synthesize them.

When you move from the skandha of synthesis to the realm of the skandha of consciousness, this is when the skandha of synthesis has been exhausted, *yang* reaches its zenith and *yin* is born, and you move one step further and enter into the realm of the skandha of consciousness. The realm of the skandha of synthesis also has ten forms of delusion. When you reach the skandha of consciousness, these are no longer called delusions, but rather, outside paths.

What are outside paths? In the Buddha Dharma, the four fruits of arhatship,[2] the path of the *shravakas*, the literalist disciples, and the path of the *pratyekas*, the solitary illuminates, are all counted as outside paths. This is because these paths do not penetrate through to realize the fruit of the path of enlightenment. Thus, from this point of view, they are all outside paths. This is based on what Buddha said.

There have been quite a few great thinkers and great philosophers who have not been able to achieve enlightenment because lifetime after lifetime they have been fond of playing with thoughts, and have gone on playing with them forever. It will take a good many eons before they will be able to turn back. Buddha was not wrong when he spoke like this. He felt sorry for them, because they have been trapped by their thoughts and knowledge, and have been revolving around within them for a long time. Still, they cannot fall into the three lower realms of existence, the realm of hell-beings, hungry ghosts, and animals. As *The Surangama Sutra* says, "With pure thought you fly; with pure feeling you fall." People who play with thoughts go upwards, but people who are dragged around by feelings and desires can fall downwards.

Therefore I always say, there are many intellectuals who do not manage too well with their wives and families, and it is always because they have gone too far in the development of their thinking. The Buddhist scriptures explain what kind of life you may fall into according to the proportion of emotion and thinking in your life. According to this, all living things, including all plants, all have attachments.

When you reach the stage when the skandha of synthesis is exhausted, can you really completely comprehend this world? The

---

[2] That is, entering the stream of enlightenment by embarking on the Buddhist Path, reaching the level of having to be reborn only once more, reaching the level of not having to be reborn again, and reaching the level where the passions are extinguished and one becomes an arhat.

phrase in the sutra, "the various planes of rebirth," means the constant ceaseless revolving through birth and death in the six planes of the cycle. At this time, because of "the retribution incurred by the karmic principle of cause and effect," you come back to settle accounts. At this time, when you have exhausted the skandha of synthesis, you can know just where the main point of your inner *yin* body is located. Afterward, this power cannot suck you in. However, the average person is gone, back into the cycle of birth and death as soon as it sucks him or her in. But, when you have reached the stage of exhausting the skandha of synthesis, you can get a long vacation from this birth and death.

Some people sit in meditation and they cannot sit for very long before they are unable to sit steady: either their legs get numb, or they feel they cannot sit steady, or they want to take a look at their watches. The function of the skandha of synthesis is sure to start moving if you sit for a long time: as the Sixth Patriarch said in the famous story, "Perhaps it is your mind moving." Whether you believe this or not, try it and see!

If you are studying Zen, every place is a meditation topic: study it, observe it, why is it so? Why is it that a person who gets up every day at six o'clock can get up on time every day? Because your nervous system has something of a grip on it. These everyday things are all occasions for learning, they are all meditation topics. A buddha—an enlightened person—can master all forms of knowledge, and penetrate to the source of the myriad dharmas. There should not be one thing you do not understand, or anything you are confused about.

When you reach this place where the skandha of synthesis is exhausted, then the power of the process of karmic influence and response to suck you in is cut off. At this point, birth and death can no longer be the master. Some people can act the master, and some people can only act the master halfway. Some people enter the womb undeluded, but become deluded as they stay in the womb. Some people are still undeluded as they stay in the womb, and become deluded when they emerge from the womb. In the past I had a friend who had some shadow memories of entering and emerging from the womb: this is the principle involved here.

When you have reached this realm, "deluded responses are cut off, and you are about to awaken to the sky of nirvana"—soon you will penetrate through to great enlightenment. Wait till the sky is about to brighten, and observe how a bit of sunlight comes forth. At this time the six sense faculties of the body and mind are pure and clean. They cannot run toward externals: instead, they enter into the realm without entry. This is the Dharma Gate of "realization via perfect fusion in the ear" explained by the Bodhisattva Kuan-yin in *The Surangama Sutra*: "Entering the stream, you forget about where you are, and the entry itself is already still."

At this time, with body and mind, you comprehend the basic root of the lives of all classes of sentient beings. You have the "basis of observing the origin," and you do not go off to be reborn. You can remain in the fundamental state of inherent nature, just as Mahasattva Fu explained in a verse:

> There is a heaven and earth before things
> Formless, fundamentally quiet and still
> It can act as the master of the myriad forms
> It does not wither along with the four seasons.

This is entering into liberation from the domain of the skandha of consciousness of living things.

# 4

# LIBERATION
# FROM THE SKANDHAS

In the last chapter we discussed the phenomenal aspects of cultivation and realization, and mentioned the fifty kinds of delusion associated with the skandhas set forth in *The Surangama Sutra*. All of these are phenomena that appear during the process of cultivating practice. I still have not finished explaining liberation from the five skandhas because in the previous chapter, I only went as far as the scope of the last of the skandhas, the skandha of consciousness. Now I will bring up an important point—the emphasis on cultivating realization. Up until now, all I have done is to explain some basic materials related to cultivating realization.

To discuss cultivating realization, I must cite a classic story from the Buddhist scriptures as an illustration. After Shakyamuni Buddha had passed away, his personal attendant and disciple, the Venerable Ananda, lived on for ten or twenty years. As Ananda grew old, he came to look like his elder brother Shakyamuni Buddha. In the past, in mainland China, the Buddhist nuns were sure to make offerings to the Venerable Ananda, because Buddha had not consented to allow women to leave home to become nuns, but Ananda insistently pressed him on this point until Buddha agreed. Buddha then rebuked Ananda, saying, "Because of this fine thing you have done, my teaching will perish five hundred years earlier." Because Ananda had previously asked on behalf of his aunt that she be allowed to leave home to become a nun, later people called Ananda the Joyous Venerable One. (This does not mean the Joyous Buddha of the Yung-ho Palace in Beijing, built by the Ch'ing emperor Shih-tsung. You should not mix them up.)

While the Venerable Ananda was still in the world, among Buddha's disciples there was a [self-styled] Dharma teacher who had studied with Buddha, and was a follower who attempted to pass on Buddha's teachings. He taught his disciples what he took to be the Buddha Dharma and this was passed on second and third-hand. There were those who thought that this is what Buddha had said.

The scripture relates: "One day the Venerable Ananda entered a bamboo grove, and he heard people chanting this verse: 'If people live for a hundred years without seeing the crane, this is not as good as living one day and being able to see it.'" The followers of this teacher were all chanting this. When the Venerable Ananda heard this, he thought "What a mess!" So he asked them, "Who taught you this?" The disciples told him that their teacher had taught this phrase to them. Ananda told them that what Buddha said was: "If a person lives a hundred years without understanding the Dharma of birth and death, it is not as good as living one day and managing to understand it." Because these misguided students had been pronouncing the verse incorrectly, they had changed it into "without seeing the crane."

After Ananda had set this band of disciples straight, they went back to their teacher to tell him. The teacher said, "You must not listen to Ananda. He is old and confused. It is my version that is right." This time there was nothing Ananda could do. Fortunately at that time there was a sagely experienced eminent man who spoke a verse:

> The verse that those people are reciting
> Is really not Buddha's meaning
> Today they have encountered the Joyous Venerable
>     One
> So they can rely on what he says and understand
>     this.

This verse states that what Ananda said was correct, and what the other one said when he taught was incorrect, and thus sets them straight.

Thus we see that not very long after Buddha's final nirvana, the Buddha Dharma had already been changed to this extent. A hundred years after Buddha's demise, because there were different interpretations regarding codes of discipline and the teachings, Buddhists had split into two factions, the party of the monks, and the party of the "Great Congregation" which included lay people as well as monks and nuns. About four hundred years after the Buddha's demise, there had already developed twenty sects. So nowadays people wrangle over their opinions and try to figure things out. Since the disciples personally instructed by the Buddha were already like this, how much the more so for us in the present day!

When you listen to the Buddha Dharma you must pay attention. You must not give rise to biases and deviations, and turn the teaching of birth and demise into a basic misinterpretation like the crane in the story above. That would really be looking at one thing and calling it another.

Now I will continue to explain the realm of the skandha of consciousness. The scope of the skandha of consciousness is very large. In fact, the scope of all of the five skandhas is very large. This is a realm to explain properly, a positive realm. If they travel the road of genuine correct cultivation of practice, everyone will have to pass through these steps. The road of cultivating practice genuinely and correctly is pretty well set.

*The Surangama Sutra* says: "If in the midst of all that calls to you, you have attained a state of equanimity and balance, and you have dissolved away the six gates, then you succeed whether the six gates are open or closed, your seeing and hearing permeate what is around you, and function interchangeably with perfect clarity."

In regard to the root source of all forms of birth and death, the sutra has already explained this very clearly in its discussion of the scope of the realm of the skandha of synthesis. Here in this passage, the "six gates" are the six sense faculties: eye, ear, nose, tongue, body, conceptual mind. For us ordinary people, if we do not rely on the eye, we cannot see; if we do not rely on the ear, then we cannot hear. Why? The beginningless force of karma in our lives requires us to rely on the individual capabilities of these organs. If we genuinely reach the point where we have success in our cultivation of practice and we are liberated from the skandha of consciousness, then we will be capable of perception without relying on these physical capabilities.

"Dissolving away the six gates" in the passage from the sutra means that the person who has succeeded in cultivating practice is not subject to the limitations and obstructions of the capabilities of the six sense faculties. "You succeed whether the six gates are open or closed, and your seeing and hearing permeate what is around you" means that the eye can function as the ear and the ear can function as the eye. When you hear this you might feel it is somewhat strange, but in reality it is not strange at all. It can be accomplished not only by people who have succeeded in cultivating practice, but in some things even by ordinary people.

For example, when we are paying attention to one thing, we are just paying attention to what is in front of us. But if someone passes by behind us, we know it, without turning around and without using our eyes to look. What modern people talk about as the sixth sense all belongs in the scope of this. However, this is just the tiny bit of understanding that average people have. When we come to what the sutra calls "succeeding whether open or closed," this is a bigger realm.

The next words in the sutra, "seeing and hearing permeate what is around you, and function interchangeably with perfect clarity," explain that the interchangeable functioning of the six sense faculties is not chaotic or mixed up, that right and wrong are always clear. We always say that the six sense faculties of people who have left home to become monks and nuns are perfectly clear. This is where the saying comes from. To say that the six sense faculties are perfectly clear does not mean that they cannot perceive sounds, but rather that they are equally clear, no matter whether listening to sounds that are pretty or ugly, or good or bad, or right or wrong. We will have to discuss this perfect clarity again later.

At this juncture, according to the sutra, "All the worlds in the ten directions, along with your body and mind, are all crystal clear, pervaded with light inside and out. This is called the end of the skandha of consciousness." When we take another step, and are liberated from the skandha of consciousness, what realm do we reach? The whole universe, along with the individual person's physical and psychological being, the whole body and mind along with the universe: everything is fused together into one whole. It is like a crystal clear sphere, illuminated all the way through inside and out, its whole body suffused with light, without any obstructions. Only when you reach this realm does it count as liberation from the functioning of the skandha of consciousness.

To be liberated from the skandha of consciousness is fantastic: we cannot even catch a glimpse of it, or imagine it. Right now if we first penetrate the principle and understand it clearly, then the phenomenal aspect of cultivating practice will be easier. Buddha said that if a person reaches this realm, "this person can then transcend the defilements of life." Having finished with the root of life in the three realms [of desire, form, and formlessness] the person can escape from the three realms. But take careful note: only after completely finishing with the skandha of consciousness can one transcend the defilements of life.

You must also pay special attention to Buddha's conclusion which follows: "When we observe where all this comes from, apparitions, empty nothingness, delusion and false thought are their basis."

To move from the skandha of consciousness and reach "the end of the skandha of consciousness" and from there "transcend the defilements of life"—when we investigate this carefully, it is still the functioning of false thought, it has still never left a moment of thought.

Those of us who study Buddhism and sit in meditation detest false thoughts, and want to chase them away and get rid of them. But look, all of you, if you want to be able to be liberated from the realm of the five skandhas, you will still be relying on them! Everyone now studying Buddhism or Zen, no matter what you are studying, you are always taking the concepts and states of consciousness in your minds that are running back and forth in your brains and making them into thought. But this is just a moment of floating thought, floating on the surface: it is not the true root of false thought and false consciousness. Therefore, at the beginning of *The Surangama Sutra*, Buddha tells Ananda: "Even if you annihilate all seeing and hearing and feeling and knowing, and maintain an inner silence and stillness, this is still the shadow events of discriminating the dust of the Dharma." He also said: "Right now even if you achieve the nine stages of meditative concentration, you will not end defilement or achieve the fruits of the arhats." Buddha is saying that if, in your study of Buddhism, you wipe away all seeing and hearing and feeling and knowing and become pure and clean, you will always still be within the states of consciousness.

The "dust of the Dharma" is consciousness. Why? For example, when you hear that the Buddha Dharma has certain realms, and so on, your subconscious has already been infected. Thus, when you sit quietly in meditation, and [seem to] reach those realms, sometimes they are not real at all: rather, what has happened is that your states of consciousness have called forth those realms. For instance, if you experience the nine states of *samadhi*, and still cannot realize the fruit of the arhats, these supposed states of *samadhi* are just the shadow events of the dust of the Dharma.

The shadow events of discriminating the dust of the Dharma—these are third level recorded images. For example, suppose I am talking. If we made a tape recording of what I say, this would be the second level. If other people take this and rerecord it, this would be the third level, or the fourth level. In the end, this would not be the real sound of me talking at all. In just this way, to reach these realms is still major false thinking, yet it is still reckoned as the correct road.

Buddha is telling you: here in this there are false roads, the outside paths. Of the fifty forms of delusion associated with the skandhas, the last one, the skandha of consciousness, is called the outside path. The approaches of the arhats, the shravakas, and the pratyekas: these are all the views of the outside paths. Buddha says these come from "apparitions, nothingness, delusions, and false thoughts."

The word "apparition" comes from Chuang Tzu. Apparitions are the same as reflected images, or reflections of reflections. Of course they are not real things; they are empty delusions. Yet these reflected images are really there, and so when *The Surangama Sutra* here puts "apparitions and empty nothingness" just before "delusions and false thoughts" it is really a very good arrangement.

Look how hard this one moment of thought is: the five skandhas are equal to this one moment of thought. Sometimes we feel that our thoughts are pure, and that our bodies and minds are pure inside and out. When you are able to reach this realm, half of it is your physiology helping you. You can reach this realm only when your psychological state is comparatively peaceful and quiet. Because these two aspects, body and mind, influence each other, this still belongs to the realm of the skandha of form.

As soon as you go off the track here, there will be a lot of problems. For example, consider our *ch'i* channels at such a time. Strictly speaking, I still haven't discussed *ch'i* channels. All I can say is that your nervous system may suddenly attain to a realm of the sort of peace and quiet you have never experienced before, over and above the realms you ordinarily sense, and the transformation that occurs because of this. When the *ch'i* channels have been opened in the back of the head, you may hear a kind of sound in your ears; when the *ch'i* gets to the eyes, the eyes may develop problems; when it gets to the teeth, the teeth may develop problems; whatever part it reaches, they all may develop problems. After you have understood these problems, you can respond to them all accordingly, and experience realization. If you do not understand this key link, then you may go into the fires of demonic delusions. In reality, there is no fire and there are no demons: these are misperceptions caused by transformations of delusory thoughts in your mind. What you recognize as pure and clear is not pure and clear. What you recognize as the light is not the light. *The Surangama Sutra* therefore explains very clearly the orderly work of gradual cultivation. Sudden enlightenment is not apart from gradual cultivation. Ordinarily, people read *The Surangama Sutra* and get so confused that they overlook what it is trying to teach.

This sutra has so many valuable instructions to offer, but using it is like trying to find precious jewels hidden in muddy wine; you have to struggle to find them. To really understand this sutra, you must read it several times until you are totally fluent in it. In this way, you will be able to extract what it has to offer.

The following is a general summation given by Buddha: "All of you should preserve your aspiration for enlightenment, and hold to the Path of the Tathagata. Take this Teaching and after I am dead transmit it to future generations. Let all sentient beings everywhere awaken to this truth. Let there be no arbitrary opinions or delusions, and do not let yourselves sink down into evil."

Buddha instructed his disciples that they must be sure to preserve their aspiration for enlightenment and make vows. Preserving the aspiration for enlightenment is equivalent to making vows. Confucians call it "preserving the mind"; Buddhists call it "making vows." It means establishing one's intent. Buddha was saying: After I have left the world, take this teaching and pass it on to people who are cultivating practice, and let all sentient beings understand this truth.

"Let there be no arbitrary opinions or delusions, and do not let yourselves sink down into evil." All [arbitrary] concepts, all mistakes in cultivating practice, all are problems of opinion. Mistaken opinions and interpretations are what are called in Buddhist terms "the defilement of views." This world of ours is spoken of as "the evil world of the five defilements"; the defilement of views is one of the five defilements. There are many opinions and ideas in this world. War, for example, arises because of a conflict of ideas. People's afflictions all are produced by opinions. I am right, you are wrong, and everyone starts fighting. When you hold tight to your individual opinions and interpretations, this becomes arbitrary opinions and delusion. When Buddha spoke of "sinking down into evil" he was saying very frankly that you yourselves create evil.

In the sutra Buddha continues: "Protect [sentient beings], nurture them, pity them, rescue them. Wipe out the causal factors of evil, and enable their bodies and minds to enter into the knowledge of the buddhas, so that from the beginning [of the Path] to its consummation, they will encounter no divergent roads." In other words, Buddha is saying: So you must tell everyone about the road of cultivating practice, so that no one will take the wrong road; if they take the wrong road, it will not work.

The sutra speaks of "pure true wondrous illumination, the perfect purity of fundamental enlightenment." "Pure and true" describes this fundamental nature, this thing that is inherent in life. *The Surangama Sutra* does not use the terminology of philosophy, like "True Thusness" [*tathata*] or "The Realm of Reality" [*dharmadhatu*] or "True Nature of Phenomena" [*dharmata*] or "Womb of the Tathagatas" [*tathagatagarbha*]. The sutra expresses itself very directly using phenomenal characteristics.

Each of the Buddhist scriptures has its own points of emphasis. The emphasis of *The Surangama Sutra* is on cultivating realization, and so it uses this clear term—"pure and true." Buddhists say that fundamental true nature is comprised of fundamental enlightenment and the enlightenment that begins [for the individual when the individual breaks through delusion]. Enlightenment to what? Enlightenment to that fundamental enlightenment. It is not a matter of attaining to something else. It is awakening to something that is fundamentally with us all along, something that is fundamentally pure.

The sutra says: "It is not held back by birth and death. All the defilements of sensory objects, and even emptiness itself, are all born on the basis of false thought." Pay attention to this line, "It is not held back by birth and death." It is not that there is no birth and death: birth is there, but birth and death do not hinder it, they do not hold it back or obstruct it, they do not make it dirty or clean, they have nothing to do with it. Therefore Chang Cho awakened to the fact that "Nirvana and birth and death are both optical illusions, flowers in the sky." Not only are birth and death the same as flowers in the sky, but so is nirvana. In other words, if you think that nirvana is a thing, then nirvana is birth and death. To say it another way: if you realize the fundamentally empty illusory nature of birth and death, then birth and death is nirvana. The phrase "is not held back" is used very well here in this passage, and cannot be changed. Look at the Chinese translation of *The Surangama Sutra*. Not a single word can be vague. . . . How much thought went into it!

*The Surangama Sutra* was brought to China by the Dharma teacher Paramiti [circa A.D. 700]. At that time in India, it was prohibited to take Buddhist books outside the country, and violators faced execution. The story goes that Paramiti cut an opening in the flesh under his ribs, sewed the sutra up inside his skin, and thus was able to bring it to China. When we read the sutra, we often overlook all the hardships that took place at that time. Thus there is a prediction in the Buddhist teachings that this sutra would be the last to be transmitted to China and the first to be destroyed when the Age of the End of the Dharma arrives.

The Age of the End of the Dharma has arrived, and some people attack this sutra as false. People in later generations will hear the theory from these critics: they will hear that this is a false sutra, and accordingly will not read it. In reality these critics are not students of Buddhism: they have done no meditation work, no cultivation, and they have no level of realization at all.

In the sutra Buddha follows up with another instruction: "The wondrous, illuminated true essence of this primordial fundamental enlightenment, because of falsity, gives rise to all the worlds that contain sentient beings." This is a big question in the realm of science, and it is also the question Purna asks Buddha in the fourth volume of *The Surangama Sutra*. You say that fundamental nature is originally pure, originally perfectly illuminated, so why then does this material world take shape? The questions discussed in the fourth volume of the sutra is precisely this: through what transformation did this world come forth? When we sit in meditation, why is it that the "field of elixir" below the navel can generate heat?

The secret is here. Buddha takes the secret and reveals it to you. That's why *The Surangama Sutra* calls itself "cultivating realization of the secret basis." Its secret lies within you, but fundamentally, too, there is no secret. "In heaven and earth, in space and time, there is a jewel within, hidden in the mountain of form." It's there in you.

*The Lotus Sutra* also tells you this: the wondrous illumination of the fundamental enlightenment of all sentient beings, because of false thought, gives rise to the worlds which contain them. The worlds which contain them are the material world. The true Buddha Dharma is purely mind only: the material world is a subordinate part brought about by transformations wrought by the capabilities of mind.

Thus Buddha said, "It is like Yajnadata, who couldn't find his head because he thought the reflection was his head." This is how the story goes: in the time of Shakyamuni Buddha, there was a man named Yajnadata living in the city. He grew up to be very handsome.

One morning he got up and looked in the mirror, and he got a shock. Thinking that the image in the mirror was his real head, he imagined he had lost his head. "Where has my head gone?" he wondered. There was a head in the mirror, but what person can see his own real head directly? Is there anyone who can see his own original face or not? When you look in a mirror, the one that is reflected back from the focal point in the mirror is not the real self. Yajnadata went looking for his head day after day until he went crazy.

This story describes things very well, doesn't it? Our real heads have been lost and what we always use are the reflections, third-level illusory reflections.

When ordinary people sit in meditation, they all want to get rid of false thoughts. After you have read and comprehended the Buddhist scriptures, you will laugh out loud at this idea. You will not try to get rid of false thoughts: the sutra says that "falsity originally has no basis!" If you sit there meditating, trying to remove false thoughts, aren't you to blame?

False thoughts are fundamentally empty. For example, suppose false thoughts come. Oh no! You think: "False thoughts, I am going to get rid of you." As soon as you start thinking like this, those false thoughts have already run away and you are still there chasing them away! False thoughts have no root. Therefore *The Diamond Sutra* tells you, "The Tathagata comes from nowhere and goes nowhere: thus he is called the Tathagata, the 'One Who Has Come From Thusness.'" This clearly tells you that false thoughts have no root.

Since false thoughts in themselves are neither cause nor effect, why do you fear them? If you have the ability, think false thoughts for three days and three nights, observe whether or not you can go without sleep, and concentrate on false thoughts. If you can do this, I will bow to you. That's right! There are people who can do this, in the mental hospital there are people who can do it, but even they cannot manage to stick with a single false thought from beginning to end. Their false thoughts also come in waves: one wave passes, and another wave takes its place. This is how false thoughts move. So what false thoughts do you want to get rid of?

The sutra says: "In the midst of false thoughts are established the identities of cause and effect." False thoughts arise on the basis of something else; they are induced by external forms. The Vijnanavada philosophy's concept of "dependent identity" [*paratantra-svabhava*] takes consciousness and the external world and puts the two aspects in opposition. But what you don't understand is that your own body is part of the external world. From the point of view of the sixth consciousness [the conceptual mind], the external world is the first five consciousnesses [associated with seeing, hearing, smelling, tasting, touching]. For example, the physical body is also the external world, a response of consciousness brought about by the transformations of the external world. From the point of view of the eighth consciousness [that is, *alaya-vijnana*, the storehouse consciousness], your physical body, your consciousness and discriminating thought, are all fundamentally the external world.

These are points you must start paying attention to. We see how all the world's people who play around with Vijnanavada philosophy are just like those who play with the *I Ching* [the Book of Changes]. Those who study the *I Ching* and play with the eight trigrams, whether ancient or modern, Chinese or foreign, all fall into the trap of the eight trigrams and never climb out. They play with the trigrams and sixty-four hexagrams, they make charts and note down numbers, they play with such things half the day. It may be all right to climb into these things to play, but if they really want to make use of them, they are unable to. It is the same with those who play at Buddhist studies without seeking cultivation and realization. They can never climb out: they are trapped by all the terminology, and they change Buddhism into a system of thought. They play around with thoughts inside it and go on playing forever. They can play all day long, without helping their own body and mind the least little bit. Therefore, it is very important that you pay attention to the real meaning and intent of the Buddhist teachings.

Many people are not clear about the passage, "Falsity originally has no basis. The identities of cause and effect are established in the midst of false thoughts." Thus in the words of the sutra, people "are deluded about cause and effect, and call this spontaneity."

You know that all cause and effect come from natural spontaneity. This is "natural spontaneity," not in the sense of the word *tzu-jan* in Chinese culture, but in the sense given to it by the naturalistic philosophers within Indian philosophy. This concept of natural spontaneity is a theoretical construct. The "natural spontaneity" of the Indian natural philosophy should not be mixed up with the *tzu-jan* "natural spontaneity" of Lao-tzu and the Taoists. In discussing the history of Indian philosophy, both Chinese and foreign works go wrong from the start on this point: there's nothing to be done about it.

This is the blind leading the blind, rolling around in a pile of dregs. It is totally wrong. There are also several masters among the ancients who went wrong in their writings on the theories of Lao-tzu and their criticisms of Lao-tzu. They lumped together the "natural spontaneity" of Lao-tzu and the "natural spontaneity" of the Indian natural philosophers, so their accounts are wrong, too.

Buddha tells us: "That emptiness seems real but is born from illusion. The natural process of cause and effect is all a judgment of the false mind of sentient beings." Buddha says, that from the point of view of the whole universe, even empty space is not something that exists forever. Earlier in *The Surangama Sutra*, Shakyamuni Buddha says: "You must realize that empty space is born in your minds, like a bit of cloud in the sky." Empty space is a construct of illusory thought. In other words, empty space belongs among the "seven elements" [fire, water, earth, wind, space, perception, consciousness]: it is a material thing, a phenomenon that is subordinate to the true nature of the mind of Mind-Only.

How much the more so with us, we who are phenomena born from cause and effect, creatures clinging to the surface of our earth in a world of empty space and matter, who call ourselves the human race. Even this name is only something our brains have thought up, so we cannot rely on it. Do you understand?

In sum, even empty space is an illusory phenomenon, to say nothing of this learning of ours, this planet of ours in space, this world of ours on the planet, these creatures clinging to this world! These clinging creatures call themselves humans, but this is no more than an illusory thought cooked up in their own brains. Therefore, as Buddha said, "these are all the judgments of the false minds of sentient beings." To make it sound good these judgments could be called inferences; speaking bluntly, they are no more than estimates or guesses.

Buddha said: "Ananda, knowing the arising of falsity, we speak of false causes and conditions. Since falsity is originally nonexistent, when we speak of false causes and conditions, these are originally entirely nonexistent."

Pay attention to this "knowing," the knowing by which you know the arising of false thoughts. At this key juncture, hold tight to the thought that is here in this. "We speak of false cause and conditions." We say that false thought is born of causes and conditions. If you clearly understand that false thought by its very nature is origi-nally empty you will know what Buddha meant when he said, "When we speak of false causes and conditions, these are originally entirely nonexistent," that is, fundamentally empty.

"How ignorant they are, those who pursue deductions from nat-ural spontaneity!" As for those who think that the psychic source of this life comes from natural spontaneity, Buddha doesn't want to say any more about them.

"Thus the Tathagata has revealed to you that the fundamental basis of the five skandhas is false thought." So Buddha says: Before I told you that these five skandhas of ours—form, sensation, perception, synthesis, and consciousness—differ when they are exercising their functions. But when we get to the root of the matter, even though they are not the same, they are all false thought.

The World Honored One follows with explanations of the nature of each of the five skandhas as false thought. Then, to sum up, he says: "These five skandhas you receive are formed by five kinds of false thought." Buddha continues: "Now you want to know the causal basis for them and the progression from the shallow to the deep." In other words Buddha says: If you want to know the causal factors and the scope of their formation, now I will tell you.

The first of the five skandhas is the skandha of form. "Forms and emptiness are in the realm of form." The appearance of any kind of "shape" or "mark" is form. The opposite of the appearance of form, that is, the absence of form, can be said to be a kind of emptiness. Since this "emptiness" is the empty space of the material world, or else the emptiness at the level of psychological concepts, strictly speak-ing, this emptiness is a kind of form: it is the form of emptiness, so it still belongs within the boundaries of the skandha of form. This is the principle in the statement "Forms and emptiness are in the realm of form."

"Contact and separation are in the realm of sensation." For exam-ple, when our hands encounter something, or let go of something, these are the two major phenomena within the scope of the skandha of sensation. This is talking in terms of big principles. If people part from their friends, the feelings in their minds are hard to bear. This is not the kind of contact we are discussing here. What we are talking about is the kind of contact connected with definitions of relatedness formed by the skandha of conception.

The five skandhas must be rolled together in layers. It is like telling fortunes in China in terms of the five elements. The five elements overlap in a complicated way: wood conquers earth, earth conquers water, water conquers fire, fire conquers metal, metal conquers wood. In this analysis, in terms of the five skandhas, the mutual influences back and forth between the body and mind are very great.

"Remembering and forgetting are in the realm of conception." Within the boundaries of the skandha of conception appear the configurations of two great functions, remembering and forgetting. When you forget, then you no longer think of a certain thing; in the world of conception, there appears a vagueness, an indeterminate form. Thus, like remembering, forgetting belongs within the boundaries of the skandha of conception. Remembering and forgetting are two opposite phenomena that fall together in this realm.

"Destruction and birth are in the realm of synthesis." Within the boundaries of the skandha of synthesis appear the configurations of two great opposing functions, birth and destruction.

"Clarity enters into and merges with clarity, returning to the realm of consciousness." This is very hard to explain. "Clarity" means clear and pure. When the mind's perspective reaches total clarity, a single empty awareness, this is the first "clarity" in this passage. "Enter" means to enter into the basic essence of inherent nature, the realm of profound clarity where there is nothing at all. This is "clarity enters into and merges with clarity." This is the area of the eighth consciousness in its true nature as the matrix of thusness, the womb of the Tathagatas.

"This is the starting point of the five skandhas, which arise from it layer upon layer." This is the root source of the five skandhas. These five skandhas are like the five elements in Chinese culture, just as troublesome and complicated to understand. Among the five elements there is mutual influence and they succeed each other in turn as cause and effect. In the Buddhist scriptures there is a work called *Treatise on the Five Skandhas*, but it still does not explain them clearly.

The Indian Buddhist theory of the twelve causal links of interdependent causation, the twelve *nidanas*, is based on the twelve double-hours of the day. It is like the schema in Chinese culture of the twelve earthly branches used to name the double-hours, as well as for other purposes. For example, the first of the twelve *nidanas* is "ignorance," which corresponds with *tzu*, the first branch that represents the time interval 11:00 P.M. to 1:00 A.M. "Action," the second of the twelve *nidanas*, corresponds with *ch'ou*, which is the second branch representing 1:00 A.M. to 3:00 A.M. This is a whole other field of study. In former times in mainland China, in the big temples when they wanted to receive disciples in the abbot's room, they would use "Bodhidharma's handful of gold" to observe the year, month, and day the candidate was born, and calculate if he could become a monk, or if he had no karmic affinity with Buddhism and should not leave home. "Bodhidharma's handful of gold" was based on the twelve earthly branches and the twelve branches came from the twelve links of interdependent causation. Intelligent, wouldn't you say? The Buddha Dharma says that everything is mind alone, so the great Zen teachers did not use this procedure.

"Birth exists because of consciousness. Demise follows from form being removed." In birth and death for an ordinary person, when form is not there anymore, it is called death. In cultivating the Path, "demise follows from form being removed," and the first thing to do is to think of a way to manage the body. If you cannot remove the obstructions of the body, if you cannot get free of the five skandhas, then what's the use? When you close your eyes and sit in meditation, you are only rolling around inside this body. You feel comfortable here, uncomfortable there; you are blocked here, and open through there; you turn back and forth, but you never get out of this body. It is like the rebuke that the masters of the Zen school addressed to people: you shut your eyes and make plans for living on that black mountain, inside the ghost cave.

"In principle, it is sudden enlightenment, and taking advantage of this enlightenment to dissolve everything away. But phenomena are not gotten rid of suddenly: they must be exhausted gradually." Liberation from the five skandhas is a step-by-step affair; it is scientific; it is a basic principle that there is no way to violate. Of course there are people who, once they get started on the process, can be liberated first from the skandha of synthesis or the skandha of consciousness: the procedure is not entirely fixed. Sudden enlightenment pertains to seeing truth; gradual cultivation pertains to cultivation and realization. If you really reach the level of seeing truth, then you are sure to reach the subsequent phenomenal level of cultivating practice. But let me say this again: when you really reach the level of seeing truth, then you must cultivate practice.

The emphasis of *The Surangama Sutra* is on cultivating realization. What I explained previously about "searching for mind in seven places" and "the eight returns" pertains to seeing truth; everything I have explained since then concerns gradual cultivation. In other words, what I have been talking about are the real methods for cultivating realization. In fact, gradual cultivation is not apart from sudden enlightenment, and sudden enlightenment is not apart from gradual cultivation.

I have a comprehensive plan that will provide everyone with a systematic explanation from the first step of beginning to meditate, straight through to cultivating practice. Right now I am still drawing together resource materials for you. Therefore, don't think that what I have said has no structure.

From reading the sutras, it is quite clear that Buddha opposed supernatural powers, but on several important occasions when he expounded the Dharma, he demonstrated supernatural powers. The first time was when Ananda had developed an illness, and Buddha ordered the Bodhisattva Manjushri to go quickly and bring him relief. In *The Surangama Sutra* it relates that Shakyamuni Buddha sat crosslegged and "from the top of his head emitted a fearless light of a hundred jewels, and in the light there came forth a thousand jewel lotuses, each with a transformation body of the Buddha sitting crosslegged within it, intoning spiritual spells, commanding Manjushri to use the spells to go protect Ananda."

Why didn't Buddha go himself and bring Ananda relief? Why didn't he exhibit supernatural powers, reach out with his two hands, and bring Ananda back? These are all cases to meditate on. The second display of supernatural powers was when Buddha emitted a light from his forehead. The third was when he emitted light from the sign for infinity on his breast. The fourth was when he emitted light from his limbs. The fifth was when he emitted light from the lump of flesh in the middle of his forehead. Each time he emitted light it was different. Why? You must investigate all of these cases.

There are some scriptures in which the designs are especially numerous. For example, there is *The Lotus Sutra*, which is entirely made up of stories. But in these stories you cannot find anything. In the first of these stories, Buddha comes into a teaching hall, and before he even opens his mouth, five thousand monks get up and leave. Why is this? There are questions everywhere in these stories. Everyone has been stumped by the philosophical thought in them, and still they say they are good. They think that these important points are fantastic.

When I was writing *A Modern Explanation of the Great Meaning of the Surangama Sutra*, I omitted everything about hell and heaven, because these days no one believes in such things, but in reality, there is a great deal to learn from those stories. For instance, why do people turn into animals? I can see myself get frightened. That is to say, when one of your thoughts or your emotions goes wrong, then cause and effect comes to you.

For several decades I have read a lot. The times are not the same; cause and effect are faster. The stories and parables in the scriptures are very important for cultivating practice. Everyone is of the opinion that the hardest part to understand is "searching for mind in the seven places, and discerning the eight returns." In reality, those concepts are easy to understand. The real learning is in the places that are the easiest to read: these are the places that are the hardest to understand.

Now I will talk about liberation from the seven elements—from earth, water, fire, wind, space, perception, and consciousness.

Before I only discussed the four elements that are related to the physical body. These days people who meditate like most of all to play with *ch'i* channels, the three channels and the seven chakras and such things. They specialize in playing inside the body. Take note! This is only the realm of the skandha of form, that's all. Here you can go on and on playing around: the patterns you can experience are numerous. You can even play around until your head is spinning, until you black out and lose all sense of direction.

If you understand things clearly, then you will know that it is not here, it is not in the physical body made of the four elements of earth, water, fire, and wind. The four elements are born in a moment of thought. Today when people talk about thought, they only know that thinking in the mind is thought; they do not know that even these four elements are also thought. This is all pointed out in *The Surangama Sutra*.

In Dharma teacher Hsuan-tsang's "Verse Guidelines for the Eight Consciousnesses," the verse on the *alaya* consciousness says:

So vast that all the Buddhist scriptures
    cannot exhaust it
Profoundly deep: the objects of the
    seven waves make wind
Subject to influences, holding the seeds
    of sense faculties, bodies and worlds
After they go, before they come,
    it is the master.

"Sense faculties, bodies and worlds" means the sense organs, the human body, and the material world. All of them come about by transformations of this moment of thought. This moment of thought is the force of karma: as thought transforms, so does the force of karma. Thus, when the Zen school completely comprehends mind, it is completely comprehending this moment of thought. This moment of thought is the five skandhas; it is the eight consciousnesses. Cultivation means cultivating this: it is not only cultivating the sixth consciousness. The sixth consciousness comes from moment of thought to moment of thought, and it also goes from moment of thought to moment of thought. Thus, if in a moment of thought you cannot completely comprehend the seventh consciousness, if you cannot completely comprehend the eighth consciousness, then you are hardly learning Zen!

Ordinarily we just get a bit of clear consciousness in our minds. This is something that has to do with only one part of mind—the sixth consciousness. This is far from completely comprehending all eight consciousnesses. When you are on the point of death, and the four elements that make up your physical body are about to disperse, then this clarity and this meditative accomplishment that you have attained through the course of your life will be totally useless, because it only exists at the level of the sixth consciousness alone and it cannot function at all.

When a baby is born, the sixth consciousness does not yet make discriminations, and when a person gets old, it becomes confused and does not function. But all through life, the seventh and eighth consciousnesses are functioning. You must realize this. Thus, when someone is about to die, you tell him to recite the Buddha-name and be mindful of Buddha, and he says, "It's not working! It's not working!" Indeed, it is really working. So what can you say then? At this moment—the moment of death—the sixth consciousness is disintegrating and can only partially function. Therefore, if in a moment of thought you cannot completely comprehend the seventh consciousness and the eighth consciousness, then you are certainly not learning Zen and you have certainly not completely comprehended the moment of thought.

So then, if you can completely comprehend the seventh and eighth consciousness, where are the four elements of earth, water, fire, and wind?

First let us talk about the element of fire. *The Surangama Sutra* says: "The fire of inherent nature is true emptiness. The emptiness of inherent nature is true fire. Pure and clear and fundamentally so, inherent nature pervades the universe. It follows the minds of sentient beings, and responds to their knowledge. It appears according to karma, but the worldly do not realize it: they confuse it with causal conditions and spontaneous nature, but it is all the mind of consciousness. Discriminating thought and judgment are only a matter of language, totally without real meaning."

When you see empty inherent nature, then it's "The fire of inherent nature is true emptiness. The emptiness of inherent nature is true fire." Thus our fundamental teacher Shakyamuni Buddha has taught us lessons in so many precious scriptures and we do not realize it. Many people meditate, and when their bodies get warm, they think it is the "clumsy fire" (kundalini) arising. I ask you to go investigate this to see if it is true. It might even be a symptom of illness. In the generation of warmth in the four intensified practices, warmth and suppleness go together. When you get the warmth, you are rejuvenated. When you see empty inherent nature, it is not just the area below your navel that gets warm; when you see empty inherent nature, then it will be however you want it to be.

When some people sit in meditation, they listen to their breathing and they count their breaths. The sutra says: "The wind of inherent nature is true emptiness. The emptiness of inherent nature is true wind." Breathing is the element of wind. It is a phenomenon that is born and perishes. To use this to regulate the body is not without usefulness, but it will be of no help at all in awakening to enlightenment. True enlightenment is: "The wind of inherent nature is true emptiness. The emptiness of inherent nature is true wind."

The material world is all appearances. It can transform into fire, into atmospheric flows, into lightning. What is hidden behind these appearances is the functioning of the fundamental essence, which is "pure and clear and fundamentally so, pervading the universe." It is the single source of both mind and things. The places that states of mind can reach, material things can reach, and the places that material things can reach, states of mind can reach, too. These two are equally important, and there is no difference in importance between them.

"It follows the minds of sentient beings, and responds to their knowledge." Everything is created by you. That's why when you are meditating, and you feel a certain part of your body get warm, you think that it is a *ch'i* channel opening. I tell you frankly, this is just an opening conjured up by your false thoughts. If we give it a nice name, it is "cultivation and refinement," but if we speak bluntly, it is your false thought acting up. That's all it is, it's not the path to enlightenment. This is inherent nature responding according to the minds of sentient beings: you seek in a certain direction, and its capability develops in that direction. This is why the sutra says "it appears according to karma." It transforms following the force of your karma. The word "appears" is used well. It is not discovered; rather, it is inherent in the universe. It is not created or made; it is just made to appear, and that's all.

Only if you are clear about this will you be good at cultivating practice. There are still a good many important points that I cannot explain fully right now. Right now I want to shift to *The Lotus Sutra*.

These days when Chinese people talk about cultivation and realization, especially in the Zen school, they mention two scriptures: *The Lotus Sutra* and *The Surangama Sutra*. *The Lotus Sutra* came to China earlier than *The Surangama Sutra*. It was transmitted to China in the Eastern Chin era (c. A.D. 4th century) of the Northern and Southern Dynasties Period. This sutra exerted a great influence over Chinese culture. We frequently see things in Chinese literature and learning that come from *The Lotus Sutra*.

The great teacher Chih-i (538-597A.D.) and his teacher, Hui-ssu, founded the T'ien-t'ai school, which reveres *The Lotus Sutra*. Many of the eminent monks of the past who studied pratyutpanna-samadhi (a meditative state in which all the buddhas of all worlds are visualized) followed the line of *The Lotus Sutra* in their cultivation of practice. Really to explain this sutra is very difficult: this is the real One Vehicle Buddha Dharma.

In my other books I have discussed why Shakyamuni Buddha held up the flower at an assembly on Spirit Peak to initiate the mind-to-mind transmission of Zen, and why the Venerable Kashyapa smiled to acknowledge it. While I was in Kuang-chung I had some thoughts about this and wrote a poem to answer an old friend who wanted to leave home to become a monk.

> Zen started with a flower held up and a smile
> Buds of the flower of Spirit Peak fill the
>     spirit platform
> What about the Hua-yen assembly in the Pure Land
> Who also say that the flower has opened and we
>     see Buddha returning?

Buddha was at an assembly on Spirit Peak, and too many flowers were offered to him by celestial devas and humans, and they filled the spirit platform. It is a strange thing, but all along Buddha's teaching was connected with flowers.

Later, I gave my friend another verse to contemplate:

Don't think falsely! You'll waste your doubts
The ascetic left and returned with his head empty
The east wind is blowing straight on, making a
    thousand trees blossom
They all open on South Flower Mountain,
    after enlightenment.

Speaking of *The Lotus Sutra*, why did Buddha hold up the flower? Why did Kashyapa smile? If you stand there and observe the flower, the meditation case will come to you. If you can understand the flower, then you will probably know how to cultivate practice. How can a seed send forth a flower? How can it produce a fruit?

The full title of *The Lotus Sutra* is "Scripture of the Lotus of the Wondrous Dharma." Like Chuang-tzu, it is made up of parables and stories. It makes a special point of saying how much merit there is in expounding the sutra. In Indian culture, they write verse after verse and pile them up into a big pile, but nevertheless, if we have patience and investigate them as we read, every line has a reason. Everywhere in this sutra are meditation cases, stories to contemplate deeply. This sutra really explains the work of cultivating practice.

Volume One, the First Prefatory Chapter of *The Lotus Sutra* begins: "In the East there appeared a good omen." Buddha emits a light and causes the earth to move, and his disciples know that this time when he transmits the Great Dharma will be very special. Yet five thousand monks withdraw from the assembly at the start, thinking that this old teacher has gone astray and has become a heretic, so they leave their places and go. Amitabha Buddha (the Buddha revered by Pure Land Buddhists) is in the West, but in *The Lotus Sutra* the light always comes from the East: "In the East there appeared a good omen." This sutra is wholly made up of stories and each of the stories is a meditation case.

Among Buddha's disciples, the foremost in wisdom was Shariputra. He gets up to ask about the Dharma. Buddha has sent forth such a great light, and set the stage on such a grand scale, and he says, "Enough, enough. My teaching is too inconceivable. I don't want to speak of it. Look at how the five thousand monks have withdrawn." In Volume One of *The Lotus Sutra*, the second chapter, titled "Expedient Means," Buddha says, "Stop! Stop! My teaching is wondrous and inconceivable. The arrogant ones who hear it are certain not to believe it." People all have an attitude of arrogance, especially those who study Buddhism, and they assume that they understand Buddha. "In heaven and on earth, I alone am honorable"—that was Buddha, not you. In this passage Buddha is saying: Many arrogant people will surely be unable to believe the teaching I am about to explain.

Buddha continues: "This Dharma is not something that intellectual judgment and discriminating thought can understand. Only the buddhas can know it." Pay attention! This is the level of seeing truth, something that we who study Buddhism must perceive correctly. The Buddha Dharma cannot be realized by relying on intellectual thought. Here Buddha tells us that the true correct Buddha Dharma is not something that can be interpreted by your thinking and discriminating. The line that follows this is extremely serious and we have not really learned it: "Only the buddhas can know it." The genuine Buddha Dharma can only be known by buddhas. We can only really understand it when we reach the realm of the buddhas. No wonder these five thousand monks withdrew from the assembly. Only buddhas can understand, so why should we study it?

Buddha continues: "What is the reason for this? All the buddhas have appeared in the world for one great mission." He says that all the buddhas appear in the world for one thing, called the great mission. In other words, Buddha says that the Buddha Dharma has just One Vehicle, just one thing, and if you understand it then you will become a buddha.

Buddha continues: "All the buddhas want to enable sentient beings to open up their enlightened perception and make it pure and clear, and so they appear in the world. They want to show sentient beings the perception of the buddhas, and so they appear in the world. They want sentient beings to awaken to the perception of the buddhas, and so they appear in the world. They want to enable sentient beings to enter into enlightened perception, and so they appear in the world."

Pay attention to this! To open up enlightened perception, to show the perception of the buddhas, to let sentient beings awaken to the perception of the buddhas and enter into enlightened perception.

Awakening means awakening to enlightenment; entering means entering into realization. The progression in *The Lotus Sutra* is thus opening, showing, awakening, entering, and at last realizing enlightenment.

Buddha continues: "In this assembly, there are no peripheral people, only those who are genuine and true." After the five thousand monks had left, the dregs were all gone, and those who remained were all genuine types—select people whose minds were pure—who could make the grade.

Buddha says: "Though I speak of nirvana, this is not true extinction." Nirvana is not the nihilistic view of going without coming. What is nirvana? A kind of appearance. Buddha says: "From the beginning, all phenomena have always inherently had the peaceful extinction characteristic of nirvana." Pay attention! What *The Surangama Sutra* just talked about, fundamental nature—if you want to awaken to it, where will you look? "All phenomena" means all the myriad forms of existence, no matter whether spiritual or material, all the phenomenal appearances of all that exists in the world, all in the midst of continuous birth and destruction, all transforming in myriad ways. Before they have transformed, after they have been transformed, while they are in the process of transformation, they are fundamentally from the beginning in nirvana. Fundamentally they are peaceful and extinct and pure. You must comprehend this first of all. This is studying Zen; the Zen school is always bringing up this phrase.

Buddha says to Shariputra: "Having traveled the Path, oh, child of Buddha, in a life to come, you must become a buddha." In other words, Buddha says that if you try in the present to carry out your vows, and cultivate realization, then in a future life, you will become a buddha. Pay attention to this. This is what Buddha said to Shariptura, who was foremost in wisdom among the assembly of monks who were followers of the lesser vehicle.

Buddha says: "The seed of the buddhas arises from causal conditions. Thus I speak of One Vehicle." There are not three vehicles, there is only One Vehicle. But what is this One Vehicle?

"This Truth abides in the station of Truth, while worldly appearances always remain." If you take the previous statement, "From the beginning, all phenomena have always inherently possessed the peaceful extinct characteristic of nirvana," and join it to this statement, "This Truth abides in the station of Truth, while worldly appearances always remain," this is a very good pair of statements, and as soon as you look at them, then you will understand the main essentials.

Where does Buddha say that enlightenment is? It is right here. If you go to hell, it, too, is in hell; if you go to heaven, then it, too, is in heaven. When you are in the paths of delusion, or revolving among the six planes of existence, it is always with you. All phenomena are in the fundamental state: this is the functioning of the basic essence. What about apparent phenomena? "Worldly appearances always remain." All the manifestations of the myriad forms of beings in the world are all just its manifestations; all functioning is just its functioning.

"Having attained knowledge at the site of enlightenment, you speak with the skill in means of a guide and teacher." After you have become a buddha, and you are sitting in that spot, the one awakening is the site of enlightenment. After you have knowledge of this, then you can preach the Dharma with skill in means and however you explain is it.

We have come to the key point in *The Lotus Sutra*. Buddha is very compassionate, and brings up the main points for us in the first two chapters. Because he is preaching to followers of the lesser vehicles, he is afraid their wisdom will not be sufficient, so the best thing to do is explain clearly.

Later on, when Buddha preaches to the bodhisattvas of the Great Vehicle, he just tells stories. He wants you to understand. "You must realize that from the stage of the supreme worldly dharma to the peaceful extinction of nirvana, because the enlightened are using the power of skill in means, although they teach all kinds of paths, in reality these are all the Buddha Vehicle." People who have consummated the Path and awakened to enlightenment are right no matter how they preach. From the supreme worldly dharma to the peaceful extinct realm of nirvana, they have awakened to this Path. Thus Buddha says that when they are preaching the Dharma, even though they introduce all kinds of methods of cultivating practice, speaking sometimes of the lesser vehicles and sometimes of the Great Vehicle, in reality these are all expedient means.

Therefore, in *The Nirvana Sutra*, Buddha says, "I have preached the Dharma for forty-nine years, but I have not said a single word." Why hasn't he said anything? Because "From the beginning, all phenomena have always inherently possessed the peaceful extinct characteristic of nirvana." From the point of view of that metaphysical basic essence, everything is skill in means and nothing more. So even though he taught all kinds of methods, this was all skill in means. The so-called worldly dharmas are just the Buddha Dharma.

*The Lotus Sutra* speaks this way, and *The Vimalakirti Sutra* speaks this way, too. Thus, at the very end, *The Lotus Sutra* says, "No form of livelihood or work is opposed to reality." Everything we do in life is the business of the buddhas. Those who have left home to become monks and nuns should pay attention to this! I am not speaking just to householders. It says in *The Lotus Sutra*, "No form of livelihood or work is opposed to reality." In this there is just a single Dharma Gate, and there is no difference between householders and leavers of home, and no difference between leaving the world and entering the world.

I will continue discussing this point later. Everyone should note that we are progressing from seeing truth to cultivating realization and carrying out vows. Now I am still talking about *The Lotus Sutra* materials related to the aspect of seeing truth, seeing inherent nature. I have not yet talked of cultivating realization. I will talk about that later.

# 5

# A TALK ON
## *THE LOTUS SUTRA*

When I was in seclusion, a friend sent me a letter, and I used two poems by the 16th century Confucian philosopher, Wang Yang-ming, to serve as a reply:

> I see that your new home is on the
>     other side of the mountain
> If I set out by morning in my cart
>     by evening I can return
> I know that for a long time
>     your fence has been down
> Why would you still close your gate
>     in such a remote village?

> Riding off searching, crossing myriad mountains
> Going by boat to the gate and then returning
> Don't make the sickness of the body
>     into sicknesses of the mind
> But where there is no barrier
>     there is still a barrier.

"Don't make the sicknesses of the body into sicknesses of the mind. But where there is no barrier there is still a barrier."

These two lines are excellent. Could it be that you are declining and don't want to see me? In these lines there is this sense of blaming.

In order to cultivate and realize the Buddha Dharma, we are not talking about Buddhist studies, nor are we talking about ordinary Buddhism. We are talking about the road to learning to be a buddha and cultivating realization. We are learning to see the truth of the Buddha's teachings, to cultivate realization, and to carry out the vows of bodhisattvas. These are three aspects of one whole. We can use these three key points in reading all of the Buddhist scriptures.

If you cannot get started in meditation work, it is because you do not see truth correctly. If you do not see the truth of the Buddha's teachings correctly, then you are incorrect in principle, and you will not be able to succeed in carrying out vows, and you will not be able to complete your merit. Why can't you arrive at seeing truth? It's because you have not succeeded in cultivating realization, and because you have not completely carried out your vows. Why can't you succeed in carrying out your vows? Why isn't your merit complete? Because of problems with seeing truth and cultivating realization. The three aspects are one whole, and cannot be divided.

*The Lotus Sutra* and *The Surangama Sutra* are the two great scriptures of the Zen school, but our lecture today is not limited to the Zen school and we will not take the line of the Zen school. We who study Buddhism must pick the road that is advantageous to cultivating realization and take it. It doesn't matter whether or not it is Zen: we must not have sectarian views, or think that Zen is the highest form of Buddhism, or that any school is the highest. The divisions among the schools of Buddhism are all caused by differences in methods. At the basic level, all are the same.

Like Chuang-tzu, *The Lotus Sutra* tells stories. Present day people think that Chuang-tzu specialized in telling boundless stories that are all illusory imagination. This is wrong. A parable is a story in which a message is lodged. They have an objective; they are not told at random.

In the last hundred years and more, the Western children's stories and novels that have been translated into Chinese have usually first followed Japanese translations and then been passed on here. For example, the Chinese term for "philosophy," *che-hsueh*, is translated from the Japanese *tetsugaku*. In these imaginative novels translated from the West, Chinese translators have made use of the parables in Chuang-tzu. Thus, when they were young, our fellow students read Aesop's fables, and later when they read Chuang-tzu, which also tells parables, they thought that this was the same as the Western imaginative novels. This is inverting cause and effect.

In *The Lotus Sutra*, one story follows another, and almost nothing else but stories can be found in it. But you must pay careful attention! Ever since the period of the Northern and Southern Dynasties, this scripture has exerted a huge influence on Chinese culture. The way the eminent monks and nuns in the biographies of extraordinary monks and nuns cultivated the Dharma is intimately linked to *The Lotus Sutra*. *The Lotus Sutra* is also connected in an important way with the Zen school.

The prefatory chapter of *The Lotus Sutra* takes the most important point and puts it at the front. The way the Buddha expounds the sutra this time is different: he emits light and makes the earth move. His eminent, illustrious disciples know that this time the Buddha is going to explain a major teaching.

But there were five thousand monks who had followed Buddha for a long time who turned away and left. They did not want to listen. They felt that on this day the Buddha would teach incorrectly and thought that only what he said in the past was correct. This was because what Buddha had taught in the past was how to cut off delusion and witness reality, how to cut off afflictions and false thoughts, and realize the inherent nature of true thusness. This is the Hinayana Buddhism. By means of the so-called Four Noble Truths and Twelve Causal Links and such teachings, one could realize the fruit of the arhats. But on this day Buddha was going to expound another different teaching, and so these five thousand monks and nuns left the assembly. In other words, they fell into the lesser vehicle, into Hinayana, and took the lesser road. They only understood emptiness, and could not bear to speak of wondrous existence. They did not understand the teaching of interdependent origination. In the Buddhist scriptures these monks and nuns are called "scorched sprouts, spoiled seeds." When the sprouts have been scorched, the seeds cannot grow, and no fruit can develop.

When these five thousand disciples walked out, Buddha was silent, and let them go without saying anything. After they had left, the Buddha said, "In this assembly there are no peripheral members, only those who are genuine and true." He meant that those people who were left were those who were capable of sustaining the Great Dharma.

The first chapter of *The Lotus Sutra* is called "An Omen Appears in the East." This is a label we have given it. The original translations of Buddhist scriptures into Chinese were not divided into chapters. For example, the thirty-two chapters of *The Diamond Sutra* were the division into chapters made by Crown Prince Chao-ming.

When the Buddhist scriptures explain a teaching, sometimes they mention the West: when they explain Pure Land Buddhism, they are sure to mention the West, where the pure land of Amitabha Buddha is located. But *The Lotus Sutra* tells of a good omen appearing in the East. What is the reason for this? This is another meditation case, another point to contemplate. What am I calling a meditation case, a point to contemplate? This is a point to contemplate.

When it comes to studying meditation cases, to contemplation points, you must not go about it in the wrong way and think that it means taking a little question, and turning it over uneasily back and forth in your mind. If you turn it over in your mind all day long and think that this is called studying a meditation case, this is ridiculous. The Buddhist scriptures, as a whole, are a great meditation case.

In *The Lotus Sutra*, why does the good omen appear in the East? Only when it talks about the realm of nirvana do the omens appear in the West. Friends who like to study *The Book of Changes* want to pay a lot of attention to the reasons for these directions. They are relevant; they are not matters of chance.

"This Truth abides in the station of Truth, while worldly appearances always remain." Therefore those five thousand monks had to withdraw; they could not keep on listening. Those monks had specialized in leaving home to cultivate the Path, but after all, Buddha says that the real Buddha Dharma is in the world, and not apart from the world. Within the world or beyond the world, there is nowhere it is absent. "This Truth abides in the station of Truth," and is in accord with the Tao, the one that is fundamentally there. "Worldly appearances always remain," and are in accord with the Tao, and it is not necessary to leave the world before one can consummate the Path and achieve enlightenment.

In the third chapter of *The Lotus Sutra*, "Metaphors," Shariputra speaks a verse:

> The World Honored One knows my mind
> To extirpate falsehood he spoke of nirvana
> When I totally removed false views
> I attained realization of the teaching of
>     emptiness
> At that time my mind thought
> I had reached the stage of extinction
> But now I finally realize
> That this was not real extinction.

First Shariputra says to Buddha: I was wrong, and the World Honored One understood the level I was at. At the time all my misguided false thoughts had been totally cleared away, and I thought that this was nirvana.

Hinayana gets this far. This is truly the highest realm of nirvana. We must not look down upon Hinayana Buddhism. Mahayana Buddhism must take Hinayana Buddhism as the basic foundation. When we talk of cultivating realization, if we do not take this first step, then it will not work! After Shariputra had reached this realm, he sought to progress further, and so he realized his error.

Shariputra says: In the course of my cultivation of practice, I have completely stopped false thoughts and I have reached the realm of emptiness. His verse says: "I attained realization of the teaching of emptiness." We always say that the four elements are all empty, but we only reach this in theory. When you are hungry, you clearly understand that the physical body composed of the four elements is entirely empty, so why do you still feel hungry? When it gets cold, you say that the four elements are all empty, and the cold is empty. In theory it is: "inherent cold is true emptiness and inherent emptiness is true cold", however, if you do not put on warm clothes you cannot bear it. What's the reason for this? So Sharipture announces: At that time I had realized that realm of emptiness, and I thought that I had already traveled the Path, and had reached the realm of nirvana, the fruit of the buddhas. Now he realizes his mistake, and realizes that this is not truly experiencing great nirvana.

From Buddhist theory, all of you understand that emptiness is also called nirvana, and that this is the realm of the arhats. When you get so you have abandoned the myriad entangling objects, and not a single thought is born, and reach the realm of absolute emptiness, that is called "nirvana with remainder." It is not the highest station. In present day terms, "station" means "effect" or "result." Why is it called "with remainder"? This means that although you have managed to abandon the myriad objects so not a single thought is born, the thought that is the root source of karmic force, and the seed of the myriad objects, is still there: it just hasn't burst forth yet. When it encounters the stimulus of other causal factors, it still may burst forth, because the seeds of habit energy are all still there.

Therefore, in the highest realm of the arhats, they can finish with portioned out birth and death, but they still cannot completely move beyond the birth and death of transformation. Strictly speaking, they cannot finish with portioned out birth and death: all they can do is take a long vacation from the process of birth and death. They can even pass eighty-four thousand great eons in samadhi. From our point of view, it is eighty-four thousand great eons; but in terms of their experience, it is no more than the time it takes to snap one's fingers.

I do not know whether you have experienced this or not: when you have been in samadhi for several hours, when you come out of it you feel that you have just closed your eyes for two or three minutes when in fact several hours have passed. Thus, time is relative. Eighty-four thousand eons are no more than the interval of time it takes to snap one's fingers.

When the great teacher Han-shan was 30 years old, he climbed Mount Wu-t'ai with Zen teacher Miao-feng and lived in a thatched hut. At the time he saw the myriad mountains covered with ice and snow, and the stillness all around, and thought it would be good for cultivating practice. Later the weather grew warmer and the ice melted, and the mountain streams turned into torrents, and their sound was like thunder. Han-shan heard the sound in the midst of the stillness, like a great army rumbling forward. He felt that it was very noisy and disturbing, so he asked Miao-feng. Miao-feng said, "Objects are born from mind: they do not come from outside." We hear that Han-shan said, "For thirty years I have heard the sound of water without transforming my conceptual mind. I will realize the perfect penetration of Kuan-yin!"

Then he went off by himself to a single log bridge across a mountain stream and sat on it day after day. One day as he was sitting on the log bridge, suddenly he forgot his body, and the sound was no longer there. From this point on he could enter the stream and forget where he was. With his mind unmoved, he felt that the sound was no longer there, and he was no longer disturbed by sounds.

One time, in the house of his disciple Mr. Hu, the governor of P'ing-yang, Han-shan said, "I'm going to rest a bit," and he sat down on the bench. He sat there for five days straight, and the servants in the house could not arouse him. After five days, his disciple, Mr. Hu, returned from a trip, and he picked up a gong and struck it, and Han-shan immediately came out of *samadhi*, but he did not know where he was. This, too, is a meditation story, a point to contemplate: indeterminancy. Nevertheless, a minute later, Han-shan knew where he was.

The great teacher Han-shan was in this realm. But this is not the ultimate. Therefore he said to himself, "It is easy to set foot in the thicket of thorns, but it is hard to transform the body under the curtain when the moon is bright." This is traveling the Zen road. What is the thicket of thorns? It is when the mind is in total confusion, and false thoughts are many. It is like placing yourself in a thicket of thorns: everywhere are thorns that prick you, but this is not too difficult. Han-shan is saying that when the mind is in a confused mess, to abandon it all at once is, of course, very difficult, but this is not what is most difficult. What is most difficult? When your meditation work reaches a certain stage, so that when you start sitting your mind feels pure and illuminated and empty clear through, you always think that this is final comprehension. In reality, you have fallen into the result of the lesser vehicle, the fruit of Hinayana. What Shariputra was talking about is precisely this realm. At this time you must want to be transformed: this is very difficult, extraordinarily difficult.

I urge you to read Han-shan's autobiography constantly, especially those of you who are monks and nuns. The course of another person's cultivation of practice, told very accurately and realistically, can stimulate your development. Of course Han-shan's learning was good, his study of Buddhism was good, his cultivation of practice was good: he was good in everything, without exception. Not only had he written a commentary on the Confucian classic *The Great Learning*, he had also written explanatory commentaries on *The Doctrine of the Mean*, *Lao-tzu*, and *Chuang-tzu*. He had also mastered calendrical calculations, geography, geomancy, *I Ching* studies, and calculating people's fates. No wonder such a Buddhist master made a big impact on his era.

These anecdotes concerning Han-shan are relevant to what Shariputra says in *The Lotus Sutra*, so I have mentioned them here and said a word about them.

In the prefatory chapter of *The Lotus Sutra*, there are a good many meditation sayings that you must study. How did those disciples who withdrew know that they could not go on listening even before Buddha had opened his mouth? It is apparent that the story of those five thousand monks is not simple. As soon as they saw that the circumstances were not right, assuming that their own world-transcending road of the study of emptiness was good, they did not want to listen to anything else. It seems they could see clearly in advance what was about to happen. What is the reason for this? Everything that Buddha said came after these monks left the assembly.

For the purpose of expedient means in this discussion, I am labeling the third chapter, "Metaphors," as the metaphor of the burning house and the three carts. The triple world is like a house on fire. This world is being burned up by a great fire, but the sentient beings living here think it is very enjoyable. Buddha says that these sentient beings, these children , are not willing to leave the burning house, so the only thing to do is to think of a way to induce them to leave by saying there are three carts. The three carts represent the paths of the three vehicles: the shravakas, the pratyekas, and the bodhisattvas. A teacher like Buddha loves sentient beings as he loves his children, but none of his children understands enough to listen to what he says. There is nothing that can be done except to trick them, to lure them out of the burning house. He lures sentient beings into those three carts.

Buddha says: "In the Dharma treasury of the buddhas, all these sentient beings are my children and I give them all the Great Vehicle. I cannot allow anyone to attain extinction in isolation." Here Buddha is saying: I love all sentient beings the way parents love their children. I cannot save only one particular person. "I give them all the Great Vehicle" means Buddha gives the Path of the Great Vehicle to all equally, regardless of how they are toward him. It is like a large cart that must carry them all, no matter whether they are good or bad.

Buddha says: "I deliver them all with the deliverance of the Tathagata." The following question therefore arises. This sentence says that Buddha uses the Dharma gate of the deliverance of the buddhas to enable all sentient beings to arrive in reality at the same realm of nirvana as the buddhas. Why doesn't he say that he delivers them all with worldly deliverance? The choice of words here has been made after a careful process of selection. "Tathagata" means the basic essence of the buddhas: that is, they all reach the realm of the metaphysical body of reality, the Dharmakaya.

Buddha says: "When all these sentient beings have been liberated from the triple world, I will give them such enjoyments as the meditative concentration and liberation and bliss of all the buddhas." Here Buddha is saying: What toys will I give to these children, the sentient beings, when they have managed to escape from the burning house of the triple world (the realm of desire, the realm of form, and the formless realm)? I will give them meditative concentration, and liberation, and all the rest. In other words, Buddha is saying that all Dharma gates, all teachings and methods, are expedient means. It is like enabling children first to attain a realm of happiness. Thus med-

itative concentration, liberation, and the rest are by no means nirvana, or the fruit of liberation; they are only methods of intensified
practice, and that's all.

Buddha says: "[All these expedient teachings] are all one form,
one lineage. Acclaimed by the holy sages, it can engender pure, wondrous, supreme bliss." According to the final, highest principle, everything is "one form," namely, the reality of the Tathagatas; everything
is "one lineage," namely, the lineage of the buddhas. Buddha is saying: This Dharma gate of mine is hailed by all the holy sages of the
past and future. Even though I take these metaphors as playthings,
you must not misunderstand. If these playthings are not ours, what
merit will we have, what results will there be? "It can engender pure,
wondrous, supreme bliss." This is the bliss of the highest Dharma in
the human world, pure and beautiful and wondrous, but this is not
the ultimate.

Buddha says: "All sentient beings are my children." He is saying:
I love all sentient beings as I love my own children.

Buddha says: "Those who are deeply attached to worldly pleasure do not have the mind of wisdom. There is no security in the
triple world: it is like a house on fire." All sentient beings crave the
temporary and unreal pleasures of the world, and they lack wisdom.
Because human beings live in the triple world, it is like burning up in
a house that is on fire. One day, one hour, one second, they will all be
burned.

Buddha says: "This triple world is all mine. The sentient beings
in it are all my children. Only I can save them and protect them from
all the afflictions and difficulties in this place." Here we have another
meditation saying, another point to contemplate. Buddha expounds
selflessness, but here he speaks of having a self. When he was born he
said he had a self: "In heaven and on earth, I alone am the honored
one." At the time of his final nirvana, he said that the things he had
been talking about all along—impermanence, suffering, emptiness,
selflessness—were all expedient teachings, and that the ultimate truth
was eternal, blissful, personal, and pure. Here in *The Lotus Sutra* he
also mentions "self," but this, too, is an expedient device to expound
the Dharma. Thus now he says, "The triple world all belongs to me."
Isn't this a meditation saying? What is the reason for this?

The second line is an expression of great compassion: "All sentient beings are my children." Why does Buddha expound this teaching? Because in the world everyone is suffering, and there is no one

who can relieve this suffering. Buddha is saying: Only I can relieve it. What "I" is this? This is a meditation saying: pay close attention to it!

Buddha says: I have said that after realizing nirvana, and realizing emptiness, then you can finish with birth and death. Now, in the Lotus Assembly, I frankly tell you that there are no such things. What can you call "extinction"? Extinction is not it: "This Truth abides in the station of Truth, and worldly appearances always remain." They are always there. What is the principle here? Isn't this a meditation saying, a contemplation point? This is also within the scope of seeing truth. Now it is still a matter of seeing truth clearly. After you have seen truth clearly, then we can begin to talk about how to function.

Buddha says: "To detach from all the bonds of suffering is called attaining liberation." There is a five-step process in the cultivation of the Hinayana teaching: discipline, concentration, wisdom, liberation, and liberated perception. Fundamentally, we study the Buddha Dharma to seek liberation. Why do we seek liberation? We seek liberation because there is pain and suffering.

Buddha said: "How can these people attain liberation? Just detach from falsity. This is called liberation." When you have detached from all forms of falsity, then you will find liberation. A question arises. The ordinary person thinks that falsity is false thought, and assumes that if he or she just gets rid of false thought, he or she will attain liberation. *The Surangama Sutra* clearly tells you that all the five skandhas are false, and that you must get free of all of them.

That is why when a great arhat enters nirvana, he smears his body with ashes and extinguishes his knowledge. In the Buddhist scriptures, it says that when a great arhat wants to leave this life, he smears his body with ashes and extinguishes his knowledge, and his mouth spits out the true fire of samadhi. That is, he sends forth fire: all that appears is a flash of light and his body is not there anymore. This is not false. It really can be accomplished. Of course, we cannot do it, because we have not cultivated practice. A great arhat can exercise the functions of earth, water, fire, and wind: as soon as he intends it, he can exercise any function. This kind of great freedom is the realm of the great arhats.

We must not think that the word "falsity" in this quote from the sutra designates only false thoughts. Everything in our bodies and minds, and also the material world, is all counted as falsity. The sutra says: "Just detach from falsity. This is called liberation." But even if you reach this realm of liberation, this is only called the ultimate fruit of the lesser vehicle.

Buddha says: "In reality, you have not yet attained total liberation." Even if you accomplish this, you are still not completely liberated. In the Zen school they record the following public case: There was a great Zen master who assumed that he had penetrated through to great awakening. But in the end, when his own teacher was about to die, the teacher did not give him the robe and bowl emblematic of succession. Instead, the teacher called another younger disciple back from a distant region and bestowed the successorship to his Dharma on him. The teacher felt that the first disciple did not fully appreciate the Tao, while the younger disciple did know the Tao.

Thus, when the teacher was about to be cremated, the younger disciple called over the first disciple and said to him very seriously, "You think you are enlightened, don't you? Right now if I took you and cremated you together with our teacher, where would the two of you meet?" The first disciple said defiantly, "So you don't believe in me, huh? Light a stick of incense, and before the incense has finished burning, I will depart from the world." In other words, the first disciple was saying, "If I want to go I go, and if I want to come I come." The younger disciple paid no attention, and took a torch and lit their teacher's pyre.

The first disciple ran off and sat down cross-legged, preparing to die himself, to show that he could meet with their teacher. This is called "[being able to die at will] whether sitting or standing." Even if you reach this stage, you are still not enlightened! The younger disciple went over beside the first disciple's corpse, slapped him and said, "Elder brother, though you do not lack the ability to die at will, you have never even dreamed of our teacher's intent." In other words: You have the ability to die when you want to die, but you have never even dreamed of the real truth of the Buddha Dharma.

"Buddha says that such people have not really become extinct." That is, this type of person has not really reached the fruit of nirvana. "Because these people have not reached the supreme Path" means that this type of person has not realized supreme unexcelled enlightenment.

Buddha says: "I do not wish to enable them to reach nirvana." This statement of Buddha's is wonderful. He says, why are these people so stupid? In fact, I do not want to teach them, they are too stupid. Why is Buddha acting so petty? His answer is very strange.

"I am the Dharma King, sovereign over the Dharma." In other words, he says: I am the King of the Dharma, and however I want things to be in the triple world, that's the way they will be. Tell me, what kind of talk is this? It really makes people get greedy and angry and ignorant. In reality, it is not so: Buddha is very compassionate. This statement is like Zen master Lin-ch'i giving blows of his staff to a student. Buddha is deliberately provoking everyone. He is intentionally not teaching us to see whether or not we will be able to reflect back ourselves, and repent, and be humble. This is Buddha's method of teaching, and it is also a true statement.

Buddha says: "I appeared in the world in order to bring peace and security to sentient beings." Buddha says: I came to this world to deliver sentient beings. How could I be unwilling to teach them? The reason I do not teach you, is because you yourselves will not accept my teaching, because you yourselves are not vessels of the Dharma.

At this point the scene concludes. This, too, is a meditation case. You yourselves must go study it, even though I have already explained it.

The fourth chapter of *The Lotus Sutra* is called "Decisive Faith." Everyone should take careful note. It is possible to attain the Path only by relying on faith. But it must be true faith, not superstitious faith. If you have faith in the truth, then you can attain the Path.

The representative of this here in this chapter is the Venerable Kashyapa, who is also a model patriarch of the Zen school. He is not the same as Shariputra. The Venerable Kashyapa was the foremost among Buddha's leading disciples in asceticism. Monks and nuns who practice austerities and live as ascetics are traveling the road of discipline. The Hinayana codes of discipline have precepts for monks and precepts for nuns; they are particularly oriented toward asceticism, and you yourselves should study them. According to the guidelines for the practice of asceticism, we are breaking the precepts as we sit here, because we desire to enjoy the experience of the Path. An ascetic does not spend three nights under the same tree, for fear of getting attached to it, for fear of the feeling of attraction. They wear rags, garments made of scraps of cloth which have been collected from the trash and cleaned.

Now in *The Lotus Sutra*, the Venerable Kashyapa, foremost in asceticism, gets up and proclaims: "We have inner extinction, and we consider this enough. We only comprehend this: there is nothing else. We feel no joy at all if we hear of purified Buddha-lands, and the teaching and transformation of sentient beings."

The Venerable Kashyapa clearly and directly announces the Hinayana realm. He says in effect: We have cultivated practice according to Buddhism and we have reached "inner extinction." We have sat in meditation until we have no false thoughts within. When not a single thought is born, this is enlightenment. Extinction is the extinction of all afflictions, and we consider this the ultimate. We think that we have already arrived home, and we care about nothing else.

As for the Mahayana realm of purified Buddha-lands, take note. A galaxy of worlds is called a Buddha-land. It is not a matter of teaching and transforming a hundred people or a thousand people: a bodhisattva must teach and transform all the sentient beings in the whole galaxy, and bring them all back to the pure land of ultimate bliss. This is called a purified Buddha-land. This is the road that the bodhisattvas of the Great Vehicle travel. How hard it is! When the Venerable Kashyapa first hears of the Mahayana Path, and hears one must purify buddha-lands and teach and transform sentient beings, he thinks, "Oh no. That does it! I am not at all happy with that. I won't do it."

In the sutra Kashyapa continues: "What is the reason for this? All phenomena are empty and still, unborn and undestroyed, without great or small, without defilements or contrived actions. Contemplating like this, I do not feel joy."

What he says is not wrong. In effect he is saying to Buddha: Isn't this what you taught us, old man? Everything in the world is impermanent, painful, empty, selfless, fundamentally neither born nor destroyed, neither big nor small, fundamentally without defilements and without contrived action. Since it is like this, why do we have to try to deliver sentient beings? If we act like this, won't it be contrived activity?

My personal teaching is for the Buddha Dharma, not for people. Once a student asked me, "You study Zen, don't you? So why do you work on something like the Ching-hua Cooperative Association?" I asked him, "Then what do you think the study of Zen should be like?" He said one must be like Han-shan. What Han-shan showed was another model, which in Buddhism is called showing the Dharma. Here is a poem by the great teacher Han-shan:

> At ease, calling upon eminent monks
> Myriad layers of misty mountains
> The teacher personally points out the road back
> Hanging a lamp from the moon.

I am very familiar with Han-shan's poems, as familiar as I am with the classic novel, *Dream of the Red Chamber*. When I mention Han-shan, I think of the *Dream of the Red Chamber*. Why? It is a meditation case. I am laughing at you, and like Buddha with the monks who left the Lotus assembly, I do not want to explain.

In the sutra, Kashyapa continues: "We pass the long nights in the wisdom of the buddhas, without craving or attachment, without any further intentions. Being ourselves in the Dharma, we consider this the ultimate."

The venerable Kashyapa is accusing himself: he is in the wisdom of the Buddha Dharma and does not seek to progress. It is like searching in the dark. He thinks he is in the Buddha Dharma and has already reached the ultimate. These are his words of repentance.

Kashyapa continues: "We pass the long nights in cultivating the teaching of emptiness, and attaining liberation from the triple world and the troubles of suffering and affliction. We stay in our final bodies, in nirvana with remainder."

He says: We really are small vessels. It is as if we are groping around in an endless night, and thinking that we have reached the realm of emptiness, that we have reached the ultimate. We think that we have leaped beyond the triple world and are moving outside the five elements.

But take note! The Venerable Kashyapa is qualified to say such things, whereas we only understand Buddhism. People who do not have the accomplishment of the true cultivation of practice are not qualified to talk like this. The Venerable Kashyapa has reached his "last body." His physical body will not come again into portioned-out birth and death, and will enter the realm of the birth and death of transformation.

What is this thing called the birth and death of transformation? It is the realm of the transformation body, but it is not Buddha's transformation body. The realm of arhats is to live in their final body. When they must go, they all say the same few sentences. I feel very happy when I read them. They say: "I forever salute the world. My life is ended, and what I have to do has been accomplished. My pure conduct has been established, and I am not subject to subsequent states of being." What we call establishing virtue, establishing merit, establishing words, and establishing a name are all present in this final statement. But this is the ultimate fruit of the lesser vehicle. It is not ultimate nirvana, it is nirvana with remainder.

Why is this chapter in *The Lotus Sutra* called the chapter on definitive faith? What is a *shravaka*? It is someone who has no enlightenment himself, who is totally dependent on a teacher's teachings. We are all *shravakas*. We talk about the Dharma all day long, but what we are talking about are all results achieved by the Buddha. To truly believe in the Buddha Dharma is to believe in these.

In the passage from the sutra Kashyapa continues: "Buddha reveals such rarely seen things, knowing they will delight the small-minded. By the power of this skill in means, he tames their minds, and only then does he teach them great wisdom. Today we have found what we have never had before. Something we had not hoped for previously, today we have attained. It is like a poor man finding immeasurable wealth."

Here there is a classic story. In the first part is the Venerable Kashyapa's repentance to the Buddha. "Buddha reveals such rarely seen things, knowing they will delight the small-minded. By the power of this skill in means, he tames their minds." Buddha has done things which are very rare and hard to accomplish. He knows that people like the lesser vehicle and like to travel on small paths. There is nothing else to do, so first he uses skill in means and gives us a lump of sugar to lick. Now he boxes our ears and tells us we are wrong. "Only then does he teach the great wisdom." We must study the attainment of great wisdom. "Today we have found what we have never had before. Something we had not hoped for previously, today we have attained." Now we understand, and we are very happy: we have gotten something unexpected, something that we had not even hoped for before. We thought that Buddha had said all he had to say, and we did not imagine that he also had this to say.

Pay attention to this! Buddha has already taken something out and given it to us, but how should we act to receive it? The Dharma-Jewel is not only there with Buddha: it is here with us, too. "In heaven and earth, within space and time, within there is a jewel, hidden in the mountain of form." As the sutra says, "It is like a poor man finding immeasurable wealth." It is like a totally impoverished penniless man unexpectedly discovering great wealth: how happy he will be then!

All these passages in *The Lotus Sutra* are meditation sayings. In the sutra, two of the most famous of Buddha's great disciples play the role of people asking for the Dharma, asking Buddha to expound this part of the great teaching. One is foremost in wisdom, one is foremost in asceticism. Both have already attained the ultimate fruit of the lesser vehicle.

Still, the designations for Shariputra's chapter and Kashyapa's chapter are not the same. The chapter on decisive faith teaches that it is right to believe in this, that we must manage to believe. Why is it arranged this way? This is a big question. First I will reveal a little bit to you. Buddha thought that the lesser vehicle is still important for the Mahayana path. After expounding inherent emptiness, he spoke of interdependent origination.

Following the two chapters we have already discussed comes the fifth chapter of *The Lotus Sutra*, "The Metaphors of Medicinal Herbs." This chapter is very subtle. Buddha says: When I preach the Dharma it is like rain; all the plants growing on the mountains and streams of the earth are medicines. This is a very big question!

In Volume Two of the Zen classic, *Record of Pointing at the Moon*, there is recorded a story that relates to the metaphor of medicinal herbs:

"One day the Bodhisattva Manjushri ordered Sudhana to pick medicinal herbs, saying, 'Pick some medicinal herbs and bring them to me.' Everywhere Sudhana looked all over the earth, nothing was not a medicinal herb. Sudhana came back and said, 'There is nothing that is not a medicinal herb.' Manjushri said, 'Pick some medicinal herbs and bring them to me.' So Sudhana picked a blade of grass from the ground and gave it to Manjushri. Manjushri accepted it and showed it to the assembly and said, 'This medicinal herb can kill people, and it can also bring them to life.'"

To paraphrase the story: The Bodhisattva Manjushri told the youth Sudhana to go pick some medicinal herbs. Sudhana then crouched down and picked up a blade of grass from the ground and handed it to his teacher Manjushri. Why did he do this? Sudhana said, of all the plants on earth, which one is not a medicine?

What is Buddha explaining in this chapter on the metaphors of the medicinal herbs? The human body is made of flesh, not of iron. We must take medicine, or else our bodies will be sick. Many people say, since I cultivate practice, I will chase away sicknesses by relying on my meditative accomplishments. Can you? If you can dispel sickness only after several decades of meditation work, these were decades not of cultivating practice, but of cultivating sickness. Was it worth it? Thus, we must consider medicine important. This is medicine that has form. Formless medicine is everywhere. The hundreds and thousands of Dharma Gates are all medicines.

After this chapter on medicinal herbs has been completed, suddenly comes the "Chapter of Prophesies." Buddha gives individual predictions of enlightenment, doing everyone a big favor. He summons all the great disciples of the lesser vehicle and rubs the tops of their heads, and tells them that after several hundred years, or several hundred eons, they will become buddhas, and they will be called buddhas. The result is that each and every one of them will become a buddha. None of them had ever imagined before that he, too, would be able to become a buddha.

What trick is Buddha playing here? He gives predictions of eventual enlightenment for all the adherents of the lesser vehicle, but he does not show his hand to the Mahayana bodhisattvas. What is the meaning of this? This is another great meditation case.

Up to here, the sutra is all like this, filled with parables and metaphors. It is very lively, but it has still not said a word about the Buddha Dharma. It is not like *The Surangama Sutra*, or *The Avatamsaka Sutra*, and it is not logical like the Yogacara scriptures. *The Lotus Sutra* does not discuss principles. It just gives a big bunch of prophesies like this. Tell me, how can we keep reading along? Up to this point is the Hinayana section of the sutra. After the lesser vehicle portion has been finished, Buddha begins to give prophesies of enlightenment. In this there is a great big meditation case.

After this, another scene begins, the chapter on the metaphor of the illusory city. Buddha conjures up a city, an amazingly wondrous illusory city. This is the road of the great vehicle. The leading character in the chapter on the illusory city is a Buddha called "Triumph of Great Pervasive Wisdom." This Buddha makes a grand entrance: he has sixteen princes who all become buddhas. Amitabha Buddha is one of his princes. Shakyamuni Buddha is the youngest of the princes, the sixteenth prince. The Buddha "Triumph of Great Pervasive Wisdom" was originally a king. Later he left home, and brought along sixteen princes who all left home, too; later they all became buddhas.

When a person manages to become like the Buddha "Triumph of Great Pervasive Wisdom," then that person has done everything that it is possible to do. What am I saying? Among worldly phenomena, the body is the king. It has good fortune, long life, happiness, and all kinds of things: the "sixteen princes" are all good. It enjoys the good fortune and rewards of life to the point that they should not be enjoyed. Then it leaves home, and again each and every one of the "sixteen princes" all become buddhas.

This is the story told by Buddha in the seventh chapter, "The Metaphor of the Illusory City." He takes us to a time many hundreds of millions of eons ago. He says that under the rule of this king, it was foreordained that he would "attain supreme perfect enlightenment in the world of Saha." (Saha, "Endurance," is the Buddhist name of our world.) What is the reason for this? Here Buddha is explaining past karmic causes, the workings of cause and effect over past, present and future.

Buddha says: "After my demise, there will be disciples who do not hear this sutra, and they will not have any knowledge or awareness of the conduct of bodhisattvas."

To paraphrase, Buddha is saying: In the future, after my final nirvana, there will be disciples who do not believe this scripture, and who do not know of the root of this teaching. They will know nothing at all about what the practices and vows of Mahayana Bodhisattvas really are, or how they should be carried out. "They will not have any knowledge or awareness of the conduct of bodhisattvas." This sentence is very serious. We must not assume that because we have studied many scriptures and read a lot of Mahayana sutras that we understand the conduct of bodhisattvas. In fact, this is very problematic. Later on, when we talk about carrying out the bodhisattva vows, we will have to discuss it further.

Buddha continues: "They will imagine, with their thinking process rooted in the realm of birth and death, that they will enter nirvana by means of the merits they have attained."

Buddha is saying: In the future, after my final nirvana, there will be some disciples who do not understand, and who moreover are arrogant, who assume that the little bit of merit they have managed to attain will enable them to realize nirvana, but this is wrong. As the Zen patriarch Bodhidharma said to Emperor Wu of Liang about his many pious acts directed to winning merit, "These are the lesser fruits of gods and men, a defiled causal basis." You donate ten thousand dollars and think that you have made merit, but in fact this is a very minor thing.

Buddha says: "I will be a buddha in other worlds under different names."

In other words, Buddha is saying: After my demise in this world, I will go to other worlds, and attain buddhahood there. Of course I will not be called Shakyamuni Buddha anymore; I will have different names. (In *The Avatamsaka Sutra* these names are mentioned: what Shakyamuni will be called in the world above, and what he will be called in another place, and so on. There are so many it is inconceivable.) Therefore, Buddha says that you must not think that after his final nirvana here on earth, he will not exist any more.

Buddha says: "Though such people have their thinking process rooted in the realm of birth and death, after they die, in other worlds, they will seek the wisdom of the buddhas and get to hear this scripture."

Buddha is saying in effect: If my disciples can understand this truth, then after they experience nirvana and leave this world, they will go to other worlds to be reborn, and there they will be able to seek the Mahayana Path, and have the opportunity to hear again the truths of *The Lotus Sutra.*

After he has finished telling this story, Buddha raises a big question, a question that is often raised in the Zen school as well. Shakyamuni Buddha says that his father at that time, the Buddha "Triumph of Great Pervasive Wisdom," was sitting in meditation studying Zen. The sutra says in verse:

The Buddha "Triumph of Great Pervasive Wisdom"
Sat in the place of practice for ten eons,
But the Buddha Dharma did not appear before him,
And he did not attain enlightenment.

The Buddha "Triumph of Great Pervasive Wisdom" took great pains cultivating practice, didn't he? He sat there in *samadhi*, not for one or two days, but for ten eons. This is quite a bit of meditation work! He sat there without moving, his work of cultivating realization and his power of concentration had reached this level, but this still does not count as enlightenment. Enlightenment was not revealed, he did not experience awakening, he did not manage to consummate the path of buddhahood.

The Buddha Dharma is not apart from *samadhi*, nor is it apart from sitting in meditation. Nevertheless, sitting in meditation and entering *samadhi* for many eons still is not necessarily going to work. This is a famous verse in *The Lotus Sutra.*

Younger students must not study sitting meditation as they please without ever lying down. What's the use of just sitting there? What's the use of never lying down? The Buddha Dharma will not appear before you, so you will not be able to become enlightened. Pay attention to this. You cannot just do as you please. If you ruin your body, then even though the whole world is medicine, you will not be able to use it and things will be spoiled even more.

# 6

# FURTHER LESSONS
# FROM *THE LOTUS SUTRA*

Earlier I mentioned the great teacher Han-shan (of the T'ang period), because there are close links between Han-shan, *The Lotus Sutra*, and T'ien-t'ai Buddhism. These days Han-shan's poems are circulating very widely. Some people do research and claim that he had an elder brother and a sister-in-law, and it was because his elder brother's wife didn't treat him well that he was forced to leave home and become a monk. They say that they have discovered this in his poems. But in Han-shan's poems he mentions a wife, too. Don't tell me he also found a wife! There is no way to account for theories like this: all we can do is laugh at them.

In *The Lotus Sutra*, it says that when the five thousand monks left the assembly, they wanted to travel the Hinayana path. What these monks followed was the road of Han-shan and Shih-teh. But there is a problem here. Sometimes Mahayana Bodhisattvas are incarnated among Hinayana monks; that is, in a congregation of Hinayana monks, there may very well be incarnations of Mahayana Bodhisattvas. But there is no way to find this out.

In Chinese poetry, it is not only the poems of monks that carry the message of the Buddha Dharma; the poems of householders frequently do so, too. This is because any poetry, from the Buddhist point of view, has a bit of the karmic seeds of wisdom, lamenting impermanence, and expressing regrets that nothing in the world can be relied on. To end up lovelorn shows the impermanence of love: thus we have such literary works as *Tea Flower Woman* and *Dream of the Red Chamber*. In Han-shan's poems the aspect of lamenting impermanence is particularly prevalent: what he is following is the Hinayana line.

All we see is the beauty of Han-shan's poetry; we do not notice his practice. I will help you pick it out. In the old days Han-shan asked Shih-teh, "When worldly people slander me, cheat me, insult me, ridicule me, slight me, denigrate me, are disgusted with me, how should I handle it?" Shih-teh said, "All you can do is tolerate them, yield to them, let them have their way, avoid them, endure them, respect them, and not pay attention to them. Wait a few years, and then see how they are." This is what's so wonderful about Han-shan and Shih-teh.

Han-shan said, "Do you have any secret way for me to avoid all this?" Shih-teh then answered with a verse from the Bodhisattva Maitreya:

> A clumsy old fellow wearing a tattered jacket
> Belly full of tasteless food
> Patching the holes to ward off the cold
> Understanding the myriad things according
>     to conditions
> Some people revile the clumsy old fellow
> But he only speaks well of them
> Some people beat the clumsy old fellow
> But he only tumbles down and falls asleep
> They spit in his face
> But he just wipes it off afterwards
> I am saving my strength
> Him nothing vexes
> This kind of going beyond
> Is the jewel in the subtle wonder
> If you know this scene
> There's no worry that you won't finish the Path.

Though we say that Han-shan's practice is in the Hinayana style, can we do as much? All we are qualified to do is to bow before him. This is traveling a path that is absolutely Hinayana.

I have spoken about the passage in the sutra that says: "The Buddha 'Triumph of Great Pervasive Wisdom' sat at the place of practice for ten eons, but the Buddha Dharma did not appear before him, and he did not attain enlightenment." Shakyamuni Buddha is telling us a story. He tells us how splendid was the meditation work of the Buddha "Triumph of Great Pervasive Wisdom." The place of practice is not necessarily a Zen meditation hall, or a T'ien-t'ai contemplation hall. All that is required is that we sit anywhere with a moment of pure mindfulness: this is the place of practice. So what does it mean, "The Buddha Dharma did not appear before him"? What does it mean for the Buddha Dharma to appear in front of us? This is worth paying careful attention to. A meditation case has come.

Broadly speaking, a meditation case is a question. You should not think that the only meditation case is "Does a dog have buddha-nature or not? No." This is a minor meditation case. The Buddha Dharma appearing before us: this is a big question, a major meditation case.

Buddha says: I love all sentient beings as I love my children. This is the same as the way the Buddha "Triumph of Great Pervasive Wisdom" loved his sixteen princes. But the children did not listen to their loving father. Though there was money in their own house, they did not want it, and instead went running around in confusion outside. All the father could do was sew a jewel into the garment of each child so that when they were impoverished and starving, they would discover it themselves and be rich. This was the father's compassion and love.

The Venerable Kashyapa is saying to Buddha: In your great mercy and compassion, you took a precious jewel and hid it in our garments, but we are so stupid we did not realize it.

This is the source of the story that is so famous in Chinese culture, the story of the pearl hidden in the poor man's garment. Every person is wealthy, but he or she does not realize it, and so becomes impoverished. This is another meditation case.

What is our garment? It is our physical body, which our mother bore us with: this is our garment. This is a borrowed house, but inside it is a precious jewel. How can we find "the pearl hidden in the garment"? Volume Four of *The Lotus Sutra*, chapter eight, "The Five Hundred Disciples," tells you: "The bodhisattva practice of the inner secret." In Chinese Taoism they speak of "using the false to cultivate the real." Without this garment, there would be no way to find the real. This thing is the "inner secret." The practice of the inner secret, "the bodhisattva practice of the inner secret," the secret within the secret, is found within your own mind.

The sutra says: "In their outer appearance, they are disciples, *shravakas*." In an assembly of *shravakas*, bodhisattvas always appear with the characteristics of home-leavers, of monks and nuns. The mental practice of the *shravakas* is "reducing desires and being averse to birth and death." Only Mahayana Bodhisattvas above the eighth stage, who have reached the realm of buddhas, are able to be absolutely without desires. "Reducing desires and being content" is the practice of ascetics. So you should not ask too much of practitioners who have left home and are cultivating the way of the *shravakas*. "Reducing desires" is already very difficult, and "being content" is even harder. "Reducing desires and being content" is one of the disciplinary practices of the *shravakas*. *Shravakas* "feel aversion to birth and death," whereas bodhisattvas "do not fear birth and death." Therefore, "reducing desires and being averse to birth and death" is the realm of the *shravakas* and *arhats*, the ultimate fruit of the path traveled by people like Han-shan.

"The jewel itself purifies the Buddha-land." This world where Shakyamuni Buddha is, the world called "Saha," is a place where ordinary and holy live together, with both purity and defilement. But Buddha says: Here where I am is a buddha-land. Why is it necessary first to concentrate the mind and cultivate realization by "reducing desires and being averse to birth and death" before you can reach the pure Buddha-land? This is the practice of the inner secret. But what is this inner secret? This is another meditation case.

The classic story of the jewel in the poor man's garment occupies a very important place in the history of Chinese literature and learning. We often encounter it in our reading. For example, when Li Hou-chu, the last king of the Southern T'ang dynasty, lost his son, he referred to this story in his verse of lament:

Eternal thoughts are hard to dispel
Alone with his pain, lamenting to himself
Deep in the rain of a lonely autumn
Sharp sadness making him sicker
Choking back sobs, longing in the face of the wind
Hazy and dim, illusory shapes in his eyes
The King of Emptiness must be mindful of me
The poor child has lost his way home.

This poem was written by Li Hou-chu before he lost his country [to the forces of the new Sung dynasty around A.D. 960.] Li Hou-chu had learned Buddhism very well, hadn't he! He understood Buddhism completely, like Emperor Wu of the Liang dynasty, but he did not do well politically. This is an important question in Chinese civilization. You should pay attention to this: Buddhism is Buddhism, and politics is politics.

There is an important connection between literature and the phenomenal aspects of cultivation and realization. When we speak of seeing truth, cultivating realization, and carrying out vows, worldly dharmas and world-transcending dharmas are all the same. In later generations, after the flourishing of the Zen school, when they wanted to evaluate a person, first they looked at his "capacity and percep-tiveness." "Capacity" meant the measure of the person; "perceptive-ness" meant farsightedness. In anything, without a farsighted view, nothing great will be accomplished. There is a close connection between capacity and perceptiveness. Capacity corresponds to the carrying out of vows; perceptiveness corresponds to seeing truth. This poem of Li Hou-chu is very fine, but it does not seem like an emperor's poem; it seems like the poem of a sour pedantic literary man.

Among the descendants of the Emperor T'ai-tsung, of the T'ang dynasty, there were several who became monks. Before Hsuan-tsung came to the throne, he was a novice monk. Because emperor Wu-tsung plotted to have him killed, he had no choice but to take refuge in a Zen monastery. In history, the emperors who had "Hsuan" in their names were all very extraordinary, like King Hsuan of the Chou dynasty, Emperor Hsuan-ti of the Han dynasty, and Emperor Hsuan-tsung of the T'ang dynasty.

T'ang Hsuan-tsung made a thorough study of Zen. He was a fel-low student of Zen master Huang-po; they were both disciples of Pai-chang. Zen master Huang-po knew he was from the royal family, but, nevertheless, whenever he was wrong, he would give him a beat-ing as he would anyone else. There are stories like this about the two men: one time, the two of them were walking in the mountains enjoy-ing the scenery. They came to the side of a waterfall, and Hsuan-tsung said, "Let's both compose a poem. You make up two lines first, and I will add the last two lines." Huang-po gave these two lines:

> A thousand cliffs, ten thousand valleys,
> we do not decline the labor
> Only when we look on them from afar do we see
> that where they come from is lofty.

When people compose poems, they unintentionally reveal their own perceptions. Later Huang-po become a great Zen teacher. How did Hsuan-tsung follow up on this? He said:

> How can we hold back the mountain streams?
> In the end they return to the ocean to make waves.

Huang-po immediately gave him a slap. "Away with you! Little monk, you won't become a buddha like this." These two lines added by Hsuan-tsung show an emperor's mettle: he, too, unintentionally revealed himself. In effect he was saying: This shaven head of mine is only temporary, and cannot hold me back. I will end up returning to the great ocean to make waves. At the time T'ang Hsuan-tsung had another fine poem:

> Sun and moon both pass over my shoulders
> I see mountains and rivers
>     all in the palm of my hand.

He was describing the realm he had awakened to in his study of Zen, and also his grandeur when he would later become emperor.

Now let us return to our discussion of *The Lotus Sutra*. After the conclusion of the story of the jewel in the garment of the poor man, Buddha does not tell you how to look for the pearl in your garment. This is "the bodhisattva's practice of the inner secret." Take note of this! Our parents have given us a precious jewel and put it in our bodies. If you cannot find it, it serves you right! What about your father? After he has passed away, the old man is not concerned with you anymore. Once you look at the sequence of the stories in this way, you will discover how very splendid the arrangement of the text of *The Lotus Sutra* is.

In the fourth volume of *The Lotus Sutra*, chapter nine, "Predictions of Enlightenment Given to People in the Stage of Study and Beyond the Stage of Study," study means cultivating and learning discipline, concentration, and wisdom. For example, arhats at the level of stream-enterer, once-returner, non-returner, which are the first, second and third fruits of arhatship, are all still in the stage of study, like the arhats who withdrew from the assembly at that time in the first scene of the sutra. When they reach the fourth stage, their meritorious conduct is complete, and they achieve the stage of results, then they are called "beyond the stage of study."

In this chapter of the sutra, Buddha summons together before him all his disciples in the stage of study and beyond the stage of study, and gives them all predictions of enlightenment. Then he says: "The True Dharma and the Semblance Dharma are all equal, with no difference between them." The Buddha Dharma is Truth, and it will abide forever in this world. When Buddha said, in the future, after he died, there will be no True Dharma, this was only an expression of skill in means, it was not the ultimate truth. In the teaching of the ultimate truth, there is no such thing as eras of the True Dharma, the

Semblance Dharma, and the End of the Dharma. Truth abides for-ever unchanging, but it is necessary for all of you to go yourselves and seek it out. That's why in the sutra Buddha predicts that both those beyond the stage of study and those in the stage of study will become buddhas.

After this Buddha expounds chapter ten, "Dharma Teachers," and says that anyone who disseminates the True Dharma of *The Lotus Sutra* is a great Dharma teacher. "No form of livelihood is opposed to reality." This is the basis of Mahayana, the Great Vehicle. Immediately after this, Buddha says that Dharma teachers are the great medicine for this world. This, too, is a meditation saying.

If we explain—according to the principles of the teaching—Buddha is the great king of physicians, who can cure the sicknesses of sentient beings. Not bad! He can cure illnesses of the mind, but can he cure physical illnesses? In the exoteric teachings, Shakyamuni Buddha does not speak of this, and he himself appears several times to be sick, showing physical illnesses. For example, at the time of his final nirvana, it appears that he caught a cold when he was practicing aus-terities in the snowy mountains during his youth, and developed rheumatism: he felt a pain in his back when he passed away. He had died and his body was already lying in his coffin, but he still could stick his feet out for you to take a look!

You tell me, could Buddha have avoided death? Yes, he could have! Too bad that at the time Ananda did not hold him back. Before he died, he had asked Ananda: "My time is coming soon. However, I have a means of living forever in this world, keeping my physical form and staying in the world: What do you think I should do?" Ananda held his tongue because he was distraught and all choked up. A little while later Buddha again asked Ananda: "My time is almost up. Do you think I should keep my physical form and stay in the world?" Three times he asked Ananda this, but each time Ananda remained silent and said nothing. So Buddha announced that he would die on such-and-such a day. Then Ananda burst out crying. Buddha said: "I asked you three times, but a demon blocked your mind, and you did not answer." Why did Buddha want to die? "The seed of the buddhas is born from causal conditions," as the sutra says, and these conditions were no longer right. The conditions had passed, and the best thing to do was to depart.

Though Buddha left, his four great disciples still kept their phys-ical forms and stayed on in the world. The first was the Venerable

Kashyapa. The second was the Venerable Pindola. Right now we must invite Pindola. He can still come, but you will only know it after he has gone. We cannot say for sure, but he may already be here with us. The third was Buddha's son Rahula. The fourth was Kundupada. All of them received Buddha's last instructions and so stayed in the world, each with a different status and a different form, to teach in this world called Saha. Why do I mention this point? Because this is connected with the Medicine King Bodhisattva. When we read this scripture there is nothing about this in it, so the questions multiply, and all of them are meditation cases.

Buddha tells you where the medicine is: "If you want to abide in the Buddha Path, and perfect spontaneous wisdom, you must always take care to make offerings to *The Lotus Sutra*, accept it and uphold it."

If you want to take up the task of the Great Dharma of the Tathagata, you must perfect fundamental wisdom. This is something inherent and spontaneously so. It is not something that anyone else can give you; each and every person inherently possesses it. Each person must search it out, "he must perfect spontaneous wisdom." How must we perfect it? We must constantly make offering to the Dharma Gate of *The Lotus Sutra*, accept it and uphold it. It is a lotus, a flower. Why did Shakyamuni Buddha hold up a flower to inaugurate the mind-to-mind transmission of Zen? Why did the Venerable Kashyapa smile to acknowledge it? Everywhere in the important scriptures they are talking about flowers: what is the reason for this?

After this chapter has concluded, a key point in *The Lotus Sutra* arrives. This is the famous chapter "A Jewel Stupa Appears." The stupa is a grave, and it is also a storehouse of jewels. While Buddha is preaching the Dharma, a jewel stupa wells up out of the ground. In it a buddha is seated, a buddha who had attained enlightenment countless eons ago. This buddha is called the Tathagata Prabhutaratna ("Many Jewels").

The Tathagata Prabhutaratna beckons to Shakyamuni Buddha, the door suddenly opens, and he calls to Shakyamuni Buddha to come in, and shares his seat with him. This is a very big question! The two of them are both buddhas, so they share the seat. Afterward, bodhisattvas from other regions arrive from everywhere. If we only explain the principles involved in this story, it could be made into a metaphor, but if we are truly explaining cultivation and practice, then these things really exist.

We could call the Tathagata Prabhutaratna a nirmanakaya Buddha or a sambhogakaya Buddha, and we could also say he is dharmakaya Buddha. We could say that Shakyamuni Buddha is one of his nirmanakayas, one of his physical manifestations. The three bodies of Buddha, the nirmanakaya, sambhogakaya and dharmakaya, are joined into one.

Those who cultivate practice and travel the road of the Zen school at best only attain the realm of the dharmakaya. If I can speak boldly, of the many people in the Zen school over two millennia, no more than a few have been able to achieve all three buddha bodies. This is because, in studying Zen, it is easy to fall into the realm of the lesser vehicle. Many people just attain a little bit of the purity of the dharmakaya and then run off: Shariputra was like this. But nowadays it wouldn't be bad if we could be as the Zen patriarch Bodhidharma said: "Those who speak of the truth are many, but those who practice and realize it are few." In later generations even those who speak of the truth no longer exist. If we really want to study the Buddha Dharma, we must pay special attention to this chapter in *The Lotus Sutra*.

Let me tell another story. The Sung dynasty prime minister Chang Shang-ying studied Buddhism, was active in politics, and also awakened to enlightenment. When Chang Shang-ying was seriously ill and near death, he said to his sons and sons-in-law: "I tell you this. In*The Lotus Sutra* it says that the jewel stupa of the Tathagata Prabhutaratna welled up out of the ground, and the Tathagata Prabhutaratna shared his seat with Shakyamuni Buddha. These events really took place, they are not theoretical. " As he finished speaking, he pushed his pillow away, extended his legs, and passed away. When he had gotten sick, he had lain down on a bed, but when he was about to die, he didn't want to die lying down, so he pushed aside the pillow. He rapped on the window frame, and the air resounded with a loud sound, and then he departed. From the words he used to instruct his family members when he was about to die, it is evident that his sons and sons-in-law were all studying Zen.

When the sutra says that Prabhutaratna's stupa welled up out of the ground, this "ground" is the mind-ground. It means that when you genuinely reach certain realms in the Dharma Gate of the mind-ground, true emptiness gives birth to wondrous being, things that well up spontaneously. Only this is called success, building a seamless stupa. This is also Maitreya's tower in *The Avatamsaka Sutra*. The jewel stupa has no door; it is also what *The Lankavatara Sutra* speaks of when it says "No gate is the Dharma Gate." This is not a theoretical statement.

When you are sitting in meditation, and you reach the state where your thoughts are even and still, and everything is pure and clear, this is only the first step of the preliminary stage of the realm of the sixth consciousness. You have not yet found the Dharma Gate of the mind-ground. Here are two lines of a verse by the T'ang dynasty master Kuan-hsiu:

> If in your cultivation of practice, you do not
>     reach the state of mindlessness
> The myriad kinds and types flow along with the
>     stream.

I'm also thinking of a poem by Tu Hsun-ho. But I am not telling all of you to study poetry! In this poem there is Zen, and there is the Buddha Dharma. As for cultivating realization, this is a whip to urge you on. Tu Hsun-ho was born in the chaotic world of the end of the T'ang dynasty and the ensuing period in the tenth century A.D. called the Five Dynasties. His poem says:

> The gate of profit, the road of fame:
>     a downpour, nothing to rely on
> In the face of the wind of a hundred years,
>     a brief blazing lamp
> I'm just afraid my intention to become a monk
>     is not complete
> If I could completely become a monk,
>     I'd totally lose monkhood.

All of you must pay attention to this. Genuine cultivation of practice requires serious reflection. Concerns for fame and profit are not easy to abandon. It is not that it is not easy to get rid of them: it is impossible to get rid of them! Only when you have really gotten rid of these concerns for fame and profit will your practice of cultivating realization be somewhat sound. If you don't get rid of these, it will not be sound or decent.

Now we come to the twelfth chapter of *The Lotus Sutra*, the chapter entitled "Devadatta. " After the Tathagata Prabhutaratna shares his seat with Shakyamuni Buddha, it becomes very exciting, and bodhisattvas from all over appear. The buddha of the eastern land comes, too. The chief disciple of this land is the Bodhisattva

Jnanakara, whose name means "Accumulation of Wisdom." Shakyamuni's chief disciple is the Bodhisattva Manjushri, who is foremost in wisdom.

As soon as the Bodhisattva Jnanakara comes to this world of ours, he sees that here things are very sad, that it is a region that has not yet been opened up to the teaching, that it is very backward. So he tells his buddha: I am going back. The buddha of the east tells him: slow down a bit! You still have not seen the pure aspect. You have not seen their pure land.

At this point, the Bodhisattva Manjushri comes forth from the Naga Palace beneath the ocean. Once the bodhisattvas standing on both sides have a look at him, they see that after all his appearance is extraordinary. The Bodhisattva Jnanakara then asks, "There are many sentient beings diligently making progress and cultivating the practice of this sutra. Will they soon become enlightened or not?" He is saying: There is much suffering and affliction in this Saha world of yours. Are the sentient beings here easy to save? The implication in his words is: the sentient beings here must surely be very difficult to save.

Manjushri speaks on their behalf: I have just returned from the Naga Palace, and the King of the Nagas has a princess, "just eight years old, endowed with sharp faculties of wisdom." Pay attention to this line! "She is good at knowing the karma of all the faculties of sentient beings." She knows how sentient beings stir their minds and set their thoughts in motion, and she is able to know the deeds of every sentient being, lifetime after lifetime. "She has already attained *dharani*." That is, she has already attained the method of total command associated with reciting mantras, she has already grasped the most crucial point.

"She can receive and uphold the treasury of the most profound secrets spoken by all the buddhas." This refers to her perfect attainment in regard to wisdom. As for her meditation work, "She enters deeply into samadhi, and totally comprehends all phenomena. In an instant she generates the mind of enlightenment and attains the stage from which there is no falling back." In that moment she is suddenly enlightened, and reaches the eighth stage of the bodhisattvas, from which there is no retrogression. "Her eloquence is unimpeded. She thinks compassionately of sentient beings as if they were babies." This is the compassion of the bodhisattva realm. "Her merits are complete, and her mental states and her utterances are subtle and wondrous and vast and great. She is compassionate, humane, and yielding, and her intent is harmonious and refined. She is capable of reaching enlightenment."

Why have I extracted this passage from *The Lotus Sutra*? To give you a model for studying Buddhism. Each line of this story contains within it seeing truth, cultivating realization, and carrying out vows.

In the end, the Bodhisattva Jnanakara does not believe in the enlightenment of the Naga princess, because according to the Buddha Dharma, no females can become enlightened. Women have the body of the five corruptions [as men do], and they also face five barriers: "They cannot be kings of the brahma heaven, they cannot be kings of the gods, they cannot be wheel-turning sage kings, and they cannot be buddhas." At this point Manjushri calls to that disciple, the Naga maiden: "Go now, darling child." When the Naga maiden sees the Tathagata Prabhutaratna and Shakyamuni Buddha, she offers them her most precious pearl. In Chinese culture there is the phrase "the black dragon's pearl." The story goes that under the jaws of the dragon there is a precious pearl. In the story of the Naga maiden, the pearl is her lifeblood, her very life, the refined essence of her cultivation. She takes this priceless pearl and relinquishes it, and offers it to these two buddhas. Shakyamuni Buddha quickly accepts it. With the offerings of other people, he has to consider whether or not he wants them!

The Naga maiden says to the Bodhisattva Jnanakara: "I have profound comprehension of the characteristics of wrongdoings and merits, extending through all the worlds of the ten directions." What she means is that she can see clearly all sorts of configurations in the minds of sentient beings, all their characteristics of wrongdoing and merit and good and evil. The power of her wisdom and perception is aware of everything in the ten directions.

"The subtle wondrous dharmakaya is equipped with thirty-two auspicious marks." Every person's fundamental nature has the thirty-two marks and the eighty kinds of good. Every person is a buddha, every person is originally a buddha, but you have not yet searched out this key link. Can there be any distinction of male and female in this?

# 7

# CULTIVATION
# THROUGH REFINING THE BREATH

Now we will discuss an important part of the phenomenal aspect of cultivating realization: the Hinayana scripture called the *Ekottara-Agama Sutra*. There are many reasons for using this sutra. One important point is this: before the Sui-T'ang period [A.D. 580-906] there were many people, both home-leavers and householders, who cultivated practice and realized the results. Especially on the monastic side, you can read of them all in the biographies of eminent monks and nuns. At that time, the Zen school and Esoteric Buddhism [Tantra] had not yet been transmitted to China. What we speak of now in Buddhism as the southern transmission of the Buddhist teaching which prevails nowadays in Sri Lanka and Thailand is based on Buddha's earliest teachings, the four Agamas of the Hinayana canon.

The *Ekottara-Agama Sutra* is part of the four Agamas. These were transmitted to China in the Eastern Han—Three Kingdoms period [second-third centuries A.D.], which was a very lively time in both Chinese and Indian culture and learning. At that time in China, the first sprouts of Buddhism were beginning to flourish and were being synthesized with the three Chinese traditions of mystic learning, the *I Ching, Lao Tzu*, and *Chuang Tzu*. In politics, the period of the Northern and Southern Dynasties, which followed the collapse of the Han dynasty and the demise of the Three Kingdoms, was a very chaotic era. Nevertheless, in the history of learning, this was a very special period of transition, which continued for two or three centuries.

At that time there were many people who left home to study Buddhism and who cultivated practice until they realized the results. No one paid any particular attention to things like the special channels and the eight *ch'i*-channels, but people with spiritual powers were very numerous. You all know stories like these:

One evening when the Buddhist adept Fo-t'u-teng was reading a sutra, he took out a piece of cotton that was blocking an aperture in his chest, and a light spontaneously came forth from his body. Once he felt a stomachache from having eaten something unwholesome, so he went to a river bank and pulled out his stomach and washed it; after he had washed it clean, he put it back in.

When Master P'ei-tu wanted to cross a river, he took a willow branch and threw it into the river, stepped onto it, and thus crossed the river.

All those who cultivated practice at that time followed the road of *The Agama Sutras*, the road of mindfulness. In terms of the eightfold path, this was "correct mindfulness." In *The Agama Sutras* there are the methods of the ten forms of mindfulness. What does "mindfulness" mean? It is a kind of training method directed toward the mind's spiritual awareness, training your own mental awareness using the method of "mindfulness."

The ten forms of mindfulness are: mindfulness of the Buddha, mindfulness of the Dharma, mindfulness of the Sangha, mindfulness of discipline, mindfulness of giving, mindfulness of heaven, mindfulness of stopping and resting, mindfulness of *anapana*—that is, mindfulness of breathing in and out—which is the same thing as the present day Esoteric Buddhist and Taoist method of refining the breath. When the Chinese Taoists talk of the channels of the *ch'i*, [the breath or vital energy], it is always because they have been subjected to the influence of the Buddhist method of *anapana*.[1] Next of the ten forms of mindfulness comes mindfulness of the body, and the last one is mindfulness of death. These ten forms of mindfulness include all methods of cultivating practice. Mahayana Buddhism has Hinayana Buddhism as its basis: if you cannot manage Hinayana, don't even speak of Mahayana!

*The Ekottara-Agama Sutra* says: "Thus have I heard. Once Buddha was in Shravasti in the Jetavana Park. At that time the World Honored One told the monks: 'You must cultivate the practice of one method, you must broadly apply one method. When you have cultivated the

---

[1] The Chinese word for breath, *ch'i*, also has the extended senses of the vital energy within the body and the energy which fills the universe at large. In this translation, the English word "breath" must at times take on these larger connotations. Many traditions of psycho-physical cultivation in China use various techniques of *ch'i-kung*, "breath-work" or "energy-work" to promote both physical health and spiritual transformation.

practice of this one method, then you will have a good reputation. You will achieve the reward of the great fruit, and all forms of good will come to you.'"

In other words, you must carry out one method well, and then your cultivation of practice will be correct, and you will accomplish all forms of good. "You will attain the taste of sweet dew"—that is, the taste of the supreme Buddha Dharma—"and arrive where there is no contrived activity, and then you will achieve spiritual powers." After a long time of profound accomplishment with the mind abiding nowhere, true emptiness spontaneously gives birth to wondrous being, and spiritual powers come. No fooling!

The sutra continues: "You will remove all confused thinking and reach the fruit of monks, and achieve for yourselves nirvana." In other words, when you have gotten rid of all false thoughts, you will reach the fruit of the arhats. Proceeding directly onward from this, you will naturally arrive at the station of nirvana. Buddha continues: "What is this one method? It is what is called mindfulness of Buddha." This one method means the method of being mindful of Buddha.

These few lines are a formula. In almost all of the ten methods these lines are present. If those of us who are studying Buddhism look down on the Hinayana scriptures, and do not study them, this is wrong. Present day people all say: "Oh, I am traveling the Mahayana path. I don't talk about spiritual powers." Don't brag so much! Everyone likes spiritual powers, but they like false spiritual powers. People who pay no attention at all to spiritual powers are almost capable of sudden enlightenment: these are people with the great bodhisattvas' perception of truth. Of the rest, who would not like spiritual powers? They may say they would not, but in their hearts they surely would. We must seriously reflect: since we would like spiritual powers, how should we seek them? If you want to attain the fruit, Buddha tells you that you must enter deeply into one gate. If you cultivate it well, all of you can attain the results.

The first method is mindfulness of Buddha [in Chinese, *nien-fo*]. This is not *nien-fo* in the sense of "reciting the Buddha-name" used by Pure Land Buddhists in later generations! The later method of reciting the Buddha-name was devised by the Dharma teacher Hui-yuan, based on three Mahayana scriptures, *The Infinite Life Sutra*, *The Contemplation of Amitabha Sutra*, and *The Amitabha Sutra*. The mindfulness of Buddha in these ten forms of mindfulness taught by *The Ekottara-Agama Sutra* is not mindfulness by reciting the name of Amitabha Buddha! I leave it to you to go study this for yourselves.

The second method is mindfulness of the Dharma. The Hinayana scriptures tell us: "All compounded things are impermanent, they are phenomena that are born and perish. After birth and death is extinct, peaceful extinction is bliss." This is the Dharma. The eight forms of suffering in human life, the twelve links of interdependent causation, the thirty-seven items that aid the Path: these are all teachings that are part of the Dharma.

What does "mindfulness of the Dharma" mean? It means that you concentrate your mind to employ these principles taught by Buddha to understand human life and all the transformations of body and mind. Even if we study Buddhism, and sit in meditation, we do not take the principles of Buddhism and join them together with the work of sitting in meditation. Is what I am saying right or not? When you are reading the sutras, you may understand a lot, but when you sit in meditation, you are still there grunting and groaning, with your *ch'i* moving here and not moving there. The Buddha Dharma does not tell you to play with your *ch'i* channels. The Buddha Dharma tells you to fully fathom the truth, to correct your thinking. It is not that you cannot think about the Dharma! You certainly can think about it. The principle of the Buddha Dharma is correct thinking; with correct thinking you can attain meditative concentration.

The third method is mindfulness of the Sangha. Don't think this means being mindful of ordinary monks. How could this be considered as mindfulness of the Sangha! Mindfulness of the Sangha means wholeheartedly taking refuge with the community of worthy sage monks and nuns, those superior people who have realized the fruit of the Path.

The fourth method is mindfulness of giving. What is mindfulness of giving? It is what the Zen school means by "Put it down!" This is inner giving, abandoning everything, taking all the miscellaneous false thoughts that are in your mind and giving them all away. If you act like this, you can get home; you can attain spiritual powers. This is what Buddha is telling you. This is the great principle for cultivating the Dharma. To extend it further, mindfulness of giving means reflecting back on your own faults from mind-moment to mind-moment, taking your unwholesome mental activities and totally getting rid of them so that there are no mistakes as your mind stirs and thoughts move. This is mindfulness of giving.

The fifth method is mindfulness of heaven. What is there about heaven to be mindful of? Shakyamuni Buddha acknowledges the existence of the Lord of Heaven, and he introduces twenty-eight heavens in the realm of desire, the realm of form, and the formless realm. You must not underestimate the heaven planes of existence. If you do not do meditation work or practice virtue, it won't be easy to get to heaven! Buddha also acknowledges the existence of spiritual immortals, who can live for several tens of thousands of years. Through what practice can this be achieved? *The Surangama Sutra* will tell you. Buddha does not say that the spiritual immortals are wrong, he just says that they have not attained true enlightenment. This is because they have not awakened to the basic essence. If they had attained true enlightenment, they would not be said to be on outside paths.

If people do not practice virtue, then no matter what meditation work they do, they will not be able to enter heaven. Buddha explains in great detail about the heavenly planes of existence: for example, he discusses how many heavens there are in the realm of desire. Of course these are not above the earth, they are in other worlds. If people want to be born in the heavenly plane of existence after they die, it is really not easy! As for how people can ascend into the heavenly planes of the realm of form, the only way is to accumulate virtue and merit, and to rely on the work of meditative concentration. If you cannot achieve the four *dhyanas* and the eight s*amadhis*, you will not be able to reach heaven. We cultivate practice all day long and still cannot even reach the first *dhyana*, so it will not be easy for us in future births to obtain another human body. In *The Surangama Sutra* it already tells you how to cultivate *samadhi* and reach the six heavens of desire.

The sixth method is mindfulness of stopping and resting. This does not mean just sleeping; rather, it means abandoning the myriad entangling objects. In fact, if you really can stop and rest, this is *samadhi*. If you really can stop and rest, you can experience the fruit of enlightenment. Why? *The Surangama Sutra* tells you in eight words: "When false nature stops, the stopping is enlightenment." By profound stopping, you can witness enlightenment. Our sleeping is a false stopping and resting. It is real stopping and resting only when body and mind are both empty and the myriad objects are abandoned. The body stops, the mind stops, emptiness stops. You take the realm of emptiness and put a stop to it: only this is called profound stopping. When in the sutra Buddha speaks of "mindfulness of stopping," he wants you to abandon everything from moment to moment at all times wherever you are, whether walking, standing, sitting, or lying down.

The seventh method is mindfulness of discipline. We will discuss this topic another time. The eighth method is mindfulness of *anapana*. This is also called focusing the mind with *anapana*. You must pay careful attention to this method! It is very important. *Anapana* means being mindful of breathing out and breathing in; it means cultivating the breath. The T'ien-t'ai school's methods of cessation and contemplation, and paying special attention to breathing out and in—a method that came later—were derived from focusing the mind with *anapana*. Focusing the mind with *anapana* was not devised by Shakyamuni Buddha: it already existed in India in the teachings of the brahmans and in the techniques of yoga. Nevertheless, Buddha used Buddhist methods and synthesized them with the *prajna*[2] contemplation practice. After *anapana* was transmitted to China, it fused with Taoism: the Taoist practices of guarding the apertures and refining the breath are related to it. The fact that so many of China's eminent monks developed spiritual powers and realized the fruit of enlightenment is all related to their mindfulness of *anapana*.

Cultivating the breath is very important. You have been born in this era when material culture is developed to such a high extent. Future generations will be even more frantically busy. The best thing to do, therefore, would be to adopt this method. If you do not travel this road, then it will be extremely difficult if you want to attain the results of cultivating practice, very difficult indeed!

First we will cite a section of the text, from volume seven of *The Ekottara-Agama Sutra*, chapter seventeen, on *anapana*. Buddha is teaching his son Rahula the method of focusing the mind through *anapana*:

"At that time, after giving these teachings, Buddha went away and retired to a quiet room." Buddha, too, is made of flesh and blood, and he needs rest. "At that time, the Venerable Rahula thought thus: 'How can I practice *anapana* now, and get rid of my sadness and worries and be free of all thoughts?' At this time Rahula got up from his seat, and went to the room of the World Honored One." In terms of personal sentiments, Buddha and Rahula were father and son; in terms of the formalities of the teaching, Rahula was one of his disci-

---

[2] The Sanskrit word *prajna* means transcendent wisdom, perfect knowledge of both worldly phenomena and the one absolute reality that pervades them.

ples. "When Rahula got to the room, he bowed at Buddha's feet, then sat off to one side." Why did he sit off to one side? Because Buddha was sitting in meditation resting; thus, after bowing to him, Rahula sat off to the side and waited. "In an instant," that is, in a little while, Buddha came out of *samadhi*, and left his seat.

"Rahula moved back from the seat," the sutra says, and quickly asked his father, "How can I practice *anapana* now, and get rid of my sadness and worries and be free of all thoughts? How can I attain the great reward, and taste the sweet dew?" The World Honored One replied, "Excellent! Excellent! Rahula, at last you are capable of coming before the Tathagata, and with a lion's roar, ask about this principle." In other words: Now you are asking me such an important question about cultivating practice. Buddha continues: "Now listen carefully, Rahula, listen carefully, and ponder well what I say. I will explain it all in full for you."

There are five words here you must pay careful attention to: "Ponder well what I say." By this Buddha means, after you understand what I say, you still must go investigate and study it. Don't blindly believe. I will teach you the method, but you must go yourself and do a good job investigating it.

The sutra continues: "The World Honored One told him: 'It is like this, Rahula. Suppose there is a monk, who takes delight in quiet uninhabited places. So he straightens out his body and makes it correct, and straightens out his mind and makes it correct, and sits cross-legged.'"

Pay attention! If you cannot sit steadily when you are sitting in meditation, if your legs do not live up to expectations, then you are not "the most honorable among bipeds."[3] If the *ch'i* circulates freely in your legs, you can add several decades to your life span.

Buddha tells us that the most important thing in cultivating practice is to straighten out our bodies and make them correct. We can make our bodies correct when we are standing up. When we are sleeping we make our bodies correct for sleeping. The Taoist method of "auspicious reclining and stretching out the corpse" is also a type of straightening out the body and making it correct.

---

[3] "The most honorable among bipeds" is a way of referring to human beings in reference to their potential to become enlightened.

If you get no results from sitting in meditation and doing meditation work, ultimately what is the reason for this? It is because you
have not "straightened out your mind and made it correct." It is
because you have reversed cause and effect, taking the conclusions of
the results achieved by Buddha and making them into your own
method of cultivating practice. As soon as you sit down to meditate,
you always want emptiness. What do you want to empty? You think
this maneuver is very good, empty clear through, but in fact, this is
precisely your conceptual mind. It is the realm of the sixth consciousness, the conceptual mind. Even if right now you manage to
forget your body, and feel that inside and out everything is light, you
still have not moved beyond the scope of the sixth consciousness. In
terms of the domains of the five skandhas in *The Surangama Sutra*,
this still belongs within the realm of the skandha of form, with "solidified false thoughts as its basis."

There are some people who sit quietly in a unified light and can
know future events. They think this is "spiritual awareness." If you
study Yogacara, you will know that this is the other side of the sixth
consciousness, this is the functioning of the shadow consciousness. So
many realms! Because you are studying Buddhism, you can only see
buddhas and bodhisattvas: this is the realm of consciousness. Talking
in terms of the Hinayana theories of cultivation and realization, your
consciousness is not yet focused and unified, you have not yet "corrected your mind."

Hinayana theory speaks of correcting the body, correcting the
mind, and correcting speech. None of these three can be lacking. In
other words, you are violating the precepts everywhere, but the ordinary person speaks of the precepts at his own convenience. How easy
it is to speak of them! Your mind and thoughts and consciousness
are not correct in the least, and you are creating the karma that is the
seed of hell all the time. The seeds created by your contrived activities
are terrible! You must pay special attention to this. That's why Buddha
says that the first thing in cultivating practice is that you must correct
your body, correct your mind, and correct your speech, and focus
your thoughts.

In China, the Taoist scriptures on how to cultivate the way of
the spirit immortals became numerous after the Sui and T'ang dynasties. Many of the issues concerning the *ch'i* channels they discuss were
born from this chapter on *anapana*. After the Eastern Chin dynasty
came the Taoist *Scripture of the Yellow Court* which discusses in detail

the "three superior medicines," *shen* spirit, *ch'i* energy, and *ching* vitality.[4] These are all phenomenal characteristics, which pertain to religious work in the realm of deliberate activity. If you cannot reach home in cultivating religious work in the realm of deliberate activity, how will you be able to reach the level where there is no deliberate activity? If you cannot focus on methods that involve deliberate activity, how will you ever empty out thoughts? All you will do is deceive yourself and deceive others. It is because of this that in the later generations of those studying Buddhism, not one in ten thousand realizes the fruit of enlightenment.

Please pay special attention to this! Besides relying on the Buddhist scriptures, I also take the experience of my several decades of searching and earnestly tell all of you this: if you can really reach the point where you have corrected your body and mind, then there is not one body that cannot be transformed, not one sickness that cannot be gotten rid of, no body or mind that cannot be healthy and strong. If you can manage to correct your body and mind, then both body and mind will be absolutely healthy and you can be rejuvenated. This is true because everything is created by Mind alone. This is "correcting the body" and "correcting the mind."

"Correcting the mind" involves breathing. In Taoism it is the same. In the Taoist *Yin Convergence Scripture* there is a line: "Controlling the bird [of thought] is a matter of the breath." This is an important formula, and it is also a method. If you cannot get hold of thoughts, they can run off in confusion. If you cannot concentrate your thoughts, it is because your breath is scattering. When your breath scatters in confusion, then your mind scatters in confusion as well.

But the breath is not the principle entity; it is something subordinate to the mind. But this subordinate entity is very fierce. If you cannot get hold of it, then your mind will not be able to stop. It is like when a person is riding a horse: your breath is the horse. In the famous 16th century novel *Journey to the West*, when the character known as the Tang monk rides a horse, it represents this breath. When a person is riding a bad horse and he wants to make it stop, he pulls the reins tight, but the horse still keeps running wildy. You cannot

---

[4] For an English language discussion of vitality, energy, and spirit, see Nan Huai-chin's *Tao and Longevity* (York Beach, ME: Samuel Weiser, 1984).

stop it, and there is nothing at all you can do about it. Therefore, even if we want our minds to stabilize, if we cannot stabilize our breath, how can we stop false thoughts? There are many people whose emotions are not good and whose physical bodies are not good: in reality, the reason is always that their breathing is not good.

"There are no other thoughts." At this time, there must be no thoughts at all in the mind: this is the principle of correcting the mind. "Tie your consciousness to your nose." Take your consciousness and focus it on your nose. This sentence has killed many students of Taoism and Buddhism. Is this some sort of "guarding the apertures?" "The eyes observe the nose, the nose observes the mind"—is that so? You can be so concerned with this that you raise your blood pressure. Are you imitating the white crane? The white crane can live more than a thousand years. The story goes that this is because when the white crane stops and rests, his nose faces his anus, and the two breaths circulate together. But our necks are so much shorter than the white cranes, so how can we imitate it? Thus Buddha says: "The stupidity of sentient beings is truly pitiful."

The phrase "tie your consciousness to your nose" is not telling you to observe your nose. Rather, the idea is to first alert you to the fact that you must pay attention to your breath as you breathe in and out. This is the first step of "mind and breath depending on each other," making the consciousness follow the breathing.

"When you breathe out a long exhalation, know how long the breath is." In your correcting mind, you must not depart from breathing out and breathing in: you yourself must be aware of how long your exhalations and inhalations last. "When you breathe in a long inhalation, know how long the breath is." Pay attention to the word "know." If on one hand you are cultivating the breath and on the other hand your brain is full of chaotic thoughts, this is not right, this will not bring results. Thinking must be matched with breathing: this is called focusing the mind by *anapana*. How can you take hold of false thoughts? You must pay attention to your breathing. Breathing is like a rope. After you have tied down this horse, that is, when false thoughts have been tied down, then you can concentrate fully on cultivating practice, and then you will be able to enter the first *dhyana*. Then the results of cultivating this practice will surely come.

"When you breathe out a short exhalation, know how short the breath is, and when you breathe in a short inhalation, know how short the breath is. When you breathe out a cold exhalation, know how cold the breath is, and when you breathe in a cold inhalation, know how cold the breath is."

Sometimes as you are breathing it is cool. There are two possibilities then: one is a form of sickness, the other is absolutely healthy. The healthy alternative is that the coolness is in contrast to your own warmth that is arising from the "warming" of the four intensified practices. In contrast to this, you may feel that the air you are breathing in from outside is cool, or you may feel that this air is not interfering with you.

"When you breathe out a warm exhalation, know how warm the breath is, and when you breathe in a warm inhalation, know how warm the breath is." When you are sitting in meditation, sometimes the arches of your feet get warm: that is the "warm breath." Even if your mind is following your breath, if you cannot unify the two of them, then they will diverge and the breath itself will run off in confusion, and wherever it runs to will get warm. If it runs into the place below your navel, and you think it is the fire of *kundalini*, you better hurry up and call the fire department!

Buddha tells his son: "Observe in full detail as your body breathes in and out, and be aware of it all." This breath is what *The Surangama Sutra* speaks of as the wind element. All of you must still remember what it says in *The Surangama Sutra*: "Inherent wind is true emptiness, inherent emptiness is true wind." But this step involves the Mahayana cultivation of the Dharma, and for the time being we will not speak of it. You should not have your heart set on climbing up too high too soon: first you must be able to watch over your breath before it will work. If you are able while doing quiet sitting "to be aware of all the movements of your breath in and out," the result produced will be that your powers of memory will be very good and your brain will be especially alert.

In general, when you are learning sitting meditation, you sit there breathing, totally unaware of your breathing, and unaware of it when you sink into a torpor. Sometimes there is a bit of empty awareness in your consciousness, and then a lot of things are there flying around in confusion. If you don't believe this, go check it out for yourselves! If at the root you have not "corrected your mind," then how can this be called meditation work! You could sit for ten thousand years and it would be useless.

Most recently a lot of people have asked me about sitting in meditation through the night without lying down. Don't tell me that not lying down is the Path. What sutra, what precept of discipline, tells you not to lie down? This is only for those who are practicing asceticism. Even Buddha himself had to sleep. In the sutras and in the precepts of discipline, it teaches you that when you are sleeping you should contemplate the solar disc in your mind for a pure illuminated sleep. You will sleep less, and this special quality will be there.

When monks and nuns sleep, it is right to get rid of many layers of covers, but it is certainly not required that they do not lie down. When I say this, I am not saying that sitting through the night without lying down is not right. It's just that you will be able to manage to sit through the night without lying down only if you have the physical ability for this. If you do not have this physical ability, the result of trying to sit all night without lying down will be that you want to cultivate the Path, but you will not be able to realize the Path. If you first make your physical strength collapse, this is not worth it at all! What I say is very serious. I am telling you this very sincerely. Buddha "speaks according to reality, speaks factually, speaks without falsity." We want to speak words with reality, speak honestly and frankly. The straightforward mind is the place where enlightenment is cultivated and realized. So pay attention to this issue.

The instructions in the sutra "to be aware of everything" in your breathing is very important. Even when you lie down to sleep, you can pay attention to your breathing. This is the same principle.

The sutra continues: "At times when there is breath, know it is there." Pay attention to this! Here the sutra has moved forward another step. Later on the T'ien-t'ai school took this method and expanded it, calling it "taming the breath," "listening to the breath," and "counting breaths." Later, in Esoteric Buddhism, it was called the "work of cultivating the breath," "cultivating the nine section Buddha-wind," "cultivating the breath in the jewel bottle," and other names. The Taoists have a saying: "The mystic pearl of heaven and earth, the root of the myriad breaths." In the alignment of body and mind, the breath has ten thousand kinds of transformations. When the Chinese judge physiognomy to determine a person's fate, they first must observe whether the breath and complexion are good or not. This is really true.

When the breathing subsides into quietude and stops, false thoughts absolutely cannot be found. Even if you want to start false thoughts, you cannot start them. But at this time do you know it or not? You are very pure and clear: this is real meditation work. This is when you reach what the sutra speaks of: "At times when there is no breath, know it is not there." But what is this "knowing?" This is another question. Of this it is said, "Aware and illuminated, it remains from beginning to end."

The sutra says: "If the breath comes forth from the mind, know that it comes forth from the mind." You must investigate this line. Coming forth from the mind does not mean coming forth from the physical heart. [The Chinese word for "mind," *hsin*, literally means "heart."] It means that the mind's thoughts have moved. When the mind's thoughts move, sometimes you feel that breath is being emitted along with light. If you happened to be passing by at that time, you would immediately be infected by this, and your own mental state would become peaceful and quiet, or else you would feel as if a warm current was flowing into your body. But this process is not a good thing; this is something created, contrived. At this point you have still not attained *samadhi*; it is still early. This is no more than the result of ordinary quiet sitting.

Nowadays science has become aware that the human body can emit light. Fundamentally, every person is able to emit light. When you get to that point, after your breath has stopped, that light shines forth more strongly. If we say there are ghosts and spirits, at that time no ghost would dare to confront you. If a demon saw you, he would flee, because your *yang* energy is at a peak.

Thus, when the sutra says: "your breath comes forth from the mind," it is not that your breath comes out of your physical heart, it is that your mind's thoughts have moved. In other words, in general when people cultivate *ch'i-kung*, energy-work, breath-work, it all proceeds from the mind: it is a deliberate creation of the mind's thoughts. It is the same when you study Esoteric Buddhism: it is a theory of your mind's thoughts constructing breath.

The sutra says: "If your breath enters through the mind, know that it enters through the mind." When you pursue the Taoist practice of "cultivating the breath in the jewel bottle," there is a breath in your "field of elixir," the area below your navel. You refine it to the point that you are able not to breathe in or breathe out, so that even if you were buried underground for a long time, you could survive for some time without dying.

You must all pay attention to this! This path proceeds from the nose, but in reality our whole bodies are breathing in and out. Only when the breathing in the body stops does it count as truly entering *samadhi*. When you enter *samadhi*, three kinds of things are still present—warmth, life, and consciousness. The *alaya* consciousness has not left the body. When you have genuinely entered *samadhi*, the breath is definitely full. In a person filled with breath, no matter how old, all parts of the body are soft and supple, and the person becomes as supple as a baby. That's why we should not touch people who have entered *samadhi*, all we can do is strike a chime next to their ears to arouse them.

If you have done your meditation work for a period of time, and your body has still not become supple, and your two legs are not firmly positioned, then you are not "the most honorable among two-legged creatures." Rather, your two legs are fighting you: when you sit in meditation, your legs are struggling, suffering. Last year a friend wrote me a letter asking questions about sitting meditation. He said that he could not sit steady cross-legged. I replied to him: how could your meditation work and your legs be at odds?

In our present efforts we do not have enough time to still be fooling around with our legs! There is not enough time! What is most important is correcting our minds. Any posture will do: when your meditation work succeeds, your legs will become supple, and you will naturally be able to sit cross-legged steadily. All you need is for the *ch'i* to circulate freely in those legs of yours, and your life span will be extended accordingly. Pay attention to this! When you feel your body aging and getting stiffer, then you had better prepare a bit in advance: prepare for your departure. Lao-tzu said: "Concentrating your *ch'i* and making it supple, can you become like a child?" So you must not take a sectarian view of this. In this branch of cultivation, Buddhists and Taoists both follow it because *samadhi*, meditative concentration, is something common to Buddhist and non-Buddhist paths alike.

There are some people who are very busy everyday. Take note! Hurry up and meditate more, don't think you are too busy to do it! You say you are tired from working too hard and don't have time to sit and meditate. You should hurry up and sit, sit until you can settle your breath. Do this for an hour and you won't be able to use it up in a day. But this will only work if you do it genuinely. There is one point you must pay attention to! Your bowels and stomach must be empty during this practice. The Taoists have a saying: "If you don't want to get old, do not fill your belly. If you don't want to die, there should be no excrement in your bowels." Of course you still must take sufficient nourishment. When your bowels and stomach are clean, then it will be easy for the breath to fill you.

In the sutra Buddha continues: "If you can cultivate *anapana* like this, Rahula, then you will have no worries or vexations or confused thoughts, and you will get the great reward and taste the sweet dew."

In this era when material civilization is so developed, it is good for both body and mind to cultivate this method, and it can extend your lifespan. When you do sitting meditation, can any of you not be in confusion? You simply must coordinate your thoughts with your breathing. Then your breathing will not be able to run off in confusion, and "then you will have no worries or vexations or confused thoughts." Speaking from the perspective of Esoteric Buddhism, for people who have opened the channel from the throat chakra to the heart chakra, false thoughts do not come, and worries and vexations are spontaneously done away with.

The sutra continues: "At that time, the World Honored One had finished explaining the subtle teaching in full to Rahula." "In full" means that the main principles were already fully covered.

After Rahula heard the teaching, "he went to an *aranya*." The meaning of *aranya* is a pure quiet place of retreat to cultivate the Path. He sat under a tree, "corrected his body and corrected his mind, and sat cross-legged, without any other thoughts, focusing his mind on his breathing." Rahula thus began to cultivate the method of *anapana* that Buddha taught him.

"At that time Rahula was contemplating like this." This contemplation was in the midst of his meditative concentration—correct contemplation, without any error whatsoever. If you think that because you must have no false thoughts, that you should also discard correct contemplation, this is wrong. Every one understands this, right? If you want to empty out and get rid of correct contemplation, this is not right.

The sutra continues: "Rahula was then liberated from the mind of desire, and no longer had the multitude of evils. He had awareness and contemplation, and he was mindful of joy and contentment as he roamed in the first *dhyana*." Rahula followed Buddha's teaching, and entered into the concentration of the first *dhyana*. Only then did he really achieve great joy and generate the attitude of genuine great compassion.

# 8

# THE CULTIVATION
# PATH OF MINDFULNESS

I mentioned earlier that after the introduction of the Buddha Dharma into China, there were so many people between the Eastern Han and the Sui-T'ang period who cultivated practice and realized the fruit of enlightenment, whereas since the Sung and Ming dynasties fewer and fewer people have realized the fruit of enlightenment. The main reason involves the issue of cultivating realization.

In discussing the question of the phenomenal characteristics of cultivating realization, it is necessary to make a special point of bringing up the Hinayana scriptures, the four Agamas. Chinese Buddhism likes to talk about Mahayana, but real Chinese Buddhism is a synthesis of Mahayana and Hinayana. Moreover, Mahayana has Hinayana as its basis. The methods of cultivation of the later exoteric and esoteric schools of Buddhism cannot get away from this basic principle, either. Therefore, I will make a special point of bringing forth the important points of the ten forms of mindfulness of *The Ekottara-Agama Sutra*. Before the Sui-T'ang period, those who studied Buddhism, cultivated the Path, and realized the fruit of enlightenment were numerous because they emphasized cultivating this aspect.

Among the ten forms of mindfulness, mindfulness of *anapana* is the most important. *Anapana* is a method of cultivating realization that was transmitted into China in the Later Han period. The "Great Scripture of Focusing the Mind through *Anapana*" was translated into Chinese by An Shih-kao in this period.

We previously talked about Buddha's son, Rahula, and how he cultivated the method of focusing the mind through *anapana* and reached the realm of meditative concentration where the breath does not move in and out. He has already told us the secret: we must be sure to reach the state where the breath does not move in and out, and only then can we enter into the first *dhyana*.

The sutra says: "At that time Rahula contemplated like this, and he attained liberation from the mind of desire." Desires such as the desire for fame, profit, wealth, food, and sleep are in the province of Mahayana. The desires in the province of Hinayana are the sexual desires. We will discuss this point again. Twenty-five hundred years ago, Buddha already knew all about the sexual patterns of modern-day people. Buddha discusses them all in the sutras. If desirous thoughts are not cut off, then you cannot reach the fruit of arhatship. These desirous thoughts even include nocturnal emissions, when, for example, semen is emitted in dreams due to desirous thoughts. At the same time, it also includes all methods of masturbation: masturbation includes lascivious thoughts and methods of masturbation through purely psychological fantasies. The meaning of the passage above is that only when you reach the point where the breath does not move in and out will it be possible to be liberated from desire. This is liberation in the Hinayana realm.

The sutra continues: "He had awareness and contemplation, and he was mindful of joy and contentment as he roamed in the first *dhyana*." Only at this time did he experience the realm of the first *dhyana*. Here "awareness" means the condition of physiological feeling and sensitivity to cold, heat, congestion, hunger, etc. "Contemplation" means the condition of psychological awareness, knowing the coming and going of every thought. At this time the breath does not come or go, but it is not that breathing has entirely ceased. The pores of the skin are still breathing and the pulse is still beating. Only when you reach the point where the breathing of the pores all over the body has "stilled" is it said that the breath is not going or coming. At this time you know that your own breathing has totally stopped: this is the realm of "contemplation" referred to here.

"He had awareness and contemplation." This comes in response to feeling and knowing: this response is called "a moment of mindfulness." As the sutra says, "He was mindful of joy and contentment." In his mind was born incomparable joy. "Joy" refers to the physical side, whereas "contentment" is a psychological indication of peace and ease. At this time, it is as if body and mind are sitting in empty space: only then do you enter the condition of the first *dhyana*.

You can experience the condition of the first *dhyana* without necessarily realizing the fruit of the first *dhyana*. When you realize the fruit of the first *dhyana*, you can be called "an arhat at the level of the first fruit." It is related many times in the Buddhist Canon under what conditions you can be called "an arhat at the level of the first fruit." You will naturally be able to know this if you are willing to spend the time and reach a comprehensive synthesis.

The part of cultivating realization is the principle essence of the Hinayana scriptures. The theoretical section is "contemplate like this." The Mahayana view of truth is slightly different: Hinayana has its own concepts of seeing truth, cultivating realization, and carrying out vows. You must be clear on this point.

In studying Zen you cannot get away from *samadhi*, but it is not always necessary to begin with *samadhi*. The Zen school emphasizes the perception of truth, and transcendent wisdom. Naturally it is still necessary to cultivate realization: without a basis in gradual cultivation, how can you talk about achieving sudden enlightenment?

From having awareness and having contemplation, the sutra takes another step forward: "With awareness and contemplation, he felt joy within, and concentrated his mind. Without awareness, without contemplation, mindful of the joy of *samadhi*, he wandered in the second *dhyana*."

From the realm of having awareness and contemplation, he took another step forward and experienced incomparable joy in his mind. This is not superficial joy. On the contrary, his mind is always happy and harmonious whenever he sees any sentient being, any person, even his mortal enemies and antagonists. Even if they are in error, they are still worth sympathizing with. His compassion is a spontaneous outflow of his inner mind, it does not have to be forced. Thus the joy of bodhisattvas in "compassionately delighting in renunciation" is very important. If you stick to a joyless condition for a long time, your whole body will stiffen and you will not be able to open the channels of your *ch'i*.

At that time Rahula "concentrated his mind." That is, he concentrated on the realm he had reached in the first *dhyana*. "He kept mindful of the joy and contentment." That is, he preserved the condition where the energy was not being emitted. His breath had stopped: this is what the Taoists call, "The absence of fire is called energy." Gradually he experienced a state "without awareness, without contemplation, mindful of the joy of samadhi." In his mind was incomparable joy. The realm of this joy is "mindfulness." At this point Rahula realized the second *dhyana*.

• • •

*The Ekottara-Agama Sutra* was transmitted to China at the end of the Eastern Han dynasty and the rise of the Three Kingdoms [circa A.D. 220]. In this period Buddhism emphasized cultivation of practice. Buddhism was very easily accepted, because once they cultivated its practices, people got results. At that time the cultural level of the Western Chin dynasty [A.D. 265-318] was rather high. If Buddhism had just relied on its theories in order to advance in China, it would not necessarily have been accepted. But once the power of *samadhi* and spiritual powers came along, the intelligentsia could not but surrender.

Nowadays, on the other hand, people who study Buddhism scarcely have spiritual powers! All they have are neuroses. If Buddhists today would begin with *samadhi*, then each and every one of them would have spiritual powers and it wouldn't be anything special.

In the tradition of the Bodhisattva Asanga [the great Indian Yogacara Buddhist philosopher], they specialize in expounding cultivation and practice from the angle of consciousness only and the characteristics of perceived phenomena. In terms of this theoretical system, what we just spoke of, "He had awareness and contemplation, and he was mindful of joy and contentment as he roamed in the first *dhyana*," is still in the realm of *vitarka* and *vicara*.[1] It is still in the range of the sixth consciousness.

When you reach the stage without *vitarka*, but with *vicara*, it is what is spoken of here as "Without awareness, without contemplation, mindful of the joy of *samadhi*, he wandered in the second *dhyana*." Then the thoughts in your mind no longer run around in confusion like electrons, and you enter the realm where you have *vicara* but not *vitarka*.

But at this point there are still objects present, and you have still not yet reached the level where there is no *vitarka* or *vicara*. You have not yet arrived at the realm of "no-mind," it is still too early. How easy it is to talk of "no-mind"! If we think that passing by the myriad things which get our minds hung up on them can be called "no-mind," everyone is capable of being like this. But the ancestral teacher of the Zen school tells us: "Don't say no-mind is enlightenment: no-mind is separated from it by a double barrier." Studying Zen provides the greatest benefits for seeing truth, but in regard to cultivating

---

[1]*Vitarka* means deliberately applied attention or consideration; *vicara* means initial, unreflective attention that registers things without deliberately considering them.

realization, it opens the way for the greatest abuses. Everything has its beneficial and its harmful aspects: this is an example of the truth of the alternation of *yin* and *yang*.

The sutra continues: "[Rahula] was no longer mindful of joy. He held to his awareness and bodily bliss, the joy which is always sought and preserved by all the worthy sages, and wandered in the third *dhyana*."

Here another transformation takes place, and Rahula reaches the third *dhyana*. The mindfulness of joy in his mind is no longer there. He abides in another kind of realm, of "awareness and bodily bliss." Everything inside his body has undergone a great transformation including all the *ch'i* structures and channels and every cell and nerve. Only when you reach the third dhyana can you get rid of disease. Thus, do not think that sitting cross-legged is Zen. To be able to reach the third *dhyana* is something that has to be slowly developed through immeasurable merit and immeasurable virtuous states of mind. Before this stage, you will only be able to achieve a slight improvement in your physical state: you will only be able to achieve less sickness. After you realize the third *dhyana*, you will look upon previous realms of joy as being the same as an ordinary person, because now you have at last reached the best joy. This is the realm of the sages.

The sutra continues: "[For Rahula] both suffering and pleasure were extinguished, and he had no more sorrows or worries, no more suffering or pleasure. Preserving a state of pure mindfulness, he wandered in the fourth *dhyana*."

At this point, he took another step forward and experienced a level where there is neither suffering nor pleasure, neither worry nor sorrow. All of you should pay attention to this: when you have reached the realm where both suffering and pleasure are extinct, this is still "mindfulness." Therefore the sutra continues and says he was "preserving a state of pure mindfulness." Body and mind, inner and outer, were fused into one whole, and he realized the fourth *dhyana*.

This is Buddha's son Rahula's own report of what he attained from his studies.

The sutra continues: "With this *samadhi*, his mind was pure and clean, and free from the defilements of sense objects, and his body was soft and supple." At this point, his body and mind had no trace of defilement, and he was in the same condition as an infant. You must reach the third *dhyana* before you will be able to experience this realm.

All the eminent monks of great virtue in the past were able to predict what day they would die, and even on the brink of death their bodies were as soft and supple as a baby's. Others who were even more lofty turned into a field of light, and their human forms disappeared. At most all they left behind were a few pieces of fingernail, or a lock of hair as a memento.

At this point wisdom arrives, you "know where you have come from, and you remember what you have done, and you are conscious of the events of countless eons of past lives." At the same time, you are liberated from portioned-out birth and death, and enter into the birth and death of transformation. You know how you came and how you will go. You attain the power to know past lives, and you can know the events of countless hundreds of millions of eons. An arhat at the level of the fourth fruit can only know five hundred past lives, while a great arhat knows more. At this point in the sutra Rahula had reached this realm.

The sutra continues: "With this *samadhi*, his mind was pure and clean, and free from flaws and defilements, and free of all bonds." All the bonds of affliction had been untied.

Next the sutra says: "Then he applied his will more, and achieved a stainless mind." Pay attention to these words. The fourth *dhyana* is a realm of the work of meditative concentration. If karmic bonds and compulsions are not yet totally cut off, then the fourth *dhyana* does not make you a great arhat, and you still have not realized the fruit of enlightenment. When you reach this realm, "apply your will more." If thoughts arise, you must intensify your cultivation of practice and "achieve a stainless mind." A stainless mind is a mind without defilement.

But, some people may say, if we cannot let our thoughts move, won't we become wooden? This is not right. In this state you arouse your minds and let your thoughts move, and after they have fulfilled their function, you stop. You have no leaks or defilements, no sticking points or attachments. For people with the power of *samadhi*, even if they are busy all day long, that fundamental mind of theirs, which is situated in the realm of *samadhi*, never moves and is still illuminated and pure. They deal with vexatious matters, and at the time show signs of vexation, but the illumination of their mental state never wavers one little bit.

The sutra says: "By performing this contemplation, he attained liberation from the mind of desire and defilement." At that time Rahula was totally freed from all "the defilements of desire, the defilements of being, and the defilements of ignorance." When he reached this realm, "his mind attained liberation, and having been liberated, he attained liberated wisdom. Birth and death were ended, and his pure conduct was established; what he had to do was already accomplished and he was no longer subject to subsequent states of being."

Only when the meditation work of the fourth *dhyana* reaches this level can it be counted as reaching liberation. All of you must take note. The sutra says: "His mind attained liberation." This "liberation" is a realm of cultivation of practice. "Attaining liberated wisdom" is seeing truth. Wisdom does not belong in the province of meditation work and it is not a realm of realization. However, meditation work, realms of realization, and wisdom supplement and complete each other. Therefore, after attaining the realms of liberation, you must continue to make efforts and slowly attain "liberated wisdom." You must also take note of this: In this process of cultivating realization, at the final stage you return to "liberated wisdom." It's obvious that Hinayana considers the liberation of wisdom as the ultimate. This is just as true of Mahayana. To use the idiom of Mahayana, this is the liberation of the perfection of great transcendent wisdom.

When you have reached this realm, the fruit of the arhats arrives. This life is then called "the last incarnation" and you won't come back again to be reborn. Where do you go? In this life, the pure fruit has already been firmly established. All your worldly debts for wrongs have been wiped away, and in the future you will not come back to the realm of desire again. This is the ultimate fruit of Hinayana, the lesser vehicle. But in Mahayana theory, with this kind of success, at the most you will go for eighty-four thousand great eons without coming back again. If you do not dedicate your mind to the Great Vehicle, you cannot completely finish with birth and death, and you will again enter the realm of the birth and death of transformation.

This section of *The Ekottara-Agama Sutra* is Rahula's report of his cultivation of realization. In the sutra it is not recorded how many years or months he worked at cultivation. Still, while Buddha was in the world, there really were people who realized the fruit of arhatship instantly: there were some who realized it in three days, and some who succeeded in seven days.

When Rahula reported on the course of his cultivation of practice to Buddha, Buddha was very happy, and he praised him and encouraged him. Then he said: "You fully abide by the precepts of discipline, and you have perfected all your faculties. Gradually you will reach the stage where all bonds and the impelling forces [of karma] are ended."

Buddha explains that cultivating *anapana* begins with the method of tempering the breath. After this cultivation is perfected, discipline, concentration, and wisdom are all fully present. You need not make a special effort to keep the precepts: you have already completely achieved the merit of keeping the precepts. All the faculties have been perfected, and you have attained liberation. For example, in Buddhism they say "the four elements are all empty." You must perfect all the faculties, and only then have you "emptied" them out. Only then have you managed to reach the level where hunger and cold and heat cannot bother you: only then is the body made of the four elements transformed.

If you want to realize the state of great arhats, you must cut off "the bonds and compulsions of the three forms of being." The "three forms of being" are the realm of desire, the realm of form, and the formless realm. "The bonds and compulsions of the three forms of being" are psychological activities, that is, psychological conditions and activities constructed by arousing the mind and letting thoughts move. Only when these bonds and compelling forces of habit energy have all been totally cut off are you capable of experiencing the fruit of the great arhats.

Among the ten forms of mindfulness mentioned by the Buddha in this sutra, the one that he says the most about is using the breath to realize the fruit of enlightenment. Buddha's son Rahula also reports on the course of his cultivation and realization of this aspect.

The eleventh and twelfth chapters of *The Ekottara-Agama Sutra* extol the path of filial piety and emphasize how hard it is to repay the benevolence of our parents. This is a point held in common by the basic cultural thought of both China and India, and so after Buddhism was transmitted to China, it was very quickly assimilated by Chinese culture, and developed further.

The ninth form of mindfulness discussed in the sutra is mindfulness of the body. The technique of mindfulness of the body here is discussed in terms of exoteric Buddhism, not the esoteric school of Buddhism. In later generations Chinese Taoists and esoteric Buddhists traveled the road of the esoteric teaching, and put special emphasis on methods of cultivating the body. But in the end, they frequently did not know how to reach liberation with these methods, and instead they went wrong by becoming attached to the cultivation of the body: this is an outside path, not genuine Buddhism. If you know how to take these methods and achieve liberation, then this is not an outside path.

The mindfulness of the body discussed here is a Hinayana method. For example, in the Hinayana "four stations of mindfulness" we must "be mindful that the body is impure, be mindful that sensation is suffering, be mindful that mind is impermanent, and be mindful that phenomena have no self, no independent identities."

When the Hinayana speaks of no self, it is in reference to the manifest forms of presently existing life; the intent is to alert people to transcend this level, and attain nirvana. But when this flowed into the world of learning, especially when it was disseminated in the West, some people thought that the Buddhist idea of no self was nihilism and that it denied the soul, and they maintained that Buddhism is atheistic. This is really a joke.

Before the T'ang and Sung dynasties in China, the people who cultivated practice and realized the fruit of enlightenment were numerous, and those who cultivated the method of mindfulness of the body were particularly numerous. For example, contemplating the impurity of the body and contemplating the skeleton were both methods of mindfulness of the body. The T'ien-t'ai school's cessation and observation used breathing techniques, and added to them cultivation of the contemplation of the impurity of the body and the meditation on the skeleton.

Dharma teacher T'ai-hsu of Ning-po in Chekiang Province had a disciple whose learning was very good. In three months of cultivation he perfected the contemplation of the skeleton. He visualized people as skeletons until he saw everyone as a skeleton, and reached the realm of the second *dhyana*. Later he told me, "Even if we leave home and become monks, desires are still there." Even though he had perfected the contemplation of the skeleton, he nevertheless felt that "even skeletons are still elegant."

Therefore, the contemplation of the impurity of the body and the contemplation of the skeleton must be cultivated to the point that there are no desires. People in the old days could do this, but modern people are not so bright. Modern people feel that even skeletons are still very good looking.

In mindfulness of the body, in contemplating the impurity of the body, the most important thing is to get rid of desire. In the Mahayana precepts of discipline, the first item is the prohibition on killing. In the Hinayana precepts of discipline, the first item is the prohibition on lust. Why are they different?

If you want to attain the ultimate fruit of arhats, you must first curb desire. But as for the contemplation of the skeleton, or the contemplation on the impurity of the body, or the contemplation of counting breaths, the numberless hundreds and thousands of Dharma Gates—almost none of them has a way to deal with lustful desires. This is how hard it is to cut off lustful desires. Only if you can first transform desire can you talk of cultivating realization, and meditative concentration.

The tenth method is mindfulness of death. Human beings all have to die. Old people, in particular, really see and understand birth and death. They finally become capable of abandoning everything, and at the same time, they spur themselves on, and hasten to work hard on their cultivation of practice. In recent times, the great teacher Yin-kuang of the Pure Land school has put special emphasis on cultivating the method of mindfulness of death.

Now let's discuss the ten forms of mindfulness and synthesize them with the basic topic "synthesizing exoteric and esoteric and master the progression of cultivation and realization."

First, mindfulness of Buddha. This mindfulness of Buddha [in Chinese *nien-fo*] is not the Pure Land school's method of mindfulness of Buddha by reciting the buddha-name [also *nien-fo* in Chinese]. Though it has the same basic principle as Pure Land, the method of cultivation is not the same. As *The Agama sutra* relates, this method of mindfulness of Buddha is a method of honoring Buddha, following Buddha, faithfully serving Buddha, and seeking what Buddha achieved, from mind-moment to mind-moment, using Buddha to alert yourself and spur yourself on.

When the Dharma teacher Hui-yuan founded the Pure Land school [around A.D. 400], using the three Pure Land scriptures, his objective was to seek eternal life and immortality. Before Hui-yuan became a monk and studied Buddhism, what he studied was Taoism. Subsequently he realized that the Taoist methods of cultivation for seeking eternal life and immortality were not the last word on the subject, so he turned and began to search within Buddhism. Finally he found the Buddhist teaching in the sutras on Amitabha Buddha that by means of a pure, sincere single-minded invocation of Amitabha, one could be reborn in the land of ultimate bliss [Amitabha's pure land in the West]. So he adopted this method and founded the Pure Land school. Rebirth in the land of ultimate bliss in the West can be said to be eternal life and immortality, but it is not thoroughly finishing with birth and death. You must be reborn there and still keep cultivating practice, and after you succeed, go on to all the worlds of the ten directions to save sentient beings. This is the Mahayana path, which at the same time includes the Hinayana method of mindfulness of Buddha.

Besides this, in esoteric Buddhism there are many, many, methods of mindfulness of Buddha: for example, Vairocana Buddha's method of cultivation, Samantabhadra Tathagata's method of cultivation, the diamond of supreme bliss method of cultivation, the diamond of joy method of cultivation, and so on. All of them are methods of mindfulness of Buddha.

The mindfulness of Buddha that I am discussing here is in the broad sense, and its implications are very wide. The narrow meaning of the word *nien-fo* is the Pure Land school's method of reciting the buddha-name, but that is just one method.

The second of the ten forms of mindfulness is mindfulness of the Dharma. This, too, can be perfected. The average person these days is unable to join together studying to become a buddha, academic Buddhist studies, and the Buddhist religion. If you can really join them into one, this would be mindfulness of the Dharma. For example, we all know of such Buddhist concepts as impermanence, suffering, emptiness, selflessness, and the twelve links of interdependent causation; we all know such Buddhist maxims as "All compounded things are impermanent," and "These are the phenomena of birth and death; when birth and death are extinct, the peaceful extinction of nirvana is bliss." These principles are the Dharma. But all we do is understand these principles, without taking them and using them on our own bodies and minds. If we do not join these principles with our cultivation of realization, then we have no "mindfulness of the Dharma."

What Confucius spoke of as "Fathoming the true principle, fully realizing our true nature, in order to perfect what Heaven has endowed us with"—this, too, is mindfulness of the Dharma. To take the principles of Buddhism, and apply it to our own bodies and minds—this is the method of "mindfulness of the Dharma."

The third method is "mindfulness of the Sangha," mindfulness of the monks and nuns who were worthy sages. For example, how did the famous Zen teachers Ma-tsu and Pai-chang leave home? How did they study Zen? How did they consummate the Path and achieve enlightenment? How did the great teacher Han-shan cultivate practice? We must honor them and model ourselves on them—this is the method of mindfulness of the Sangha. What road did the worthy sages in earlier generations take? What success did they have? When we cultivate practice according to their example, this is "mindfulness of the Sangha." But people today do not read the records of how earlier generations cultivated practice, and they do not emulate the way they cultivated practice. Even if they read their records, they use a supposedly objective point of view to study them, and even go so far as to criticize them. This is not the attitude people who are cultivating practice should have.

The fourth method is "mindfulness of discipline." Mindfulness of discipline is not at all easy. In the past in mainland China on the first and fifteenth days of the lunar month, monks and nuns had to recite the precepts of discipline very solemnly. Every monk or nun who had violated the precepts had to repent these violations one by one and express the hope that he or she would not violate them again. Mindfulness of discipline is different from reciting the precepts: for mindfulness of discipline, each and every precept must be recorded in your mind so that even if you go for a walk, or do anything whatsoever, you will always be mindful of discipline. If you act this way, then your behavior will conform to the regulations in every respect. Can you do this every moment, in every state of mind?

In the disciplinary precepts, there is the distinction between secondary precepts and primary precepts. Those precepts which can be changed according to differences of time and place are called secondary precepts. The primary precepts are the precepts like the three great precepts against murder, robbery, and sexual excess, which can never be violated.

Mindfulness of discipline tells you seriously at all times that you yourself must keep the precepts of discipline. You must keep watch over your thinking and only allow virtuous thoughts to arise. To avoid violating the precepts, you absolutely must not allow bad thoughts or evil thoughts to stir at all.

If young people can really manage to be mindful of discipline very strictly for seven days, they will certainly be able to realize the fruit of *shramanas*, of real monks. After they have realized this station, they will be good at traveling the road of cultivating practice. Nevertheless, there have been very few people in the later generations who have cultivated mindfulness of discipline.

The four boundless minds—the mind of boundless compassion, the mind of boundless sympathy, the mind of boundless joy, and the mind of boundless renunciation—are also within the scope of discipline. The sutras and the disciplinary codes are joined as one. People studying Esoteric Buddhism must be even more strict and diligent in regard to maintaining the precepts of discipline. Every time you cultivate some method, you first cultivate the four boundless minds. You take upon yourself the burden of all the sufferings of sentient beings. You do not cultivate Buddhist Methods for your own sake; you hope that after you have succeeded in your cultivation, you will be able to save sentient beings. All the merits you attain you dedicate to sentient beings, you do not want them at all for your own sake. Generating the mind of enlightenment, and the four boundless minds, and so on—this all belongs to the method of being mindful of discipline.

In recent times esoteric methods are in circulation everywhere, east and west, but the basic principles are absent. This makes me feel that, as the Zen saying goes, "Where there is no barrier, there is nevertheless a barrier." I cannot bear to watch this anymore, I really cannot go on looking at it. The real esoteric teaching is very, very strict in terms of psychological conduct and moral reflection. But when the average people hear of Esoteric Buddhism, they all think of indulging in sexual practices. They have ruined the esoteric school, and they have also ruined the Buddha Dharma. There is no school of Buddhism that is this simple.

The fifth method is "mindfulness of giving." Giving means giving things away and giving things up. Mindfulness of renunciation means you must renounce everything. For example, Shih-teh quoted the Bodhisattva Maitreya to make a verse:

Some people rebuke the clumsy old fellow
But the clumsy old fellow just wishes them well
Some people beat the clumsy old fellow
But the clumsy old fellow just lies down and
    sleeps.

This is giving charity. How can you say it is easy to be mindful of giving! In Mahayana Buddhism the first thing they talk about is giving, but giving is the hardest to cultivate.

In Chinese culture, they talk about the wandering warriors who traveled around fighting for righteous causes and distributing wealth. They gave away wealth without thinking anything of it. They themselves had no money, but they wanted to give money to other people. This, too, counts as giving.

In general when we give, there are strings attached. We are either seeking to acquire merit, or seeking reputation and profit. If you can renounce everything, and give everything up until at last you are empty, then you will experience emptiness. This method of mindfulness of giving also contains a lot within it.

The sixth method is "mindfulness of heaven." In the Western religions they speak of heaven. This is truly cultivating the heavenly path. It is not wrong, and we must not look down on this Western method. People who study Buddhism must not be biased against Western religion. In *The Diamond Sutra* it says: "All the worthy sages use the [absolute] uncontrived truth and yet still make distinctions [in particular provisional methods]." The inner truth of all religions is correct; it's just that they differ in terms of the depth or shallowness of their process of realizing enlightenment and their styles of expressing it are not the same. This is certainly true for Hinayana, the lesser vehicle of Buddhism, and its method of mindfulness of heaven.

How can we cultivate "mindfulness of heaven"? To speak of this is hard on our feelings. Whether or not we will be able to go to heaven after we die is an issue for us average people as we cultivate practice. Let us say no more about being reborn in the West in Amitabha's Pure Land. Su Man-shu said:

> How can I ascend to heaven
> or become a buddha?
> In dark dreams with nothing
> to rely on, I regret I
> cannot prevail.

Speaking in terms of "mindfulness of heaven," this has an extremely vital connection to us. Even at the highest station of the four *dhyanas* and the eight *samadhis*, we still have not escaped from the heavens of the realms of desire, form, and formlessness. Therefore, if we really want to become enlightened, and leap beyond the triple world, this will really not be easy.

# 9

# BREATHING AND
# VARIOUS RANKS OF
# CULTIVATION ATTAINMENT

If we sum up the essential points of the Buddha Dharma, we will understand that Mahayana and Hinayana are inseparable. The cultivation of practice advances together with seeing truth, cultivating realization, and carrying out vows, and through this we seek to realize the fruit of enlightenment. It is certainly not a matter of quiet sitting and meditation work and that's all: that would just be playing around. Therefore, we must first bring up the ten forms of mindfulness in *The Ekottara-Agama Sutra* as a foundation for cultivating practice. The method of the ten forms of mindfulness are the great basic principle: from this developed the eighty-four thousand types of methods for cultivating practice.

In *The Ekottara-Agama Sutra*'s teaching of the ten forms of mindfulness, mindfulness of Buddha comes first. This includes all the methods of contemplation of all the buddhas and bodhisattvas of Pure Land and Esoteric Buddhism. The second of the ten forms is mindfulness of the Dharma, while the third is the mindfulness of the Sangha. All we can do is give a simplified explanation that captures the key points and hope that all of you will make a deep study of these points and learn them for yourselves. You must not act as if you are listening to stories. This would be unworthy of my explanations, and unworthy of yourselves.

The word "mindfulness" [in Chinese *nien*] in the ten forms of mindfulness is different from the word *nien*, meaning "thought," in the expression *wang-nien* ("false thought") in *The Surangama Sutra*'s account of liberation from the five skandhas. They shouldn't be confused.

Except for mindfulness of the body, the rest of these ten methods of mindfulness all belong in the area of the cultivation of spiritual methods. Mindfulness of the body includes the contemplation of the skeleton to liberate us from the vexations this physical body causes us. Mindfulness of *anapana* matches up breathing and spiritual states.

When you read a book, you cannot use only your physical eyes. You must also possess the eye of wisdom. You need to have another eye on your forehead, the eye of wisdom, so you can read with wisdom. *The Ekottara-Agama Sutra* puts special emphasis on mindfulness of the breath. Thus, it relates Buddha's son Rahula's special report on his own personal experience in realizing the fruit of arhatship. The sutra does not contain special reports on the other methods, and because of this, the importance it assigns to mindfulness of the breath is obvious.

Our spirits and bodies differ greatly. When it comes to doing meditation work, very few people set off on the journey. Even in [Confucian] quiet sitting, there are few who are able to purify their false thinking. In other words, if you can employ the method of refining the breath, the same as Rahula, then it will be comparatively easy to achieve results. This point is very important.

Before the Buddha Dharma was transmitted to China, there was a sage who had already brought out the principle of refining the breath. That was the great Confucian teacher Mencius [372-289 B.C.]. In his account of nurturing the breath, in the chapter titled "Kung-sun Ch'ou (first part)" [2 A 2], it says: "I am good at nurturing my flood-like breath. This breath is extremely vast and strong. I nurture it with straightforwardness and do not injure it, and so it fills everything between heaven and earth."

Those who study Buddhism must not look down on other traditions. The truth is common to the whole world. Those who study Buddhism should be even more clear about this, because they know that the Great Vehicle bodhisattvas appear in all sorts of different physical embodiments and use all sorts of different teachings.

The nurturing of the breath mentioned by Mencius is very reasonable. Those who are cultivating the method of *anapana* should pay attention to the words of Mencius [2 A 2]: "When will is unified, it moves the breath. When the breath is unified, it moves the will." If you cannot coordinate your spirit with your breath, then even if you do not want to give rise to false thoughts, you definitely won't be able to do it. In the chapter entitled "Fully Realizing the Mind (second part)" [7 B 25], Mencius brings up the sequence of doing the work of nurturing the breath. He says there is an orderly sequence from being an ordinary person to becoming a sage: "Being wanted is called being good. Having [goodness] in oneself is called being true. Extending and fulfilling it is called being beautiful. Extending it and fulfilling it until it shines forth is called being great. Being great and being transformed in it is called being a sage. Being sagely and unknowable in it is called being a spirit."

When we speak of Mahayana and Hinayana, where is the difference between them? There is no use talking about studying the path of the Mahayana Bodhisattvas if you do not take Hinayana as the basic foundation. There is a big fault with modern people studying the Buddha Dharma: they immediately start talking about the Great Vehicle. But in reality, they haven't even been able to do a proper job with the basis, the vehicle of humanity. The five vehicles are the vehicle of humanity; the vehicle of the *devas*, the celestial beings; the vehicle of the *shravakas*, the literalist disciples; the vehicle of the *pratyekas*, the isolated illuminates; and the vehicle of the *bodhisattvas*, the enlightening beings.

Mahayana, the Great Vehicle, is not that easy. We are not even talking about whether modern day would-be Mahayana Buddhists have properly cultivated the lesser vehicles of the *shravakas* and the *pratyekas*; generally they have problems even cultivating the vehicle of humanity. You must first get the foundation of the vehicle of humanity right. Go study the Confucian classics which focus on the vehicle of humanity. The distinction between Mahayana and Hinayana lies in their different ideas of seeing truth, cultivating realization, and carrying out vows.

The ten forms of mindfulness are methods of cultivation and refinement. As for how to realize the fruit of arhatship, it is not possible by relying only on refining the breath. Why can't you realize the fruit of arhatship this way? It is because your mental practice is still not sufficient, because you have not transformed the psychological basis of vexations and false thoughts and habit-energy, and you have not reached the stage of seeing truth. How can we say it is easy to cultivate practice to the point that you reach the fruit of arhatship, which is the ultimate fruit of Hinayana! It is not easy, after we die, to prevent falling into lower planes of existence, or to attain another human body again. As it is described in the Buddhist scriptures, attaining a human body is like "a blind tortoise happening to poke his head up through a hole in a piece of wood floating in a vast ocean."

In part two of chapter one of *The Nirvana Sutra*, the chapter on Buddha's life span, Buddha speaks a verse:

It is difficult to be born in the world as a human
It is even harder to be born in a world where a
    buddha is present
It is like a blind tortoise in the ocean
Coming upon a hole in a floating board.

A blind tortoise is swimming in the ocean and he happens to bump into a floating board, and there is a hole in the board. This tortoise happens to stick his head into the hole. What a rare coincidence this would be! Our birth as human beings is just as rare and hard to come by as it would be for a blind tortoise in the ocean to happen to stick his head through a hole in a floating board! If you want to be born in the realm of the *devas*, this is even harder!

Becoming a *deva* is the result of cultivation of the four *dhyanas* and eight *samadhis*. After you have successfully cultivated the four *dhyanas* and eight *samadhis*, you are reborn in the plane of the *devas*. But you have still not gone beyond the triple world: you are still revolving in the triple world. We have just mentioned leaping beyond the triple world, and not being among the five elements: how can this be called easy!

Sitting in meditation and cultivating concentration is a method common to both Buddhist and non-Buddhist traditions. It is not present only in Buddhism. Every religion talks about meditation, even the non-Buddhist paths and the deluded paths. When you do meditation work successfully, you can sublimate into the heavens in the realm of desire, or into the plane of the *asuras*, the demigods. It is by no means easy to ascend to the heavenly realms: to do so, you must see truth.

"The delusion of views" means affliction in regard to thinking and concepts, that is, afflictions in regard to seeing truth. In the famous Hinayana philosophical treatise by Vasubandhu, *The Abhidharmakosha Shastra*, the delusion of views is summed up into eighty-eight bonds and compulsions. They are like knots in a cord which cannot be untied. People who study Buddhism have emptiness in their lips, but from beginning to end they cannot untie their mental bonds. The word "bonds" was translated very well from the original Sanskrit. Why can't you untie what binds you? Because of your *ch'i*, because you cannot transform your body of energy and matter: that's why you cannot loosen your bonds.

"The view of the body": This means your clinging and attachment to your body. This includes all kinds of bodily pain and suffering. Lao-tzu said: "The reason I have great troubles is because I have a body." We are busy all through our lives on account of this body, and in the end it will still decompose, and change into a puddle of pus. Nevertheless, is there anyone who does not love this body? So much pain and suffering is all due to the fact that we cannot get free of the view of the body.

"One-sided views": All philosophical thinking falls in the category of one-sided views.

"Misguided views": There are many schools of thought, like the American hippies and the recent loosening of ideas about sex, that are all misguided views. Misguided views are biased views.

"Views that cling to precepts and discipline": This means the aberrations of giving rise to clinging and rejections based on the precepts of discipline.

"Views that cling to views": The different subjective fixed views that various people are attached to.

"Doubt": This means not trusting anyone else. Arrogance and doubt are linked together: in both cases it is the psychological attitude of considering oneself right and other people wrong. This is arrogance and doubt. These are present in everyone.

I will pass over other examples of the delusion of views, such as craving, anger, and arrogance. All of you should investigate them for yourselves. These ideas all belong to Buddhist psychology.

Ordinary psychology presents analyses and investigations at the level of manifest appearances. The more it has developed, the more detailed these have become. Buddhist psychology, like the Abhidharmakosha's schema of the eighty-eight bonds and compulsions and the Yogacara school's *Treatise on the Gate for Illuminating the Hundred Phenomena*, is a moral psychology. In it there is a prerequisite, that is, the idea that only the psychology of people who realize enlightenment is correct, and all the others are not. This is a psychology that is completely and purely good. The Yogacara philosophy of consciousness only[1] is really remarkable. The principles of mind I am

---

[1] The Yogacara philosophy was often epitomized in the Sanskrit term *vijnaptimatrata*, meaning the doctrine of "representations only." The Yogacara adepts observed that ordinary unenlightened people are generally not in touch with reality-as-it-is. Instead, what they perceive is a system of mental representations which they have been trained (by their acculturation) to project upon the outer world of interdependently originating phenomena, phenomena which have no independently existing identities. This process of projecting imaginary categories on the outer world leads to the deluded perception that is typical of sentient beings: the perception of the world in terms of self and others, and independently existing objects. The Chinese translation of *vijnaptimatrata* is *wei-shi*, and this is often translated into English somewhat misleadingly as "consciousness only."

talking about here are only the main principles. If we wanted to analyze them all point by point, it would be impossible to cover them completely.

People who have their hearts set on promoting Yogacara theory should keep this in mind. Don't "close your gate and proclaim yourself emperor," with the attitude that only Buddhist things are wonderful. Ordinary psychology also has some truth to it.

When we cultivate practice, we need to investigate our own psychology. This is a matter of seeing truth. If our mental practice is not done well, then we will not be able to change our behavior in regard to how we treat people and deal with things. We may think we have done our meditation work, but it will be useless. At most we are still no more than blind tortoises in the ocean.

This seeing truth also involved carrying out vows. To cultivate practice of the Hinayana vows, you must realize the fruit of arhatship. Not only must you do your meditation work well, you must rid your mind of these delusions of views and thoughts.

"The nine stages": the triple world, the realms of desire, form, and formlessness, is further divided into a ninefold progression. People in this world are in "the stage of miscellaneous abodes in the five planes" of the realm of desire. The five planes are the planes of *devas*, of human beings, of animals, of hungry ghosts, and of hell. They all dwell here, the place that is the common abode of ordinary people and sages. Added to these are four stages each in the realm of form and the formless realm, to make up nine stages all together.

"The delusions of thought" means the further developments of the aspect of thinking. For example, some people write essays on various aspects of Buddhism, of which it could be said that "the essays are flowery and beautiful, and the research is fine and detailed." Nevertheless their defects fall into the delusions of thought: that is, their thinking has not been clarified. Another example is this: when we are sitting in meditation, sometimes by chance we encounter the realm of *samadhi* and that part of us which can think then thinks: "Aha! This is probably enlightenment!" It does not know that this bit of thought is the delusion of thought. Therefore, the delusion of views and the delusion of thought are two different parts.

Before you have experienced enlightenment, you are always revolving around in the triple world. You should try to investigate this yourself, and report what you have learned from your efforts.

This chapter is very important, because as soon as there are aberrations in our view of truth and in our thoughts, then we have already fallen into the realm of ordinary people, even if we ourselves do not know it.

Among the four fruits that come with cutting off delusion and witnessing reality, when you cut off the afflictions of coarser ideas in the delusion of views, this is the fruit of the one who has "entered the stream," which is also called in Sanskrit *srota-apanna*. This is the first fruit.

"The once-returner": the first through fifth stations in the first stage of cutting off the delusion of thought is called *sakrdagamin*. This is the candidate at the stage of one more rebirth before arhatship. This is also called the fruit of *sakrdagamin*. There are two explanations of *sakrdagamin*. One is in terms of "five returns to the human realm": it says that they go five times through the cycle of ascending to the plane of the devas, and then coming back down to the human realm, and then they do not return again to the human world. The other explanation is that after they die, they ascend to the plane of the devas, and come down once more to the human realm, and then do not return again.

Therefore, in terms of the principles of this teaching, we recognize that it is impossible to become a buddha instantly. It is not at all easy to realize the fruit of arhatship: it depends on our own work in cultivating practice.

In *The Abhidharmakosha-Shastra* there are many references made to the delusion of views and the delusion of thinking, as well as the nine stages of the triple world, and cutting off delusion and witnessing reality. You can consult this work. When it says "shastra," this means that it was not expounded by Buddha: it is a record of the experience of some bodhisattvas in cultivating realization and achieving the results that is reported to us.

When Buddha was in the world, society was not as complicated as it is now. Thus, when Buddha taught these few methods in *The Agama-sutras*, many of his disciples were able to realize the fruit of arhatship on the spot. But why is it so hard for later people to achieve enlightenment?

If we want to cultivate the Path and realize the fruit of enlightenment, we cannot be unclear in seeing the truth of the Buddha's teachings. It will be useless only to try to cultivate the Path without comprehending its principles. Even if we perform the meditation work well enough, if we do not comprehend the principles, it will still be useless. These days there are many so-called teaching masters who can do meditation work very well and can produce all kinds of experiential realms. But when they die, they still have strokes and diabetes. These people have all concentrated on doing meditation work, but they have not yet mastered the true principles of Buddhism.

On the other hand, people who only comprehend the principles and do not do the meditation work are either worried or sick every single day of their lives. Even though this body is detestable, and is an empty illusion, it is very hard to make arrangements for these few dozen pounds of flesh. Therefore, it will not work if you only do meditation work and do not manage to see truth, or manage to carry out vows. And it will not work either if you only see the truth and do not cultivate realization successfully.

Only if you do the work of meditative concentration properly will you be able to ascend to heaven, to the plane of the *devas*. The average person doesn't even take the first step toward going to heaven: why? Because he does not cut off sexual relations. Thus we must first explain the fruit of the Hinayana from its basis. Not only are sexual relations not permitted; even nocturnal emissions, masturbation, and all methods of self-gratification, along with lustful thoughts, are all not permitted. That is why the first item in the Hinayana precepts is a prohibition on lust.

Not leaking vital energy *ching* does not mean not leaking seminal fluid. Men who are cultivating practice must transform it away before the seminal liquid has moved. The Taoist Kuang Ch'eng Tzu says: "When sentiments stir within, it is sure to disturb your vital energy." [The Chinese word for semen, *ching*, also denoted vital energy in Taoist terminology.] As soon as there is a thought in your mind, as soon as your emotions stir, your vital energy has already scattered. This is the meaning of this *ching*, vital energy: it is not the *ching* meaning semen. If even this leakage of vital energy is wrong, how much the more so with nocturnal emissions (which the Taoists call letting the elixir leak), masturbation, self-gratification, and so on. As the basic foundation, you must maintain this discipline. But to my knowledge, ordinary people cannot do this. After sitting in meditation for several days, they collapse again.

Next is the matter of food and drink. There are many people who do the meditation work properly, but they have trouble with their bowels and stomachs, and so their work is spoiled.

After letting us know all the principles of how to remedy these problems, the Buddhist scriptures tell us that Buddha's disciples realized the fruit of arhatship within three or five or seven days. These are things that positively occurred. Thus, immediate sudden enlightenment can be accomplished: the crucial point is to pay attention to maintaining discipline.

Volume 8 of *The Surangama Sutra* mentions ten kinds of immortals. A common reason for attacking *The Surangama Sutra* as a forgery written in China is that in India they did not have the way of the immortals, only in China. In reality the Brahmanical religion of cultivating the path of the immortals in India preceded Buddhism. For example, there are people almost all over the world, even in South Africa and South America, chanting the mantra "Om mani padme hum," but this certainly did not come from China. In this era people who concern themselves with learning and culture often, "make the cart behind closed doors" [without checking to see if it will work in the real world] and "shut their doors and proclaim themselves kings." How lamentable!

Speaking of these ten kinds of immortals in Volume 8 of *The Surangama Sutra*, Buddha says: "All of them cultivated their minds while in the human realm. They did not cultivate correct awakening. Instead they found another principle of life: they live for a thousand or ten thousand years. They rest deep in the mountains, or on the islands of the ocean, far from the abode of humans. Thus they still revolve in the stream of false thought and do not cultivate *samadhi*. When the longevity which is their reward is exhausted, they are reborn and enter into the various planes of existence."

These ten kinds of immortals only cultivate themselves on the level of mind: they do not have a great penetrating awakening and witness enlightenment. They have grasped in their hands the key to life and existence, and they can achieve lifetimes that last a thousand or ten thousand years. But this is the flow of cycling thought: they have not illuminated mind or seen true nature, and they can still fall back into lower realms of existence.

If you can illuminate mind and see true nature, this is correct. If you cling to a method as the ultimate, this is not correct. If you do not illuminate mind and see true nature, then nothing is right. If you succeed in realizing enlightenment, then everything is right.

Buddha speaks again of the heavenly plane: "People in the world do not seek eternity, and they cannot relinquish their love for their wives and concubines." Some people can avoid being sentimentally attached to this world. They are not like the people on the path of the immortals who want to live for a thousand, or ten thousand, or several tens of thousands of years. But they cannot relinquish their love for their wives. Many people think like this.

But the sutra tells us that some people can do it: "their minds do not run off into excesses of misguided lust." The method of the Confucians is also like this: no matter what you do, your mind must not scatter in confusion. Such people, the sutra says, "become clear and radiant and give forth light, and after their lives end, they approach the sun and moon." After they die, people like this, who have cultivated themselves to this extent, can transcend this world of ours, and be reborn in the four *deva*-king heavens in the heavenly plane of existence. But this is still within the realm of desire: these are called the six heavens of desire.

The *devas* in the six heavens of desire have a longer life span than we do, and they are free from the sufferings and afflictions of this world of ours. The rewards are very great, so it is always people who do good things, cultivate good practices, and do meditation work who are reborn there. They are called the devas of the heavens of desire because they are not detached from sexual desire. Although the devas who dwell there are not detached from desire, they have sublimated desire to a high extent, and so they can ascend to the six heavens of desire.

In Volume 5 of *The Yogacarabhumi Shastra*, concerning the second of the three stages of deliberate attention and investigation, it says: "None of the *devas* of the realm of desire are born from wombs. The *devas* of the heavens of the four *deva*-kings come forth by transformation from the shoulders or the breasts of their parents like 5-year-old children."

In *The Creation of the World Sutra*, Volume 7, part two of chapter eight, entitled "The Thirty-Three Heaven," it records the following: "O monks, in heaven the *deva* children come forth suddenly from the knees or from between the legs of the male and female *devas* when they are sitting. When they are first born, they are already like 12-year-old children in the world of humans. If they are *deva*-boys, they are born from the knees of the male *devas* as they are sitting. If they are *deva*-girls, they are born between the legs of the female *devas*."

As for the *devas* in the heavens of the realm of form, they are born from their fathers: the tops of the fathers' heads split open, and they come forth. All the *devas* have a crown of flowers on top of their heads. Before they die, the crown of flowers first withers. At this time the male and female *devas* all weep: this *deva* will soon die, and will have to descend into lower realms. When *devas* reach the lower realms, they change into humans like us. And yet we humans still think we are so great!

Human beings rely on sexual relations to propagate themselves. When the *devas* in the realm of desire engage in desire, as it says in *The Creation of the World Sutra*, part two of chapter eight, "The Thirty-Three Heaven": "When the *devas* in the heavens of the four *deva*-kings and in the Thirty-Three heaven engage in desire, their sense faculties reach a state of contentment, and they all give out a breath of wind. All the *devas* in the Yamadeva heaven consummate their desire by holding hands. In the Tushita heaven they consummate their desire by thinking. In the Nirmanarati heaven they consummate their desire by an intense look. In the Paranirmita-vasavartin heaven they consummate their desire by speaking together. In the Mara heaven they consummate their desire by looking at each other." The *devas* in the heavens of the realm of form can communicate their feelings to each other with a glance. The *devas* in the heavens of the formless realm do not even have to look at each other: all they have to do is think of each other to give birth to the next generation.

If we collect together the references in this section of the Buddhist scriptures that describe the *devas* of the three realms, it would make a novel. It turns into a view of life in a new universe. Certainly it would be very popular and very worthwhile.

Only when you cultivate practice to the point that you reach the first *dhyana* can you be reborn in the heavens of the realm of desire. Why so? Because people in the first and second *dhyana* have still not totally cut off desires. In the end those desires belong to the delusions of thought. They are refined, not crude. They look at themselves and feel that they are very beautiful, that they have no misguided thoughts. These sentiments belong to the delusions of thought: they too are craving, anger, and ignorance.

Speaking of ignorance, here is a poem by a very brilliant literary man of olden times, Kung Ting-an of the Ch'ing dynasty:

> The sunset red is not an unfeeling thing
> It changes into spring mud and protects the flowers.

Sympathy for the flowers: what a beautiful line! Then, too, there is the poem by Huang Shang-ku of the Sung dynasty:

Before dawn, returning from a dream a thousand miles away
In a single day, thinking of my parents all twenty-four hours.

From the point of view of the Buddha Dharma, both these poems are the delusion of thought, they are the vexations of feeling and thinking, the root of birth and death, the root of *samsara*, cyclic existence. Of course in these verses feeling and thinking have already been greatly sublimated.

Desire is very crude, so if desire is not cut off, you cannot realize the fruit of enlightenment. How can you cut off desire? First Buddha teaches us not to eat after noon. There are several great merits to not eating after noon: first, it makes it so it is not easy to sink into a torpor; second, it cuts off the tendency to get sleepy; third, it cuts off emotional desires; and fourth, it makes the body pure and bright.

Buddha taught no other method than this for cutting off desire. Still, cutting off desire is very very difficult. When young people sit in meditation, just when they are managing to do the meditation work well, emotional desires come on. If emotional desires are absent, when they start to sit in meditation, they are half torpid and half asleep. How should this be handled? They should rely on refining the breath. That's why "mindfulness of *anapana*," the eighth of the ten forms of mindfulness, is so extraordinarily important.

There are two great schools within Buddhism that put special emphasis on refining the breath in order to seek *samadhi*. One is the T'ien-t'ai school with its practices of tempering the breath, counting breaths, and listening to the breath. (Reference works for this are Chih-i's books: *The Great Cessation and Contemplation, The Greater Cessation and Contemplation, The Lesser Cessation and Contemplation,* and *The Six Subtle Gates of the Lesser Cessation and Contemplation.*) The other is the Gelugpa sect of Tibetan Esoteric Buddhism. Its founder Tsongkhapa, in his *Great Treatise on the Stages of the Path of Enlightenment*, emphasizes that in doing meditation work we must pay attention to tempering the breath. The various schools of Taoism pay even more attention to refining the breath. They say that you can realize enlightenment only after you have properly refined yourself by cultivating the breath, and the *ch'i* channels, and the bright points, and the kundalini.

Why is the breath this important? The four elements of life are earth, water, fire, and wind. Bones and muscles belong to the earth element, and are not very good for beginning the work of cultivation and refinement. To the water element belong blood and the bodily fluids: to begin the work of cultivation and refinement from this point is also very difficult. However, after meditation work is done properly, the water element in the body is totally purified: at this stage, when blood flows out, it is a white milky liquid. As for the fire element, when meditation work reaches the proper temperature, the true fire of *samadhi* comes forth, all sicknesses are removed, and you can live forever without dying.

In sum, the most important of the four elements is the wind element, that is, the breath that moves in and out as you breathe. If you cannot take a breath, you may die, so the breath is most important. There is an important link between thoughts and breathing. The more thoughts scatter in confusion, the more disturbed the breathing becomes. When thoughts become fine, the breathing becomes fine along with them. When the nose is not breathing in or breathing out, this is called "respiration."

Therefore, if you cannot properly temper your breathing when you are sitting and doing meditation, then you cannot talk of reaching *samadhi*, and you cannot talk of the T'ien-t'ai cessation and contemplation. At most you will have only a bit of a shadow of this, that's all. After sitting meditation, when your body changes for the better, this is by no means because you have properly cultivated this technique. It is because while you were sitting quietly, you were tempering your breath in the formlessness, and your breath became finer, so your body changed for the better. If we concentrate our will on cultivating practice, then the results will be even greater.

From the first step of beginning cultivation, to realizing the fruit and becoming an arhat, and going on to become a buddha, no matter whether Mahayana or Hinayana, none of it departs from this method of *anapana*. In *The Ekottara-Agama Sutra*, by means of Rahula's report, Buddha has already given us the news. It's just that we have not paid enough attention to it.

For the time being let's not talk about attaining enlightenment. If while we are alive we can have few sicknesses and few afflictions, if as we go along we can be skillful and straightforward, not troubling ourselves and not being a burden to others, we will be first class human beings. If we rely on refining and cultivating the breath, it will be very easy to attain this goal. Refining the breath is the first step because the true breath is not the physical breath. The method involved in this first step is like taking a burning brand to light something and making it catch fire. Thus in Esoteric Buddhism they call it "the method of igniting." We rely on our mundane breathing to ignite that inborn, inherent, original "breath" and make it begin to exercise its function.

When some people sit in meditation, their bodies may spontaneously begin to shake. This is because there is a problem in their bodies. When the breath moves, it goes to the place that has a problem, and that plate spontaneously begins to shake. Take advantage of the present time when you are still healthy to start refining your breath. Don't wait until the sickness has become grave to start, or there won't be enough time.

In the teaching of the T'ien-t'ai school's *Lesser Cessation and Contemplation*, there is a verse naming six different kinds of breath associated with the heart, liver, spleen, kidneys, the triple warmer,[2] and lungs.

In places where the air is clean, use one of these six sound forms, and exhale, without making a sound: exhale until you cannot exhale anymore (pulling in your stomach), shut your mouth, and let the breath spontaneously be drawn in. Keep on refining the breath until you get tired, then stop and do the meditation work of tempering the breath. This point is what the *Lesser Cessation and Contemplation* calls "having awareness and having contemplation." You feel that you are not breathing in and out any more, that you are very light, and that miscellaneous thoughts have been reduced. Slowly keep on practicing, and there will be all sorts of transformations within your body.

To help transform the body there is also the yoga technique of washing the stomach by swallowing a long strip of gauze. Swallow one end, and pull on the other end with your hand. Swallow it into your stomach and then pull it out. People who feel sick to their stomachs when doing this should immediately consult a doctor.

There is also the method of washing the brain where you inhale clear water up through your nose. When you first practice this, your head will hurt as if it is being pierced by ten thousand needles. But

---

[2] The "triple warmer" *san-chiao* is an anatomical term from traditional Chinese medical theory that has no English equivalent. It is now a well-known term for students of acupuncture.

after you have gotten used to it, you will be able to inhale the water in and blow it out through your mouth. After you have perfected this practice, when you inhale breath, it will not only go to the lungs, but at the same time it will also be able to go into the brain. The breath will pervade the whole brain, and at the same time reach to the soles of the feet. Chuang-tzu said: "The true person breathes with his feet; the ordinary person breathes with his throat." This is not at all incorrect.

Another method of washing the stomach is to lift your head back and reach back with the tip of your tongue to the top of your uvula. Retch as if you are going to vomit and you can cleanse the filth from your stomach. Best of all is to fast one day a week, drinking only water: it will purify your bowels and stomach, and your body will become healthy.

All of these methods we've reviewed are deliberate, contrived methods. Esoteric Buddhist methods, like the breath in the jewel bottle and the nine section Buddha-wind, follow the road of yogic technique.

If the four elements of the body are not tempered, it will be absolutely impossible to attain *samadhi* by sitting in meditation. If the breath is not properly tempered, the body will not be healthy. At the same time, we must understand nutrition and medical science. The Confucians say: a Confucian is ashamed if there is anything he does not know. Therefore, you must set your mind on knowing about all branches of learning. This is the Mahayana spirit: all forms of essential commonsense learning are the bodhisattva path. Conversely, if you do not understand and do not study, then you are an ordinary person.

The better you do your work with breath, the more vigorous your spirit will be, and you will be tireless. If your mind does get tired nevertheless, investigate the reasons for this later.

At this time, false thought has been reduced to a minimum: if you temper and adjust the breath properly, false thought is fundamentally absent. When false thought is no longer there, the delusion of thought arrives. So when you are sitting in meditation you will feel like this: "Hey! I have already sat for a very long time. It's not that I have not cut off false thought: it's that delusion is not yet cut off." These two levels are not the same, though their basic substance is not very different. Therefore, if people who study Zen have not even discovered these two principles in their studies, how can this be called Zen? It is nothing but a useless meditation case. In studying Zen, you must open up to enlightenment. A person who has been

enlightened already has the wisdom that has no teacher and spontaneously understands these principles.

When you get to the point that you don't want to work on the
breath, take note of what Rahula said: "When the breath comes in, I
know that the breath comes in. When the breath goes out, I know
that the breath goes out." The breath inside the body is like energy in
motion. The Taoists have the theory of the two channels for the vital
breath, the *ch'i*, which are called *jen-mai* and *tu-mai*.[3] In reality, this
is the functioning of the breath. The theory of *jen-mai* and *tu-mai* is
an example of the delusion of views.

When they get to the situation where they know when the breath
comes in and goes out, and they have awareness and contemplation,
some people feel that their bodies are still there and think that this is
because they have not emptied out false thought. In fact this way of
thinking is contradictory, and even if they do ten more years of meditation work, it will be useless. This feeling that the body is still there
is a natural phenomenon at the first stage of having awareness and
contemplation. To think this is false thought is a confusion about
principles. If you stake your life on thinking of a way to get rid of
false thought, how will you be able to attain *samadhi*? How will you be
able to get on the road? You will be acting in vain. When you reach
this point in your meditation work, you should consult this report of
Rahula's.

After you have reached the point where the breath really fills
you, you can forget your body and advance to seek the Mahayana
Path. You can advance further and reach the point where "the wind
of inherent nature is true emptiness and the emptiness of inherent
nature is true wind, the pure fundamental state, pervading the realm
of reality."

Buddha has told us the secret. The coming and going of the
breathing is a phenomenon belonging to birth and death, an apparent
phenomenon. Our lives are all within birth and death. Yet we can
make the breath go and make it come, and make that thing which
belongs to birth and death so that it is not within birth and death.
That is the basic essence: illuminating mind and seeing true nature is
seeing the essence of this mind. Therefore, when refining the breath,

---

[3] See Nan Huai-chin's *Tao and Longevity* (York Beach, ME: Samuel Weiser,
1984).

if we are following the Mahayana road, in *samadhi* there is wisdom, and "the wind of inherent nature is true emptiness and the emptiness of inherent nature is true wind." Then we reach "the pure fundamental state, pervading the realm of reality." This achieves the same subtle, wondrous result by different means as Mencius's saying: "This breath is extremely vast and strong. I nurture it with straightforwardness and do not injure it, and so it fills everything between heaven and earth."

Refining the breath is very important because by refining the breath you can cut off desires and achieve the stage where you do not let the elixir leak away. By refining the breath, old people can make their *yang* energy come back again. Sick people can use this method to get rid of their ailments, restore their health, and extend their lives. In sum, all the wonders of the hundreds and thousands of Dharma Gates are all right here in this method.

# 10

# REFINING THE VITAL ENERGY

We discussed the importance of the mindfulness of *anapana*, which in common parlance is called refining the breath. *Anapana* means cultivating the breath as it moves in and out. It includes many techniques belonging to both the exoteric and esoteric teachings of Buddhism, but the fundamental principle is the same. If we add to this Indian Brahmanism and yogic techniques, and Chinese Taoism, there are at least several hundred kinds of methods. Although there are many methods, in the final analysis they are all methods of refining the *ch'i* and refining the breath. One must remember, however, that the work of refining the breath and realizing the fruit of enlightenment are two different things. Unfortunately, everyone likes contrived methods and students of Buddhism pass these methods on to others in such a fashion that they get them wrong. Pay attention to proper method.

If you can hear the sound of your breathing even when you are in a very noisy place, you have accomplished stable, still meditation. When the Zen patriarch Bodhidharma entered *samadhi* on Mount Sung, he heard the sound of the ants under the stairs fighting as loud as thunder. Such things really happen.

A great disciple of Hsuan-tsang was the Dharma master K'uei-chi, who was also called Master San-ch'e. He went to Mount Chung-nan to visit the Vinaya master Tao-hsuan of the Vinaya school [the school that concentrates on discipline]. Vinaya master Tao-hsuan had perfected the merit of maintaining the precepts of discipline, and so male and female *devas* often came to his abode to make offerings of food to him. When K'uei-chi tried to look up at those *devas*, the *devas* did not appear, and so all he and Tao-hsuan could do was endure their hunger.

At night as he slept, Vinaya master Tao-hsuan sat up and did not lie down. K'uei-chi paid no attention to this, and lay down and fell asleep. His appearance as he slept was not very good and he also snored. The next day Vinaya master Tao-hsuan said to him:

"According to the guidelines for monks, if you do not sleep sitting up, then you must lie down in an auspicious posture. You sleep in a way that goes against these guidelines, snoring and tossing and turning, and you bothered me all night with your noise."

K'uei-chi said: "I did not sleep well the whole night, and I was bothered by the noise you made. I slept fine until midnight, but then something happened. You had a flea on your waist, which bit you. You stretched out your hand, intending to swat it, but then you thought it over some more, and you could not kill a living thing, so you took it and put it down on the ground. You had to put it down with all your strength, and putting it down from so high, you snapped off one of its legs, so it cried in pain all night long, and made so much noise I could not sleep well."

Vinaya master Tao-hsuan did not dare say anything. He thought to himself: "Since this really happened, how did he know?" After K'uei-chi left, the *devas* came again at noon with offerings of food. Vinaya master Tao-hsuan asked the *devas*: "Why didn't you come at noon yesterday?" The *devas* replied: "We did come yesterday at noon, but we saw the whole mountain peak covered with auspicious five-colored clouds, and we could not find your thatched hut. Moreover, on the outside of the auspicious clouds there were many diamond spirit protectors of the Dharma. We knew for certain that there was a great bodhisattva on the mountain, and we minor *devas* from the heavens of the realm of desire could not approach. When Vinaya master Tao-hsuan heard this, there was simply nothing he could say.

How is it that K'uei-chi could be aware of such a small sound while he was asleep? What power of *samadhi* is this? When the Zen patriarch Bodhidharma entered *samadhi* on Mount Sung and he heard the sound of the ants fighting under the stairs as loud as thunder, it was the same principle.

When you are in a noisy place, it is very difficult to hear the sound of your own breathing. At the beginning you can hear the sounds of the pulse moving, the sounds of the heart, and the sound of the blood circulating. People who have accomplished stable, quiet meditation can hear if something is not right in the sound and then know where the body has developed a problem.

A student came to me with the following comment: "When I try to practice the method of *anapana*, after six or seven days the following situation develops. As soon as I sit down, because I have studied Buddhism for many years, it spontaneously changes to counting breaths. Then I focus my attention on my nose, but I am not aware if my breaths are long or short or cool or warm. Later I gradually adjust and become aware of this. But after I have counted about three breaths, I forget to focus my attention on my nose, and I again forget whether my breaths are long or short or cool or warm. Then a strong light suddenly appears. I clearly realize that I cannot covet it, or this would be clinging. After I become aware of my mistake, I gather in my mind again, and again resume focusing attention on my nose. The more I do this, the more disturbed I become, and it changes into doing breath-work, not cultivating practice. Later I may count breaths, or I may see this light, but the more I try to bring myself to order, the more chaotic I become."

If you are in the midst of counting breaths, like this student was, as soon as a thought stirs—as soon as miscellaneous thoughts diverge from your breath—you must begin counting again. No miscellaneous thoughts are permitted: you should go straight along. Lu Fang-weng's poem says: "Count a thousand breaths at one sitting." This indicates that one sitting is at least several hours. In their time, famous men like Lu Fang-weng and Su Tung-po did meditation work.

Anyone who eats too much, or who has high blood pressure, or who cannot sleep, or has a lot of miscellaneous thoughts and extravagant desires, must count the breaths going out. Anyone whose body is feeble, or who has low blood pressure, or whose brain and nerves are weak, must count the breaths coming in. This is the way to deal with what ails them. Buddha is the great king of physicians: he can cure the illnesses of sentient beings. The first step in cultivating practice is to understand medical principles. You cannot cultivate practice properly without understanding medical principles. People whose bodies are neither good nor bad should divide the day into before and after noon, and count breaths as they go out before noon and breaths as they go in after noon.

We have discussed liberation from the eighty-eight bonds and compulsions. When I explain the methods of refining the breath, students think they have gotten a great secret. They think they have gotten a precious jewel, and that this is the Buddha Dharma. Rather, the real Buddha Dharma is a matter of mental practice, of liberation from the eighty-eight bonds and compulsions.

The student who asked this question has not been able to coordinate seeing the truth with his meditation work. His knowledge is not clear, and he has not penetrated the true principle. Tempering

| Realm | Taoist Correspondences | Esoteric Buddhist Correspondences |
|---|---|---|
| Desire | Vitality (*Ching*) | Bliss |
| Form | Energy (*Ch'i*) | Illumination |
| Formlessness | Spirit (*Shen*) | No-thought |

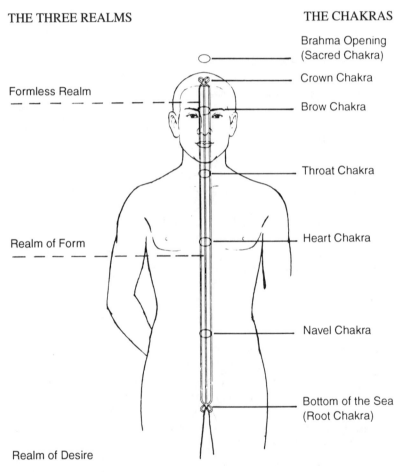

THE THREE REALMS      THE CHAKRAS

Brahma Opening (Sacred Chakra)

Crown Chakra

Formless Realm

Brow Chakra

Throat Chakra

Realm of Form

Heart Chakra

Navel Chakra

Bottom of the Sea (Root Chakra)

Realm of Desire

Figure 1. The three realms and their correspondence to Taoist and Esoteric Buddhist concepts.

the breath and stopping the breath are no more than elementary techniques for getting rid of miscellaneous thoughts. Once miscellaneous thoughts are gone, these techniques are of no further use. In *The Diamond Sutra* Buddha says: "You monks know that the Dharma I expound is like a raft to be abandoned when you have crossed to the other shore of the ocean of affliction. You must relinquish even the Dharma, to say nothing of all that is not the Dharma." Thus, to cross a river you use a boat. But after you have crossed the river, if you put the boat on your back and walked off, wouldn't that be very stupid? This student's question arises because he has done too much tempering the breath. It is like taking too much nutrition, which also may produce sickness.

When light appears before your eyes, you must temper your breath properly. When the breath fills you, an inner light will certainly arise. At that point, without using a lamp at night, you will be able to see as clearly as you would with a lamp. This is the effect of the breath, but it is not the fruit of enlightenment.

In the illustration (on opposite page) the region below the heart cavity belongs to the realm of desire, the region from the heart cavity up to the eyes belongs to the realm of form, and the region above the eyebrows belongs to the formless realm, joined to empty space.

What the Taoists call *ching* (vitality), *ch'i* (energy), and *shen* (spirit), and what Esoteric Buddhism terms bliss (if the vitality does not descend, bliss is not born), illumination, and no-thought, are other formulas for expressing the three realms. Thus, Rahula's route of cultivating the breath in Buddhism is a method of cultivating the realm of form.

The achievement of a buddha's body of bliss, buddha's *sambhogakaya*, is an accomplishment in the realm of form. If you do not move beyond the realm of desire and reach the realm of form, you cannot become a buddha. If you cannot sublimate and reach the realm of form, you cannot achieve *sambhogakaya*, the body of bliss. Vairocana Buddha is *dharmakaya* buddha, the body of reality, the ontological absolute. *Dharmakaya* is the essence; *sambhogakaya* is the appearance. Shakyamuni Buddha represents *nirmanakaya* buddha, a physical manifestation of buddha: this is the function.

By studying Zen and the other methods of exoteric Buddhism, it is easy to achieve the *dharmakaya*, but it is very hard to achieve the *sambhogakaya* and even harder to achieve the *nirmanakaya*.

When you have properly tempered the breath, it is very easy to produce a realm of light. But once the realm of light arrives, it is easy to produce a contradiction. That is when your knowledge of Buddhism must come in to say to you, "How can you be attached to form? This is false thought." In fact, whether you are attached to form or not, you must forget your body and not become attached to the light, but just be spontaneous within the light. At this point, if you feel it is not correct, this is because you have too much knowledge of Buddhism. While you are in the light, you forget about your body, about the four elements, about your breathing: you don't pay attention to anything. Then the light changes into peaceful stillness, pure peaceful stillness, and it also may change into other realms. What it's like after this transformation, I'll tell you when you get there.

People who have succeeded in cultivating this technique are all very optimistic. They have no worries or afflictions. There are also many other advantages. For example, it is easy to reach the realm where

Waves fly in the great ocean but the mind does not dwell on them
Clouds arise on the shore of delusion and you soar in dreams.

Your body may be especially hale and hearty. When your meditation work reaches this point, your saliva is sweet, indescribably sweet. This is due to the pituitary hormones coming down. The glands in your chest and the sexual glands in the lower part of your body corresponding to the realm of desire are completely transformed.

However, this vigor of the nervous system can easily bring on desires, so it is just as the line in the poem says: "Waves fly in the great ocean but the mind does not dwell on them." When the breath is too vigorous, when you have nurtured it too well, if you do not understand the Buddha Dharma, if you have not set to work on the Dharma Gate of the mind-ground to deal with the eighty-eight bonds and compulsions, then it turns into a spirit of reckless, overexuberant heroism. When this happens, "clouds arise on the shore of delusion and you soar in dreams," and people all feel that they are about to fly away. (Immortal swordsmen must pass through this process before they are completely refined.)

If you return from this state to the Dharma Gate of the mind-ground, then you can realize the fruit of arhatship. As for the Taoist spiritual immortals, they, too, go forward from this.

When you eat your fill, you cannot do breath-work, because to do breath-work your bowels and stomach must be clear. When we study Buddhism, we are following the Dharma Gate of the mind-ground. When we make use of refining the breath in our practice, this is only an auxiliary method. It is not that we concentrate on doing breath-work.

After you have really managed to refine the breath, the Taoists have a few lines for you based on their experience: "When vitality (*ching*) is full, you do not think of lust. When energy (*ch'i*) is full, you do not think of food. When the spirit (*shen*) is full, you do not think of sleep." After your spirit has become full, if you still talk about not giving your all, it is correct. When your energy is full, you will feel your body to be like a burst of energy. It will really be that "clouds arise on the shore of delusion and you soar in dreams." Walking on the road will be like stepping on cotton, and you can cultivate a feeling of lightness.

But people who have studied Buddhism will not be drawn to these aspects. They know that everything is created by mind alone, and that if the mind concentrates on making things in that area, it will become that way.

When your meditation work reaches a certain level, and you want to experience the result and enter *samadhi*, it will be impossible if you do not stop eating grain. At most you will eat a little fruit: your bowels and stomach will not need anything else. If monks and nuns can refrain from eating after noon, and in the afternoon do all they can to make efforts and cultivate their breath, they will get great advantages. After you have a basis in your meditation work, nutrition won't matter anymore. Men and women differ in this.

Another issue to consider in regard to cultivating the ten forms of mindfulness are sexual impulses, for they form an obstruction to cultivating practice. The reason why people cannot realize the fruit of enlightenment is because of sexual desire and the desire for food and drink. If you cannot transform these, you will have no basis for cultivating realization. In terms of doing breath-work, if you let the elixir leak away it will not work.

For women, just before and just after their menstrual periods, the relationship of the physical state and their breath-work is very close. If they can cultivate practice properly, their menses will gradually be reduced, until they completely stop, and their bodies will return to a youthful state. Men take on the characteristic of Buddha, whose penis was hidden inside his body. After they have become like this, the pressure of desire is reduced seventy percent. The other thirty percent is very difficult to be liberated from. At that point it is not that your mind wants something, and it is not that your sixth consciousness is setting thoughts moving. Rather, it is what Yogacara theory calls the seeds of habit energy in the storehouse consciousness. If you can transform these seeds of habit energy, then you can transcend ordinary life and enter into the realm of sagehood.

For the desire between men and women, the Chinese language uses the word *hsing,* which in modern Chinese is the usual word for sex. In the Zen formula "illuminating mind and seeing inherent nature" the word *hsing* is also used, but in its classical meaning of "inherent nature." This usage is very wondrous, because the *hsing* of sex and the *hsing* of inherent nature are almost the same thing, and very hard to distinguish. Desire is the ultimate item of ignorance. If you cannot finish with this item, then you will not be able to leap out of the realm of desire.

By following the path of cultivating breath, it is easy to ascend to the heavens of the realm of form, a level higher than the realm of desire. If you cultivate practice according to the Zen school's path of "no-thought," you can ascend to the formless realm. But each of the three realms has its biases. If you only follow the method of cultivation that belongs to any one of them, you will never be able to experience the fruit of enlightenment or consummate the path of enlightenment.

If you refine your vitality and attain bliss, your whole body will feel comfortable beyond compare. This is called a bodhisattva's inner contact with wondrous bliss. Every cell is happy with the finest, most subtle feeling of happiness. You must be this way before you can attain *samadhi.* But it is very easy to fall from this state, and sink down into the realm of the bliss of desire.

These states all belong to the four intensified practices. Intensified practice means to add effort. If you add effort without adding it right, don't even talk about studying Buddhism or cultivating the path of enlightenment. First comes attaining bliss. Bliss is born from vitality. If the vitality does not descend, bliss is not born. But for the ordinary person, once the vitality descends in the form of semen, he is letting the elixir leak away. If it is not nocturnal emissions, then it is desirous thoughts: he seeks out sexual activity, and his semen is lost. Afterward, he begins again to do meditation work. This cycle is repeated over and over: this is the realm of the ordinary man. That is why, out of ten thousand men who cultivate practice, not one realizes the fruit of enlightenment.

If the breath does not fill you, then the light will not arise. Once the breath fills you, then there will spontaneously be a single light inside and outside. If you just stay in the realm of wondrous bliss, you may fall into the realm of desire. If you just stay in the realm of light, you may fall into the realm of form. If you go the way of the empty mind and no-thought of the later generations of the Zen school, you will fall into the formless realm. Pay attention to this! If you persist in no-thought for a long time, it becomes indifference, and it is then easy to fall into the plane of the animals. Thus the great teacher Tsongkhapa, in his *Great Treatise on the Stages of the Path of Enlightenment,* repudiates no-thought and avers that it makes it easy to fall into the animal plane. He was entirely correct.

I'll say it again. If you do not attain bliss, then you will not be able to attain *samadhi.* If you do not attain the light, then you will not be able to engender wisdom. If you do not enter no-thought, then you will not be able to attain emptiness. Even so, if you want to attain emptiness, you also must be fully equipped with discipline, concentration, and wisdom. It will not be possible if you are lacking any one of these. If there is any aberration, you will fall into the three realms of desire, form, and formlessness, and you will not be able to leap out.

After vitality and breath fill you, the first response is that desire comes on. Several years ago I had a friend who wrote a treatise called "Sex is not Evil," and asked me to evaluate it. It said that sex in itself is without so-called good and evil. It is like a knife, which can save people, and which can also injure people, though in itself it has no distinction of good and evil. This principle is not easy for ordinary people to understand. Sexual desire is a form of ignorance, but ignorance is not necessarily evil: all we can say is that it is ignorance. Ignorance is linked to the karma of delusion. Whether or not the karma of delusion is good or evil, that is another function. The karma of delusion can only be counted as affliction, and there is good and bad affliction. However, without the force of this ignorance, we would not be able to experience enlightenment. When this force comes on, if we cannot transform it, then we become ordinary people in the realm of desire. Thus the Taoists call it "the gate between the two realms." When desire comes on, if we turn it upward, then it is heaven, but if we turn it downward, then it is hell. In truth it is not easy to get a hold on this.

The Buddha Dharma talks all the time about discipline, concentration, and wisdom. In fact, in the exoteric teachings they only mention them and stop at that: they rely on you, yourself, to try to awaken to them. But in the esoteric teachings, there is another set of explanations. In reality this is also there in the exoteric teachings, it's just that we never notice it. Thus I make a special point of emphasizing what it says in Volume 4 of *The Surangama Sutra* about transforming the material world, about the link of mind and objects having one source and its account of hell and heaven. Buddha has hidden the secret in this, to make us sublimate according to the Dharma and cultivate practice according to the Dharma.

• • •

It is very easy to succeed in cultivating *anapana*, because the root of life is in the breath. But the breath is also a phenomenon in the realm of birth and death. As I mentioned before, Rahula cultivated practice until he reached the realms of the four *dhyanas*. In this there is another key link. It is definitely not that you can reach the four *dhyanas* by only cultivating the breath. You also must totally rid yourself of craving, anger, ignorance, arrogance, doubt, and all the eighty-eight bonds and compulsions. Only then can you realize the fruit of arhatship.

If you only cultivate the breath, and only follow meditation work, this is an outside path, a non-Buddhist path, because this is seeking the Dharma outside of mind. I have discovered that no one pays attention to the importance of the Dharma Gate of the mind-ground. In reality, meditation work is just an illusory city; it is not the objective, the storehouse of precious jewels.

In the Sui-T'ang period [A.D. 580-906] there were many monks and nuns and Buddhist laypeople who realized the fruit of enlightenment. In those times, when the average person cultivated practice, he or she always held to one method and tried to cultivate it very rigorously. As time went on, there were more and more translations of the Buddhist scriptures, and more and more people had a theoretical knowledge of Buddhism. In addition to this, social circumstances became more complicated. People's propensity to doubt what Buddha said increased, and arrogance and doubt became more severe. Craving, anger, and ignorance toward worldly phenomena also got more serious. So of course fewer and fewer people realized the fruit of enlightenment.

In the period of the Northern and Southern Dynasties the great teacher Chih-i founded the T'ien-t'ai school. The T'ien-t'ai school was founded earlier than the Zen school. Among the ten schools of Buddhism in China, the earliest was the Pure Land school founded by the Dharma teacher Hui-yuan during the Eastern Chin dynasty.

In the T'ien-t'ai school's method of cessation and contemplation, the first step is to cultivate the breath. It then progresses to the cultivation of the three forms of cessation and the three forms of contemplation correlated with the emptiness of all phenomena, the relative existence of all phenomena, and the mean between emptiness and relative existence. Cultivating cessation is cultivating *samadhi*, meditative concentration. Cultivating contemplation is cultivating *prajna*, wisdom. This is the double cultivation of concentration and wisdom.

The T'ien-t'ai school uses the three methods of counting breaths, tempering the breath, and listening to the breath in order to cultivate cessation and contemplation. After you have really attained *samadhi*, then you immediately enter into "the contemplation of emptiness." That is to say, when you have properly tempered your breathing, to the point where the breath is not moving in and out, and the breath fills you, at that point false thoughts become few. At this point, if you do not take the road of contemplation, and just keep on refining your meditation work, then you can attain spiritual powers, and you may go toward the Hinayana fruit, or even travel the route of the outside paths.

Thus, at this point, you must immediately contemplate mind, and turn around and contemplate emptiness. You understand that your breathing has been tempered to the point that the breath is not moving in and out, and that your body and mind are peaceful and still and happy, and then you stop. At this point, it is still a moment of thought. After this, you abandon this moment of thought, and again empty out, no longer paying any attention to body and mind: this is called the contemplation of emptiness. But take note! This emptiness is still a moment of thought, so it is still within the sixth consciousness.

Therefore, when you are sitting in meditation, when you feel that there are no thoughts present at all, and it is very pure, this one that is aware of the purity is itself a thought.

When you become aware of purity, it is already not pure anymore—it is a moment of thought. It is like a sheet of glass. Whether you use a white pen or a black pen to make a mark on it, this mark is still something. You cannot say that the black pen is something bad and the white pen is something good. Therefore, in the Buddhist scriptures it says that you cannot put bits of broken rock in your eye, and you cannot put diamond dust in your eye either. It doesn't matter whether it is good or bad, you cannot put anything in your eye. But the T'ien-t'ai teaching of cessation and contemplation does not discuss this.

At this point, the realm of the purity you are aware of is existent, but this existence is "relative" existence. Thus, "emptiness itself is existence, and existence itself is emptiness." When it comes to the essence of the Path, neither emptiness nor existence abides, so it is called the Middle Path, the Path of the Mean between emptiness and relative existence. This word "Mean" is taken from the Bodhisattva Nagarjuna's *Prajnamula Shastra*, also known as the *Madhyamika Shastra*. Thus in T'ien-t'ai they call these the three forms of cessation and the three forms of contemplation linked with emptiness, relative existence, and the mean.

Sometimes those who entered samadhi in the realm of the contemplation of emptiness could stay in *samadhi* for eighty-four thousand great eons. We cannot even manage to stay in *samadhi* for eight hours, to say nothing of eighty-four thousand great eons. But if you can enter *samadhi* like this in the correct contemplation of emptiness, that's not bad, and afterward it will be easy for you to progress into the cultivation of the contemplation of relative existence, and contemplation of the mean.

At that time it was very good to cultivate the practice of the line of cessation and contemplation devised by the T'ien-t'ai school. In the Sui-T'ang period, as there came to be more great bodhisattvas and great men of knowledge who had realized the fruit of enlightenment, the principles of the teaching thus multiplied accordingly. Even as the principles became clearer, the number of people doing meditation work decreased, and naturally the number of people realizing the fruit of enlightenment also decreased. Moreover, after the Zen school developed, it was Zen everywhere. At the verbal level it was all terrific, and the principles were all understood very clearly, but the number of people who really cultivated practice was not many, and accordingly the number of people realizing the fruit of enlightenment naturally became fewer and fewer.

When the northern transmission of Indian Buddhism was transmitted to Tibet, it was called Tibetan Esoteric Buddhism. At the beginning was the Nyingmapa sect, and this developed into the Sakyapa sect and the Kagyudpa sect, and these in turn developed further into the Gelugpa sect, which was founded by Tsongkhapa [1357-1419].

Tsongkhapa's *Great Treatise on the Stages of the Path of Enlightenment* discusses cultivating samadhi and cultivating contemplation, and is almost identical to the T'ien-t'ai school's method of cessation and contemplation. It's just that the scriptural teachings it quotes are not the same. Chih-i's work *The Great Cessation and Contemplation* follows the principles of the Bodhisattva Nagarjuna's Mahaprajna school, the line of the Madhyamika school.[1] Tsongkhapa follows the line of the Yogacara school of the Bodhisattva Asanga.

In cultivating Esoteric Buddhism, the principle emphasis is on cultivating the breath and cultivating the energy channels, in order to attain buddhahood and realize the fruit of enlightenment. If the breath is not cultivated until it circulates freely, and the network of energy channels is not transformed, then you will not be able to attain *samadhi*. Of this it is said, "If your inner channels are not opened through, but you say you have attained *samadhi*, this is impossible."

As for sitting meditation, you can sit for several days and nights, but it is by no means certain that your channels will open through. Opening the channels and sitting in meditation are two different things. But when your channels have opened, if you want to sit, you sit. Not only can you sit for several days and nights, you can sleep for several days and nights, or stand for several days and nights, and always be able to enter *samadhi* just the same: entering *samadhi* has no relation to your posture.

The minds of modern people are too complicated. That's why it is best for them to cultivate deliberate contrived forms of meditation work; cultivating the method of *anapana* is best of all. When you cultivate the breath, your body will be well. If you want to use the cultivation of the breath to seek to realize the fruit of enlightenment, you must understand medical principles before it will work. Thus you must first investigate medical principles and medicines.

---

[1] Nagarjuna was an Indian Buddhist philosopher and adept of the first century A.D., the founder of the Madhyamika school. In his writings, he refuted all conceptualizations and pointed out the arbitrary, self-contradictory nature of language and its inability to reach absolute reality. His philosophy is called Madhyamika, the school of the Middle Path, because he emphasized that all phenomena are devoid of any absolute independent identities, and thus are neither absolutely existent nor absolutely non-existent.

If you study Buddhism and cultivate the Path, you must be absolutely selfish: you must first be able to take charge of and take care of your own body and mind. If you do not even know the transformation of your own body, can this be called cultivating the Path? To cultivate the Path you must be clear about the inner transformations of your body, and the transformations of your mental states. When you arouse your mind or your thoughts move, you must always know it. That is to say, you should just take care of yourself, and be completely selfish, but without interfering with other people. Then there will be peace in the world. In other words, you must always be very clear about any changes that occur in your own body and mind: only this can be called cultivating the Path. The Path of studying Buddhism means first seeking your own salvation and your own benefit. You must pay attention to this point.

When we mention any of the transformations of the body, the purification of desire, the proper handling of eating and drinking, the transformation of the condition of the breath, and so on, all these are matters of learning that you should give thought to. The great enlightened teachers of olden times, no matter whether Taoist or Buddhist, all had a thorough mastery of medical principles. They had reached high levels of their cultivation of practice and meditation work, and they had discovered these principles entirely from their own personal experience with their own bodies and with the Dharma Gate of their own mind-ground, not from reading books. A person only lives a few decades, and frankly speaking, there is not that much time or energy to read very many books. All we have to do is open up the precious treasury of the mind-ground, and then we will understand everything.

Esoteric Buddhism emphasizes the cultivation of the breath, but before cultivating the breath, you must first understand these principles. When you cultivate the breath to the point that it no longer moves in and out, to the point that breathing stops—the esoteric school calls this "the breath in the jewel bottle," and in yoga this is called "the breath in the bottle." The person is like a jewel bottle. When the state of *samadhi* is about to arrive, the breath fills you, and breathing in and out stops. Your stomach is pulled back in, and your body spontaneously straightens up, becoming perfectly upright and erect and stable. At this moment you are very comfortable, and even if you were told to leave your sitting position, you would not do it.

In this context, when we say you are neither exhaling nor inhaling, this in no sense means that there is really no breathing, just that it is very rarefied. At this point there are no more miscellaneous thoughts. After a long time, it seems there is a bit of breath coming in, and after another long interval, it seems there is a bit of breath going out. When you reach this realm, then you must begin to cultivate the channels. This is the teaching of the esoteric school from the T'ang dynasty on.

Knowing whether the breath is cool or warm is the realm of cultivating the *ch'i* channels. It does not mean knowing whether the breath is cool or warm in the nose, but inside the body. At this point, you know where in your body it is getting warm, and where it is getting cool. This is what the later generations of the esoteric school called channels. This more or less corresponds to responses of the nervous system. At this stage, each cell feels clearly where the breath is circulating freely, and where it is not. In fact, the channels take the breath a step further.

Why do your legs get numb when you sit in meditation? Because the channels in your legs are not opened through, because the channels in your whole lower body are not opened through. The hardest to open are in the buttocks.

When we reach the point in sitting that we do not want to sit any more, there are two reasons for this. One pertains to the mind and one pertains to the body. Usually, when we do not want to sit, is it that our minds do not want to sit? No, usually it is because when the *ch'i* reaches the buttocks it cannot move any lower, and at this point the breath can influence our mental state adversely. The minds of ordinary people cannot transform things. Materialists think that people's thinking is under the influence of material things, and this is not wrong. It's just that this explanation only applies to the realm of ordinary people. The *ch'i* is also a thing. Thus, when we reach a certain stage in our sitting, because the ch'i reaches the buttocks and cannot descend any further, our brains and nerves intangibly tense up, and mentally we cannot sit still anymore, so the only thing to do is to stop sitting. If the *ch'i* can move on from the buttocks and pervade the thighs and kneecaps, and keep on moving through the legs section by section, you will experience pain, itching, numbness, swelling, cold, heat, and even festering of the legs. Finally, when the *ch'i* moves all the way through freely, suddenly everything will get better.

The spirit of the people in olden times who cultivated practice was very admirable. As the *ch'i* forced out all the filth from within their bodies, to the point where their bodies were suppurating, they still managed to look upon the skandha of form as empty, and they did not mind at all. When modern people have this blessing, they have to take medicine to relieve the inflammation and get acupuncture treatments to endure it.

When the *ch'i* reaches the arches of the feet, then you can begin to talk of the three channels and the seven chakras. When the *ch'i* channels have been opened, you will surely attain *samadhi*, but what kind of *samadhi*? There are hundreds and thousands of kinds of *samadhi*, and they are all different. But we still think there is just one "Zen," one form of meditative concentration. There I say, how is it that after the Zen school there was no more Zen? Zen has really misled quite a few people!

After you have really opened up your inner channels, you will be in *samadhi* as soon as you sit down. With your eyes closed, you will be able to see all the stars in the sky clearly. What the esoteric school says is all true. The feeling of this is like sailing into space in a spaceship. This is the mystery of the universe, the mystery of life. Throughout this whole process of sailing into space in the spaceship, at every moment we are aware of all the transformations, and our attention is focused on the laws of the universe. Are they the same as the human body or not? In the end, we discover that they are the same. By this means we prove again that the experience of the cultivation of practice explained by Esoteric Buddhism is entirely without error. The error lies in us not making the effort, and not cultivating practice until we experience it.

# 11

# TEACHINGS OF THE
# ZEN PATRIARCHS
# AS A BASIS FOR CULTIVATION

We have discussed the aspect of seeing truth of the Path in the study
of Buddhism, and emphasized the phenomenal aspect of cultivating realization and doing meditation work. What you must pay special attention to—among the ten forms of mindfulness—is the
method of cultivating the breathing. There are some differences in the
method of cultivating the breathing due to the differences in individual physiology and psychology. The mindfulness of *anapana* spoken of by Buddha is a general principle. Of course, in everything
Buddha said about this method, the contents are very complex. If
you can cultivate it properly, you will positively be able to reach the
point where you are healthy and can extend your life span. If you
cannot do this, it is because you have not found the method, or
because you do not persevere.

After you take the first steps in cultivating practice, then you
will definitely be able to advance further and attain *samadhi*, develop
wisdom, and attain spiritual powers. As for the detailed methods of
doing this, of course they are not simple. Esoteric Buddhism's four
divisions—of cultivating breath, cultivating channels, cultivating
bright spots, and cultivating kundalini—are developed from cultivating the method of *anapana*.

At first let's not discuss awakening to the Path and becoming
enlightened—we will just discuss cultivating and nurturing meditation work. You must investigate old Mencius's principle of nurturing
the *ch'i*. There is also the statement in *The Hundred Word Inscription* by
the Taoist immortal Lu Ch'un-yang:

> Nurture the *ch'i*, forget words, and hold to it
> Subdue the mind and act without acting

This is also very important. Lu Ch'un-yang was a Taoist, and he also
studied Zen. In his *The Hundred Word Inscription*, he included the phenomenal aspects of his cultivation and realization, especially the

process by which he succeeded in the refinement of his breathing. It is very much worth studying, but you will have to rely on an enlightened teacher to understand it properly. Without someone's guidance, you may go into many wrong byways, but if you follow the pointers of an experienced person, half the work will be done.

Now let me turn aside from the topic of the breath and introduce again the road taken by the practice of Buddhism in China. From the Eastern Han period, into the Northern and Southern Dynasties period and up through the Sui-T'ang period, there were many people in China who succeeded in cultivating practice, especially before the Sui-T'ang period. They all followed the Hinayana methods of cultivating practice. In later times, a problem developed. As soon as people heard of Hinayana, the lesser vehicle, they looked down on it. But, if you haven't properly prepared a basis in Hinayana, how can you even read a Confucian classic with Mahayana overtones of universalism like *The Great Learning*?

During the T'ang and Sung and thereafter, the Zen school flourished. Nevertheless, fewer and fewer people realized the fruit of enlightenment, even though more and more people expounded its principles. It has been like this all along until the present. In general, as soon as people study meditation sayings and meditation cases, or "contemplate mind," or practice "silent illumination," they call this Zen, but it is really all a joke, all a case of inverting cause and effect.

In the Eastern Chin period [318-420A.D.] a great wave of Mahayana and Hinayana scriptures were introduced into China. There were many translations of these scriptures, the principles of the teaching developed more and more, and this influenced the people of the time who were doing meditation work. *The Lotus Sutra* and *The Diamond Sutra* (translated by Kumarajiva) had an especially large influence on China, an incomparable influence. So did *The Vimalakirti Sutra*.

The three centuries and more after the Eastern Han dynasty, including the Wei-Chin period and the Northern and Southern Dynasties period, was the most glorious and vigorous period in the history of Chinese culture, learning, and philosophy. In the area of metaphysics, it was more brilliant than the classical period of Chinese philosophy (when a hundred schools of thought contended during the Spring and Autumn period) and the Warring State period from the sixth to third centuries B.C.

Regrettably, however, in general people who study Buddhism today only understand Buddhist studies and do not investigate the history of the Northern and Southern Dynasties period. All they know is the cliche that at that time the philosophical movement known as "Pure Conversation" *ch'ing-t'an* led the nation into error. They have no real understanding of what the Pure Conversation was about, or whether or not it really led the nation into error. In reality, Pure Conversation never led the nation into error. On the contrary, those in power at the time damaged civilized culture. Thus, when you read history, you should not just repeat what others say; you must do some real research of your own.

This was the period when the Zen patriarch Bodhidharma came to China. At that time, there were many people who cultivated the Path and attained the fruit of enlightenment. They used the Hinayana path of meditative concentration in their cultivation of practice: it was all the Dharma Gate of deliberate, contrived activity. Though these methods were all correct, they nevertheless still lacked the turning point that transformed deliberate, contrived action into the Path of uncontrived activity beyond form. In general, although the great teachers of that period, like the Dharma teacher Kumarajiva, had introduced the lofty profundities of the metaphysical Path in the Buddhist scriptures they translated, the road of practice they followed still employed the Hinayana methods of meditation and contemplation, methods from among the ten forms of mindfulness—like the contemplation of the skeleton and the contemplation of the impurity of the body that are mindfulness of the body meditations. At that time, when it was very hard to seek the metaphysical Path beyond form, the Zen patriarch Bodhidharma came to China and started the Zen school.

Strictly speaking, the Zen school is the school of mind. That's why Bodhidharma directed that *The Lankavatara Sutra* be used to seal the mind. The message of *The Lankavatara Sutra* is in this statement: "Buddha said that mind is the source." The question of mind arose from this. The later talk of illuminating mind and seeing true nature all went wrong here. At that time the Zen patriarch Bodhidharma pointed out two directions: one was "entering through principle" and the other was "entering through practice."

"Principle" here means the ordinary sense of studying theoretical principles. It means to progress from cessation and contemplation and observing the principles of mind, to awakening to enlightenment. "Entering through practice" included the ten forms of discipline, and the bodhisattva's vows. It also means that in the midst of being a human being and dealing with things you must pay careful attention to every move of your mind and thoughts. By these means, you experience enlightenment and awaken to the Path.

The main teaching of the Zen school puts special emphasis on entering through practice. But people in later generations who investigate the Zen school make one big mistake. They take the playful, humorous teaching style, which the adepts of the Zen school used to guide people, and conclude that this in itself *is* Zen. They see the classic Zen teachers using a shout here and a slap there, and they think that Zen means awakening to the Path by having someone play tricks on you. They do not realize at all that these are the chance workings of a didactic method, not the true heart of Zen. The true heart of Zen is what Bodhidharma pointed out—entry through practice.

Studying meditation cases means doing a careful study of the process by which the people of old awakened to enlightenment, and then transferring it into your own mind-ground for direct experiential understanding. How should you pursue this? How must you be before you can reach accord with the Zen message? You must always understand it in mind.

When the Second Patriarch [Hui-k'o, 486-593] went to see Bodhidharma, he cut off his arm. We all know this story, which illustrates how sincere he was in seeking the Path. But very few people pay attention to the fact that before he left home to become a monk, the Second Patriarch was already a great scholar. He lectured on the *I Ching* in the Shantung region, and many people admired him. Later he came to feel that this learning could not solve the problems of the universe and human life. After he read *The Great Prajna Sutra* again, he knew that the real truths of the universe and human life were in Buddhism, and at that point he left home and became a monk.

After the Second Patriarch left home, he did sitting meditation on Mount Hsiang in Honan for eight years; for eight years he cultivated meditative concentration. Because there is no way for us in later generations to obtain any sources on this, it is impossible for us to know what route the Second Patriarch took at that time in his cultivation of *samadhi*—whether he cultivated the breath or he contemplated mind. Here we must note that it is far from easy to cultivate meditative concentration for eight years. What we do know is that the Second Patriarch was equipped with first rate learning and cultivation and that later he followed Bodhidharma.

The books record that when the Second Patriarch came to see Bodhidharma, he stood in the snow for three days and three nights, but Bodhidharma paid no attention to him. Instead Bodhidharma said: The Buddha Dharma is the supreme truth attained after long eons of energetic effort. What does it accomplish to stand in the snow for a few days seeking the Dharma? At this point, the Second Patriarch cut off his arm and presented it to Bodhidharma.

When people in later times study this, it seems they feel that what Bodhidharma demanded of him was very unjust. In fact, the religious fervor and zeal with which the people of the past sought the Dharma is not something we modern day people can understand. You can read about comparable cases all the time in the biographies of eminent monks. When I was young, I saw real cases of people burning off fingers to offer to Buddha, and piercing themselves till the blood ran to copy out the sutras in blood, and other such things. There have been many situations like this. In the opinion of modern day people, this is ignorance and superstition. But is it they who were ignorant or we ourselves? Past and present are not the same. Do not casually pass judgment on the people of olden times.

Later on, Bodhidharma asked the Second Patriarch: "What are you seeking?" At the time, the Second Patriarch was hungry and cold and in pain, but all he said was: "What is the method for pacifying mind?" If it had been us, we would have said, "Teacher, I cannot get rid of my thoughts." The Second Patriarch was far superior to us. He had done sitting meditation for eight years, and in addition to this were all his previous efforts. He did not speak of whether or not his thoughts were pure. What he asked was how to pacify mind. This is a very big question.

*The Record of Pointing at the Moon* is a wonderful book, an excellent book, but it is very hard to read. You must project yourself into it as you read, as if you are watching a television play. In this passage that describes how the Second Patriarch sought the Dharma from Bodhidharma, Bodhidharma was sitting facing a wall. When the Second Patriarch cut off his arm, Bodhidharma naturally wrapped a tourniquet around it and applied some medicine. If you say that Bodhidharma was absolutely indifferent, then Bodhidharma would not have been a Zen Patriarch, and it would not have been the Buddha Dharma. In this story as it has come down to us, the details are not recorded. The Second Patriarch standing in the snow, cutting off his arm, and asking for the Dharma—this did not all take place at once. Each one was a separate event, but in the book these three incidents are arbitrarily joined together.

What is the meaning of pacifying mind? What mind is pacified? At that moment, with his arm cut off, cold and hungry, the Second Patriarch's mind was of course not at peace. So Bodhidharma answered him: "Bring your mind here, and I will pacify it for you." At this point Bodhidharma stared with his big Indian eyes open wide, and with his coarse whiskers, he certainly frightened the Second Patriarch to death. With this rebuke, the Second Patriarch's heart dropped. It's not that he was a coward. This question of his was enormous, and the answer was very special, too, and it made his heart sink. After this he answered: "When I look for my mind, I cannot find it." Bodhidharma then said: "I have already pacified your mind for you." And that was it.

After the Second Patriarch had been with Bodhidharma several years, Bodhidharma told him: "By putting to rest all external entangling objects, and not agitating your inner mind, and making your mind like a wall, you can enter the Path." If you are following the road of cultivating practice, no matter whether it is Mahayana or Hinayana, no matter what school of Buddhism it is, or whether you are a householder or a home-leaver, if you do not follow the road according to these few lines, it will not work.

"Putting to rest all external entangling objects" means we must drop all external circumstances. If we do not succeed in our study of Buddhism and our cultivation of realization, it is because we have not been able to do this. Our minds are all minds that cling to entangling objects. When we finish with one thing, we go grab onto something else. We never finish doing things, and we never can put external entangling objects to rest.

"Not agitating the inner mind" means entering the realm of the four *dhyanas* and the eight *samadhis* via the method of being mindful of *anapana*, and doing it until the breath is not moving in or out.

"Making the mind like a wall" means totally cutting off inside and outside, so that the mind does not move no matter what happens in the outer world, and no false thoughts appear, and no false thoughts arise.

Pay attention to this. When you manage to act like this, then you can enter the Path, you can experience and awaken to enlightenment, and you can realize the Tao.

When Bodhidharma told the Second Patriarch this, it must have been something that happened before the Second Patriarch asked him about the method for pacifying mind. Bodhidharma judged the Second Patriarch's accomplishment in meditative concentration and taught him another route of meditative concentration. When the Second Patriarch told Bodhidharma his mind was not at peace, this must have been something that happened after he had accomplished his meditation work. Suppose a man had been able to "put to rest all external entangling objects, and not agitate his inner mind, and make his mind like a wall." Would he dare to say he had become enlightened? Would his mind be at peace or not? Would he have awakened to the Path or not? Even at this point, he still was not clear about what buddha ultimately is and what enlightenment is. Therefore he was not able to pacify this mind.

Later the Second Patriarch passed on the Dharma to the Third Patriarch Seng-ts'an [d. 606]. After he had given him the robe and bowl emblematic of the succession, the Second Patriarch went everywhere eating and drinking and acting wild. A great scholar like him, who had become a monk and then concentrated his mind on his religious efforts, who had been given the Dharma and the seal of approval by Bodhidharma—but after he had passed on the robe and bowl, in his later years his life was completely different, he drank wine and ran around like crazy in the brothel districts. People would ask him, "You are a patriarch of the Zen school. How can you hang around in the wineshops?" The Second Patriarch would say, "I am taming my mind. What business is it of yours?"

The question arises: what he had been seeking was the method to pacify mind, and Bodhidharma had taken him and given the method of pacifying mind to him, so why in his later years did he still have to tame his mind? His mind still was not pacified, so when the Second Patriarch talked about the Zen school's pacifying mind, there is obviously still a big question about what this mind is. Before becoming a buddha, nobody's mind can be pacified. Not even arhats and bodhisattvas can ultimately pacify their minds. Except with great penetrating enlightenment, no one can pacify his or her mind.

In terms of present day learning and thought, there is a struggle between the idealist and materialist schools of thought. We know that mind and matter have the same source. But no one can give a definitive answer as to how ultimately mind is able to create matter, unless he or she reaches the realm of becoming a buddha. Therefore, though everyone can discuss this on a theoretical level, in actual fact, the mind still cannot be pacified.

This was the Zen school. From this point on, in reality, the Zen school was virtually nonexistent.

When we in later generations study the Zen school, we always pay attention to the southern school, the line of the Sixth Patriarch Hui-neng [638-713]. We do not join both the southern school and the northern school together in our investigation.

The time of the Fourth Patriarch Tao-hsin [580-651] was precisely when the T'ang period was about to inaugurate a new era in Chinese history. It was also the time when Dharma teacher Hsuan-tsang [600-664] was studying in India, and was soon to return to China. At that time, the Zen school had still not begun to flourish on a grand scale, and it was still a single line of transmission. One man would look for one disciple, in order to continue to carry this burden and see to it that the line of the Dharma would not be cut off. The Fourth Patriarch and those who came after him would develop several disciples. Later on in the T'ang dynasty, several great national teachers, and even patriarchs of the Hua-yen and T'ien-t'ai schools were all descended from the line of the Fourth Patriarch, which is senior to the line of the Sixth Patriarch.

After Dharma teacher Hsuan-tsang had introduced the Yogacara classics to China, the principles of the Buddha Dharma became ever more complete. Later on, the great Zen master Lin-chi was also a great teacher of the Yogacara philosophy; he did not only study Zen. This was also true of the great Zen masters Ts'ao-shan and Tung-shan. They mastered various kinds of Buddhist teachings. They were not like the average people today who do not study the scriptures and the principles of the Buddhist teaching, but just take a meditation saying and think they understand Zen.

The great Zen patriarchs of the past proceeded like this: after they had thoroughly mastered the whole Buddhist canon, then they abandoned the principles of the teaching and pursued a simple and direct method, entering into that one method deeply. Just as Confucius said, "I broaden myself with culture, and restrain myself with proper standards of behavior." The great Zen masters moved from the broadening influence [of theoretical learning] to the restraining influence [of disciplined practice]: first they studied on a broad scale, and after they mastered the principles contained in the Buddhist scriptures, they concentrated on pursuing a single path.

By the time of the Fifth Patriarch Hung-jen [602-675], it was the period of Emperor T'ai-tsung of the T'ang dynasty [r. 627-649]. Zen was still a single line of transmission, and it did not occupy a very large place in Chinese culture. Before long, the T'ien-t'ai school gradually emerged. Naturally the form of Buddhism that was most widespread was the principles of the teaching. Soon the Dharma teacher Hsuan-tsang returned to China, and helped to bring about a flourishing period for the Buddha Dharma.

In the T'ang and Sung periods, the most talented, most intelligent people in China often put their strength to work for the Buddha Dharma. These days the most intelligent and talented people all go into industry and commerce. So how can the Buddha Dharma exist? These two eras are totally the opposite. At that time, studying Buddhism and studying Zen were as much in vogue as the study of science is nowadays. The current fashion made it that way, and so the principles of the teaching flourished to a high degree for a time. Moreover, the leader of society, Emperor T'ai-tsung, was no ordinary man. He was good at writing poetry and good at calligraphy; he had military success and was proficient in the study of Buddhism; he was good at all sorts of things. Certainly no one else could have written the Imperial Preface that he wrote for the collected works of Dharma teacher Hsuan-tsang.

The heyday of the Zen school was from the middle T'ang onward, in the later T'ang and the Five Dynasties period [eighth through tenth centuries]. At the time, Buddhist theory was developed to its highest peak, and the Sixth Patriarch's Zen had just appeared at that period. At that time all sorts of Buddhist theories—like Yogacara and Hua-yen—reached all through society and almost everyone who had read a book could say a few phrases of the Buddha Dharma. In this period, Hinayana practices had already disappeared and everyone followed Mahayana methods of cultivating practice. But they still could not find the right road. At this point, the mind-seal of the Zen school transmitted by Bodhidharma, the method of "directly pointing to the human mind, enabling people to illuminate mind and see true nature," emerged in response to the needs of the time, in the period of the Fifth and Sixth Patriarchs.

The method of cultivating practice first transmitted by Bodhidharma at the level of theory directs everyone to pay serious attention to *The Lankavatara Sutra*. At the time of the Fifth Patriarch there was a change, because the principles of *The Lankavatara Sutra* were too lofty and profound for the people of the time. In order to enable an easier entry in this Dharma Gate, the Zen teachers switched to using *The Diamond Sutra*. In fact, they had already begun to use this method at the time of the Fourth Patriarch, but it only began to really flourish more at the time of the Fifth and Sixth Patriarchs. *The Diamond Sutra* speaks of the principle of inherent emptiness, and is very simplified.

It's as if Buddhist theory in this period had reached the highest peak of a pyramid, and could not go any further. How to integrate it with the ordinary reality level of body and mind, and how to seek realization immediately became difficult. According to the principles of the teaching, for an ordinary person to become a buddha would take three great immeasurable eons. Since enlightenment was thus something for some remote and dateless future, how could a person cultivate realization?

Once the Mahayana scriptures were in circulation, people felt that the methods of Hinayana were not worthy of being considered the Path to enlightenment. The Zen school's "directly pointing to the human mind, enabling people to illuminate mind and see true nature" catered more to the needs of the times. In the era of the Sixth Patriarch, it reached a peak of popularity.

The Zen school of the Sixth Patriarch began in the South, in Guangtung Province. In that period South China was a culturally backward region. The original base for the flourishing of Buddhism was in the Central Plain of North China [which was the economic and political heart of the T'ang Empire]. The great national teachers and great Dharma teachers had all been active in the region of the Central Plain, in the area of the imperial capitals Hsi-an and Lo-yang. Because in the backward South, the Sixth Patriarch used vernacular language to communicate the Buddha Dharma, it spread widely very easily.

If we make a careful study of *The Sixth Patriarch's Altar Sutra*, we see that the Sixth Patriarch still put a heavy emphasis on "practice" and was still teaching entry into enlightenment through the gate of "practice." The unfortunate thing was that, from the time that such works as *The Sixth Patriarch's Altar Sutra* and Master Ta'chu's *Treatise on the Essential Gate for Entering the Path through Sudden Enlightenment* were in wide circulation, Buddhism and Zen were finished.

Everyone knows that mind itself is buddha, but what is "mind"? People don't have any idea what this really means. Thus some people do not believe in religion. They think that even though they do no good works, all they have to do is have a clear conscience, and then they will be buddhas. As to what "mind" is, they don't care at all. This problem originated from books like *The Altar Sutra*.

The development of Sung period Neo-Confucianism *li-hsueh*, "the study of principle," "the study of the inner design," came about because of the abuse of the Zen saying that "mind itself is buddha" and the resulting neglect of practical application. What was expressed by the Neo-Confucians was, despite everything, an attitude of the Zen school, the Zen school that came from the gate of "practice." The practice of the Path of Humanity and Heaven that the Neo-Confucians propounded was the equivalent of the Buddhist Vinaya school [with its emphasis on precepts of discipline]. The Taoists after T'ang and Sung who continued the thought of Lao-tzu and Chuang-tzu were equivalent to the Zen school in Buddhism, the Zen school of the road of liberation. The interrelationships between these three religions were very subtle.

As for the principle of "directly pointing to the human mind, seeing true nature and becoming buddha," the more clearly it was explained, the duller Buddhism became, and the more the meditation work of cultivating realization lacked a real basis. In fact, as unwieldy and impractical as it was, it was not as good as cultivating cessation and contemplation, or practicing the method of contemplating mind. At least by doing this it was still possible to get half the fruit. By following Hinayana methods it was still possible in the last analysis to seek realization, but enlightenment in the Mahayana sense must be discussed separately.

Let me reiterate: after the Zen school began promoting *The Diamond Sutra*, because *The Diamond Sutra* expounds inherent emptiness, it was easy to lead people into "crazy Zen," a lip-service Zen with no real substance. Though this sutra was very easy to understand theoretically, it was no help at all in regard to seeking realization.

Of the books of the Zen school, the best one is *The Record of Pointing at the Moon*. It collects together the essential points from all sorts of Zen records, and includes material on seeing truth, cultivating realization, and carrying out vows.

When I first published *The Record of Pointing at the Moon* in Taiwan, because sales were not good, I had to sell it off by the pound to butchers to use for wrapping meat! But that is another story. If you really want to study the Zen school, if you make a thorough study of *The Record of Pointing at the Moon* it will be enough. To read this book not only will you need a thorough knowledge of the principles of the teaching, but you will also have to have a basis in cultivating realization; otherwise, there will be many parts you do not understand when you read them.

For people in the later generations, as soon as we mention the Zen school, to them it means studying meditation sayings (koans), whereas, in fact, what the Zen school really emphasizes heavily is seeing truth.

For example, Zen master Yang-shan of the Kuei-Yang school was called Chinese Buddhism's "little Shakyamuni." Yang-shan [813-890] lived in the late T'ang period. *The Record of Pointing at the Moon* records this story:

"There was an Indian monk who appeared out of empty space. Yang-shan said, 'Where did you come from?' He said, 'From India.' This Indian monk also said, 'I came to this eastern land especially to pay homage to Manjushri, but instead I meet a little Shakyamuni.'" Then he gave Yang-shan some Sanskrit books. After he had bowed to Yang-shan, he departed into empty space. From this point on everyone called Yang-shan "little Shakyamuni." Indian arhats appeared out of thin air to seek instructions from Yang-shan more than once, as we know from his disciples who saw this and asked him about it.

One day when Yang-shan was pursuing his studies with Kuei-shan, his teacher Kuei-shan asked him, "Of the forty volumes of *The Nirvana Sutra*, how many were spoken by Buddha, and how many by Mara [the demon of delusion]?" Yang-shan said, "Master, what I have read was all spoken by Mara." When Kuei-shan heard this he was very happy and said, "In the future, no one will be able to cope with you." Yang-shan also asked his teacher Kuei-shan, "I know the things of one period: where should I practice?" By this he meant: though my words are correct, this mind is still not at peace. The things of one period I already know, I have arrived at the stage of seeing the truth of Buddha's teachings, and have a bit of experience, but what should my practice be?

Here the word "practice" includes mental behavior, the mental activity and thought involved in being a person and doing things, and it also includes meditation work and religious effort. Kuei-shan answered him with a famous line: "All that's important is that your eye is correct. I won't talk about your practice." In other words, all that's necessary is that your perception of the truth of the Buddha's teaching is correct. I will not ask about your subsequent work of cultivating realization, because once your perception of truth is correct, then your cultivation of realization will certainly be on track. If your perception of truth is wrong, then even if you do your meditation work properly, your practice will still be wrong.

On the basis of this saying of Kuei-shan's, later generations mistakenly passed along the idea that the Zen school emphasizes seeing truth, but does not think meditation work is important. In fact, every one of the great Zen teachers equally upheld seeing truth, cultivating realization, and carrying out vows. If any one of these were lacking, it would not work. This line of Kuei-shan's was said by a talented teacher to a talented disciple. Since we are not Yang-shan, this line does not necessarily apply to us.

Most of the people in later generations who study the Zen school take a casual stroll past the Sixth Patriarch and Ma-tsu and that's all. They do not study the later Five Houses of Zen, like the Lin-chi school, the Kuei-Yang school, the Ts'ao-Tung school, the Yun-men school, and the Fa-yen school at all. How can this be counted as studying Zen?

For example, among the teachings of Lin-chi, he talks about the "three mysteries and three essentials" and the "four selections." These are teaching methods, and they also include seeing truth, cultivating realization, and carrying out vows. Lin-chi said: "In each statement of mine there are three mysterious gates, and in each mysterious gate there are three essential truths." For example, in the one word "tea" when spoken by Lin-chi, there are three mysterious gates, and in each mysterious gate there are also three essential truths. He was not just talking theoretically. Another example is the famous Zen master Ta-hui Tsung-kao: within every sentence he said, he made forty-nine turning words.[1]

Lin-chi's "four selections" means selections of meditation materials. In the "four selections" there are guest and host, and there is a method. But the man of old did not explain this method: you must awaken to it on your own. If he had clearly explained the method, it would have turned into an inflexible transmission, and everyone would have become attached to it. Sentient beings cannot get free of their fundamental attachments; if you add attachment to religious methods on top of that, they are sure to go to hell.

---

[1] "Turning words" are sayings with many levels of meaning, designed by Zen teachers to interact with and transform the mind of the listeners.

In the "four selections," what is the guest and what is the host?

For example, you hit a sounding board, and it makes a sound. There is nothing under the sounding board. Your thoughts are emptied by the sound of the board, and they aren't there any more: it wouldn't be bad if you could maintain this state forever. Using the method of the sounding board is, in a word, "blowing on the cooking water to see the rice." Those who know will laugh—this is a trick to fool people. But it is not fooling people—it is using an outside force to cut off the false thoughts in our consciousness, and make us experience a purity we have never before experienced in our ordinary lives. But if you think this is "illuminating mind and seeing true nature," this is very wrong. But it is also possible to make progress in awakening by means of this shadow. At this moment, you must use transcendent wisdom, and in the sound of this sounding board, penetrate through and awaken. That is called Zen.

Here are Lin-chi's four selections. Sometimes "he takes away the person but not the objects," and your meditation work reaches the realm of purity. Sometimes "he takes away the objects but not the person." Your meditation work progresses a bit, and he hopes you will take another step forward. The previous realm was not right, so you discard it, and you are still yourself. Lin-chi is calling upon you to go investigate this for yourselves. Sometimes "he takes away both the person and the objects," so that whatever you do is not right. But we cannot use this method. Just as the ancient Zen worthies said, if we really upheld the Zen school, there would not be anyone around us, and the weeds in front of the Dharma hall would be three feet deep, and no one would come. Sometimes "he takes away neither the person nor the objects."

Zen master Lin-chi was by no means only talking about teaching methods. The process of doing meditation work is also present here in the four selections.

Sometimes you have done your meditation work properly, and there are no miscellaneous thoughts in your mind, and it is pure and illuminated and empty all the way through. This is "taking away the person but not the objects." You are still yourself, sitting there, but with your mind empty clear through: this is the realm of the sixth consciousness. Since you have taken away the person, the person does not move; since you have not taken away the objects, there is still an experiential realm. Of course this realm is still liable to change. Why? Because it is the guest, not the host. A guest cannot stay forever:

how could he not change? This is the secret of the Zen school. But at the first stage we must let the guest play the host: we must allow this experiential realm, and the longer we preserve it, the better. But in fact this is not easy to accomplish.

As for "taking away the objects but not the person," this is difficult. If I may speak boldly, there is no one in the audience who can accomplish this. Because you have not reached the stage of seeing the truth of Buddha's teaching, you cannot reach the level of cultivating practice or carrying out vows either.

Some people will ask: We are fundamentally pure and illuminated, but we can't quiet down in a couple of days. I say, if you are studying Zen, why don't you go try to investigate this for yourselves. At this point, you have taken away the objects, and the objects are not there anymore; you have not taken away the person, so the person is there as usual. Is it the guest? Is it the host? Is it the host within the guest? Is it the guest within the host? Is it the host within the host? Is it the guest within the guest?

Sometimes we employ the method of tempering the breath. Sometimes we see light. The jewels of the Dharma are many. The Zen masters have taught them all in books. If you do not understand, you can ask me. If you do not understand the higher level teaching methods, we can have a talk in the weeds, and make progress step by step.

Doing energy-work *ch'i-kung*, and cultivating *samadhi* is letting the guest act as the host. When the four elements of the physical body are not properly attuned, and the body is not in good shape, the *ch'i* channels are the guest, and they make the body shake. If you forcibly suppress this, it will not be good for your health. Wait until your body is properly attuned, and then you won't have to use the guest anymore, and you can let the host be the host.

It's also like this with thoughts. Sometimes you cannot subdue them, so just recite the buddha-name, or if there is no other way to cope with them, then sing a song! Tempering the mind is like this: this mind is very hard to tame. Sometimes as soon as your meditation work gets a little bit better, immediately your emotions get worse. At this time all you can do is let the guest be the host—the host has temporarily moved out.

When some people study Buddhism and do meditation work, they become filled with contradictions. They become aware of their *ch'i* channels and they are afraid of getting attached to them, so they want to empty them out. After the *ch'i* channels are not there anymore, they want to open up the *jen-mai* and *tu-mai* channels.[2] When they discover the light, they are afraid of getting attached to delusions. When the light isn't there they think, "What kind of benighted ignorance is this?" When they reach emptiness they think, "Won't I probably fall into clinging stubbornly to emptiness?" Don't worry about stubbornly clinging to emptiness. In several decades I have never met anyone capable of stubbornly clinging to emptiness. Stubbornly clinging to emptiness means being totally insensate and unaware of anything.

If you are this way, there are contradictions everywhere, and no way to resolve them. When you first become aware of the *ch'i* channels, simply work with your *ch'i* channels: there will be no error in letting the guest act as the host for the time being. When you first become aware of the *ch'i* channels, every part of your body is painful. So what—pain is pain! Think to yourself: "This is the guest's [it belongs to the body, it does not belong to the true self], it is not mine. At this point I do not act as the host, I let the guest act as the host."

The more you look at it, the more this body seems like a little child. As the proverb says: "When the child sees his mama, he cries three times for no reason." The more you pay attention to the body, the more severe the pain will be. If you do not pay attention to the body, it will start to behave itself. If you can really do this, it will work right away. But people do not do this: once they become aware of the *ch'i* channels, they always want to try to guide them, and they always go round and round within the realm of the skandha of form. They can talk theory well enough, but when the actual situation arises, then they are totally baffled.

Studying meditation sayings is a method thought up where there is no method: it is not Zen. There is also "silent illumination." You close your eyes and observe your thoughts, and sit with the mind very pure and clear. The great Zen master of the Sung dynasty, Ta-hui Tsung-kao repudiated this as misguided Zen. In *The Surangama Sutra* there is this line: "Preserving vacant silence within is still a shadow phenomenon of discrimination belonging to the dust of the Dharma."

Because most practitioners of silent illumination did not clearly understand the true principle, in terms of the great path of enlight-

---

[2] For diagrams of the *jen-mai* and *tu-mai* channels see Master Nan's *Tao and Longevity*, translated by Wen Kuan Chu, Ph.D. (York Beach, ME: Samuel Weiser, 1984), pp. 66-67.

enment, of course it was misguided Zen. But for people who were clear about truth and had awakened to the Path, silent illumination was Zen. This was Zen master Lin-chi's "illumination and functioning." It was both illumination and functioning at the same time. But the ordinary people did not know this; they just held on there in still silence. This kind of silent illumination became misguided Zen.

Yang-shan asked: "Where is the abode of the real buddha?" Kuei-shan said: "By contemplating the subtle wonder of having no thought, and thinking back on the inexhaustibility of the flames of awareness, thought is exhausted and returns to the source, essence and forms abide forever, phenomena and inner truth are not two: this is the thusness of the real buddha." At this time Yang-shan had just penetrated through to great enlightenment. But Kuei-shan did not box his ears or give him a kick. Instead he just explained principles to him.

"Contemplating no thought"—the Zen school calls this study, and in Buddhism in general it is called the practice of contemplation. It means fathoming and penetrating inner truth, and arriving at the wonder of having no thoughts. At this point the capacity to be able to think and feel arises, and all sorts of spiritual powers and wondrous functions arise, too.

"Thought is exhausted and returns to the source." When the thinking function of the mind's consciousness withdraws to that fundamental state, "essence and forms abide forever." After this, essence and forms appear, and all the myriad apparent phenomena in the universe all are displayed in the fundamental state, without moving from it. "Phenomena and inner truth are not two." Meditation work *is* inner truth and inner truth *is* meditation work. At this point it is the "thusness of the real buddha." This is the realm of being the same as buddha.

Because of these few sentences from his teacher, Yang-shan was enlightened. After his enlightenment, he carried on with his practices very diligently for fifteen years. For fifteen years he kept inquiring about his teacher's experience in cultivating practice, and he was always seeking realization. After fifteen years, he set forth to transmit the teaching and act as a great Buddhist teacher.

Why was it that these few sentences were able to cause Yang-shan to penetrate through to great enlightenment? Let us put ourselves in Yang-shan's place, and try to see through direct experience.

# 12

# CORRECTLY
# CONTEMPLATING MIND

Whenever people start to discuss the Zen school, they always mention studying meditation sayings.[1] In reality, studying meditation sayings is a method that was developed from lack of alternatives as the Zen school developed in the Sung and Yuan periods. Why do I say from lack of alternatives? Because from the T'ang and Sung on, there were really very few people who were genuinely able to realize the fruit of enlightenment by following the route of cultivating practice. The main reason for this was the fact that Zen was in vogue. From the Sung and Yuan onward, there was too much lip-service Zen. Everyone knew how to discuss its principles at a verbal level, and everyone engaged in displays of wit and repeated Zen sayings. But despite all this, they got further and further away from Zen. This is why the practice of studying meditation sayings was devised.

The so-called *hua-tou*, or meditation sayings, are questions. For example, "Where did you come from when you were born," and "where will you go when you die?" "Before my mother and father gave birth to me, where was I?" "Does a dog have buddha-nature or not?" "What is buddha?" The Zen master Yun-men answered this by saying, "Something to wipe your ass with." Why did Yun-men talk like this? Here is another example: "When not dreaming and not thinking, where is the master?" You might respond: "I am asleep." Well then, when you are sleeping, where are you? If at such a time someone killed you with a knife, where would you go?

[1] One practice in Zen circles was to meditate on certain classic sayings and stories of the early Zen teachers. These were called *hua-tou* (literally, "sayings," here translated as "meditation sayings") or *kung-an* ("public cases," known in English by the Japanese name *koan*) or *yin-yuan* (stories of the circumstances of enlightenment). Quotations from the sutras were also used as meditation sayings. Famous Zen books like *The Blue Cliff Record* (*Pi Yen Lu*) and *The Book of Tranquillity* (*Ts'ung-jung Lu*) are collections of meditation sayings.

These questions are divided into two types. One is "statements with meaning." They have reasons that can be explained. The other kind is "statements without meaning." They have no reasons that can be explained.

Studying meditation sayings means taking the questions that have provoked the most doubts in you throughout your life, and coming to grips with them and investigating them. Don't bother with verbal explanations of Buddhism. This method of studying meditation sayings is a method of cessation and contemplation, but it is better than ordinary cessation and contemplation, because you concentrate all your doubts on one point. No false thoughts can arise. If you have not resolved one question, you will not be able to resolve any other questions.

In the past, in the Zen halls there were some people who studied meditation sayings as if they had gone crazy. They studied until they were unaware of anything, until no false thoughts or miscellaneous thoughts were present. They concentrated solely on the meditation saying. This was a form of cessation. After they had encountered an opportunity, and suddenly opened up, they wholly resolved this question. This was a form of contemplation.

But after studying meditation sayings became fashionable, the Zen school declined. In recent times in mainland China, there have been many people who became mentally ill from studying meditation sayings. The minds of modern day people are too complicated, and the questions that concern them are already too numerous. If you add to this the business of studying meditation sayings, it would be strange if they did not go crazy!

Real, genuine Zen is very simple. The Zen masters prior to the Five Dynasties period used "directly pointing to the human mind, seeing true nature and becoming buddha" as their method of contemplating mind, and everyone could do it.

As the first step, first we understand that all people think and have thoughts. For example, when someone else is talking, we hear his words. This is a concept, a thought. This thought follows the other person's words: as he keeps talking, our hearing function keeps going, too.

When we sit quietly and contemplate mind, this mind is not the mind referred to in the formula "illuminating mind and seeing true nature." Mind in this case stands for the process of thinking, and the thoughts that afflict us. These thoughts come like this: "So-and-so is coming to see me this afternoon. He's coming at three o'clock. I will get ready to invite him to a coffee shop." In this way, three or four thoughts go by. You keep on thinking: "Well, it will be all right to invite him for a cup of tea, or to eat a bowl of noodles. Actually, it would be best if he did not come at all. It's too much trouble. I haven't got the money. . . ." The thoughts keep jumping up one after another. This mind is like this.

We must observe this clearly. When the thought that is in front of us runs off, and the subsequent thought has not yet arrived, there is an interval in between that is empty all the way through. We preserve this emptiness in between thoughts. This is called the method of contemplating mind. In this way we will be able to accomplish the first step.

Thoughts are phenomena in the realm of birth and death, phenomena that are born and that disappear. In the Buddhist scriptures it says: "All compounded things are impermanent, they are the phenomena of birth and death. When birth and death are extinct, the peaceful extinction of nirvana is bliss." Compounded things are all actions, including mental activities. When all of you sit in meditation, you rein in your six sense faculties, and observe these thoughts. You should not repress them, or make a special effort: just observe these thoughts as they pass by. For example, when you chant "Hail to Amitabha Buddha," the sound "Hail to Amitabha Buddha" cannot stay: it flows along from moment to moment with each repetition. When the previous thought has flowed away, before the next thought arrives, the interval in between is "the present thought." Fundamentally, the present thought is not there, it is pure and clear. If you can be like this, the longer you can maintain it the better. In terms of the principles of the teaching, this is the method of contemplating emptiness.

Both the T'ien-t'ai school and the Zen school term this interval of emptiness in between thoughts "emptying past, present, and future." The previous thought has gone, the subsequent thought has not yet arrived, and the present thought is empty then and there. For example, when we say "present," it is already past, it no longer exists, it is empty then and there. *The Diamond Sutra* says: "The past mind is ungraspable, the present mind is ungraspable, and the future mind is ungraspable." The interval in between is empty. If we say "in between," it immediately falls into the past moment.

There are two roads we follow in studying Buddhism. One is adding, and the other is subtracting. Making yourself empty out is subtracting. Other methods of cultivation, like the methods of Esoteric Buddhism, are all adding. When you cultivate the methods of the esoteric school, you place a lamp in front of you, and you need incense and flowers and some water and fruit: you are busy all day long. After that you put on a cap, and put on Dharma robes, and sit there contemplating an image of Buddha. Your lips are chanting mantras and your hands are ringing bells and holding vajras, and when you put them down you perform mudras with your hands.[2] You do this for a long time, until your whole body is covered with sweat. After three hours go by, you can stop and rest.

The methods of cultivating practice in Esoteric Buddhism are very numerous. If you want to get rich, there is the method of the god of wealth. If you want to get promoted, there is a method for getting promoted. If you want children, there is a method that will send you children. If you want to die earlier, there is a method for that. These methods make you add all day long, add till you are tired out, and the only thing you can do is rest. This, too, is emptying out past, present, and future.

The minds of modern day people are too complicated, and they cannot be emptied out. The best thing to do is use methods of adding, and add on until you cannot carry the weight, so that the only thing you can do is let go: then you will succeed. This is the reason for using adding methods.

The Zen school does not let you add and it does not let you subtract. It requires us to see clearly that the thoughts of this mind are fundamentally empty. Once you see this, what else would you want to look for? Why would you need to look for illuminating mind and seeing true nature? We are fundamentally very clear, but because the Buddha Dharma exists, it makes us unclear instead. We don't have to seek. If we let go it will be right. It is very simple, very natural and spontaneous.

Is emptying out past, present, and future Zen? It is not! What's the reason? Because this stage is only emptying out the contents of the consciousness. In reality, all we have to do after we sit down to meditate is shout out "Bah!" Then conscious thought is not there anymore, it is empty. This is the great Dharma Gate of Esoteric Buddhism. In years gone by I studied this sound "Bah!" and spent more than a

---

[2] Mantras are sequences of syllables chanted by practitioners of Esoteric Buddhism. Vajras are ritual implements that practitioners manipulate during Esoteric Buddhist ceremonies. Mudras are special configurations of the hands and fingers used by practitioners of Esoteric Buddhism.

hundred thousand dollars in the process. The method is this: The first step is to sit properly, straight and erect, and temper the breath. Then shout "Bah!" and you are finished.

Of course it does not work for us. After we shout "Bah!" there are no thoughts for a few seconds, but afterward thoughts come back again. After they come back, we shout "Bah" again! Later it stops working altogether. More "Bah's" cannot chase thoughts away. This is the way it is for ordinary people. Worldly people like the false, not the real. "Don't look on what is easily attained as commonplace."

The truth in this is summarized in the following phrase: "You must activate your mind without dwelling anywhere." The Sixth Patriarch awakened to the Path by hearing this line from *The Diamond Sutra*. For example, when we hear someone else talking, aren't our minds born? After we have finished listening to them talking, our minds drop it, and we are fundamentally "activating mind without dwelling anywhere," aren't we? So why do we need to preserve mind?

If you can manage to observe clearly from thought to thought, that will do. You do not need to cultivate any energy-work, or do any sitting meditation, or seek any path. People with the ability will believe this now. People without the ability will come again. At the first stage, it will be fine if you can maintain the realm of emptying out past, present and future.

In *The Record of Pointing at the Moon*, Volume 7, it records this story: One day a certain Master Lou-tzu was passing by a house of song, and he heard the sound of someone inside singing the words: "Since you have no mind, I'll quit too." At the time he was tying his shoe, and when he heard this line of the song, he was enlightened. What did he awaken to? Fundamentally we have no mind: after every sentence we say, it does not remain anywhere. Since you have no mind, I will quit, that's it! This is also the truth of emptiness.

Even though emptying out past, present and future still does not reach the final destination, almost no one can cut off past, present, and future and consistently maintain this. The basic reason is that people have no clear recognition of "subject" and "object." I will talk about this question again later when I introduce Yogacara philosophy.

The next issue concerning studying meditation sayings is this. In the present era, studying meditation sayings is really not appropriate. Following the method of contemplating mind is more normal, and easier. Using the method of studying meditation sayings is not as good as cessation and contemplation, or cultivating *samadhi*. In reality, people can cultivate these methods both before and after enlightenment. I will tell you all about this issue when I reach the conclusion.

Nevertheless, studying meditation sayings also has its advantages. In the past my teacher Master Yuan Huan-hsien talked about this issue with me when we were in seclusion in Szechuan. He said the people at that time who were doing seven-day meditation sessions should be pitied. In the hall there were more than a hundred people doing a hundred days of intense seven day meditation sessions, so they could not talk for more than three months, and at the same time they could not listen to any discussions of Buddhist principles. It was really terrible.

Later my teacher had me read several poems on "The Fragrant Beautiful Body," which spoke of reciting the buddha-name and studying Zen, and explained these methods very well. One of the poems was the following:

> It's deceptive to say that the struggle for
>     worldly power is decided by Heaven
> Children's games, success and fame are
>     fundamentally decided by chance
> But give me rivers and mountains beyond the saddle
>     and bridle
> A blow of the whip at sunrise and the steed
>     outruns the wind.

To make the effort to learn to become a buddha, you must have the mettle to refuse to become emperor and to abandon the whole empire. People who study Buddhism give constant lip service to emptiness, but with every move they make they practice existence: they are unwilling to abandon their concerns for fame, for profit, for their children, for their wives. "A blow of the whip at sunrise" means to imitate Shakyamuni Buddha stealing away from his family in the middle of the night, and riding off on the route of a leaver of home. Here is another one of his verses:

> The sound of the horse departing passes by
>     beyond the bamboo
> Whose daughter is the red-cheeked maiden
>     who looks on?

> She calls to the carriage that's taking him away
> > so many times it's hard to leave
> How wondrously she joins together
> > you, me, and him!

This is a poem of beauty. It describes a young woman from some family who is very pretty, so pretty she beguiles men, and leaves them standing there foolishly.

This describes how when studying meditation sayings, it is good if you truly exert effort and reach the point where "she wondrously joins together you, me, and him." "You" means the meditation saying, or the phrase "Amitabha Buddha" [if you are focusing on buddha-name recitation]. "Me" refers to the person sitting there [meditating]. "Him" refers to the false thoughts that keep coming [to the meditator]. [In other words—when the study of meditation sayings is done properly, the meditation saying, the person focusing on it, and the false thoughts that come to the person are all joined together.]

You may say that without sitting, you feel full of the flavor of the meditation saying. In reality, this feeling is a shadow, a little bit of meditative accomplishment that has come to you. You say you enter *samadhi*, but you cannot keep it going. In that case, if you cannot keep your *samadhi* stable, you are not cultivating it properly. You are not cultivating it properly, and yet you cannot bear to give it up—it's that you have a bit of the shadow (of genuine *samadhi*). But you cultivate it, and you cannot cut off false thoughts—they are "wondrously joining together you, me, and him." What will you do about it?

We are all revolving in this situation. It is not necessarily a matter of being unable to abandon male-female relationships. We cannot abandon any worldly things. We say to ourselves: "In another two or three years, when I've made arrangement for my children, then I will cultivate practice." This sort of worldly concern also "wondrously joins together you, me, and him." You cannot abandon worldly entanglements. In principle, you know you should abandon them. You are about to leave, and they are still calling to you from behind, "Get going." Some people who study Buddhism like to go everywhere listening to lectures which call upon them to do their meditation work properly, but they still do not get started on the journey. This, too, "wondrously joins together you, me, and him." Here's another of my teacher's poems:

The palanquins line up together east of the willow
    brook
The shadow of the swords, the light flashing off
    the halberds, confusion in the sunset light
So many gossamer threads floating in the air:
    they cannot tie them down
Rolling up the curtain, the people are in a
    painting.

Emptying out past, present and future is the realm described in this poem. At this stage, all the false thoughts running back and forth cannot hold you back. At this time, it seems as if you have awakened, but you have not yet penetrated all the way through. You have not awakened: there is really a bit of the flavor. It is like when we pull aside a curtain at a window: we can only see the shadows of the people there, we cannot see the real people. You may say they are not there, but there they are, though you cannot grasp them: "Rolling up the curtain, the people are in a painting."

If you can get to be like this in studying meditation sayings, this is the first step. But this still belongs to the states of consciousness. Why? Because there is still a "you" there. You feel that your body is sitting here. Your body is a moment of thought: all the five skandhas are a moment of thought. You are able to comprehend this aspect of your consciousness, and you have reduced out past, present and future to pure emptiness, but the state of feeling and sensing is still there, and you cannot get free of it.

Whenever you feel that your *ch'i* channels are circulating, or the water wheel (of the circular movement of the *ch'i*) is turning, this is the condition of feeling making ghosts for itself. You have not yet emptied out the moment of thought of the five skandhas.

There are many people who cultivate practice until they are very pure, but their bodies are all sick. Can we say they do not have any achievement in their meditation work? Their meditation is very stable, and their minds are empty all the way through, but in several decades of effort they have not even been able to transform sickness. When they really get to the brink of death, they cannot completely empty out that one moment of thought, and so they sink down into oblivion following it. So the moment of purity that they attained, frankly speaking, is something material, something that is linked to their physical health. Can something like this be relied upon? It cannot.

In the previous lecture I gave a general summary of Zen master Lin-chi's "four selections." Now I want to add a further explanation. Lin-chi's "four selections" are a teaching method, and they are also a method for us to exert ourselves and understand ourselves. At the same time, they tell us about the methods of cultivation of the Three Vehicles, the vehicles of the *shravakas*, the *pratyekas*, and the *bodhisattvas*.

*The Record of Lin-chi* says: "At a small evening gathering, Lin-chi said: 'Sometimes I take away the person but not the objects. Sometimes I take away the objects but not the person. Sometimes I take away both the person and the objects. Sometimes I do not take away either the person or the objects.' K'o-fu asked, 'What is taking away the person but not the objects?'"

K'o-fu was a man who helped Lin-chi start his school. At the time Lin-chi was only in his 30s, and he did not dare to teach publicly. His teacher Pai-chang told him, "Go now. There will be someone to help you." Lin-chi's eventual assistants (K'o-fu and Master P'u-hua) were both older than him, and both had awakened to the Path. These two older men acted as his assistant teachers. They deliberately asked mistaken questions, and when Lin-chi used his staff to beat them, both men obediently endured his beatings. Once everyone saw that these two men of the Path listened to Lin-chi, naturally there was nothing they could say, and in this way Lin-chi was acclaimed as a teacher. Thus, even if his learning and his virtue in the Path were lofty, if no one had sung his praises, it would have been to no avail. As the proverb says: "A short man needs other people to lift up his sedan chair."

K'o-fu saw that no one in this audience was going to make a sound, so he deliberately asked, "What is taking away the person but not the objects?" Lin-chi said:

The bright sun shines forth, spreading the ground with brocade
The infant's hair is hanging down white as silk.

This was a teaching for the moment, an extemporaneous verse. At that time this would have been considered colloquial language.

What is "taking away the person but not the objects"? For example, a person who succeeds in emptying out past, present, and future by shouting out "Bah!" totally forgets his body, and is very pure and clear there. Here among us there are some people who have blundered upon pure emptiness like "blind cats bumping into dead rats." Many people have had this kind of experience: this is comparatively central to the four intensified practices. People forget, but this experiential realm does exist. If you do your meditation work to the point that you really reach such a realm, no matter whether you are a Taoist or a Pure Land Buddhist or a Zen Buddhist, it is never easy.

This realm where the person is taken away is like the sun on a spring day, shining on the myriad things, with a vigorous potential to give life. Even if a person's outer form weakens with age, the pure illumination of his inherent nature never moves. If you preserve and maintain this realm forever, this is "taking away the person but not the objects." If you move from being an ordinary person to the realm of Hinayana *samadhi*, and preserve emptiness, even if your physical body changes, this thing does not change.

K'o-fu asked Lin-chi: "What is taking away the objects but not the person?" Lin-chi said: "The royal decree already runs everywhere in the realm, for the generals beyond the frontiers there is no smoke or dust." If the objects are not there anymore, I am still myself, the mountains are still mountains, and the rivers are still rivers. At this point there are no vexations in the mind, and no false thoughts. This is what Zen master Pai-chang spoke of: "The light of spiritual awareness shining alone, far removed from sense faculties and sense objects." Inherent nature, fundamental nature, is pure and illuminated and independent: it sends down its command, and the whole world is at peace. In the mind there is no conflict or disorder, no thoughts. But I am still myself, without the objects [of dualistic subjective experience]. Only then can it really be counted as a little bit of a semblance of entering the gate of enlightenment.

K'o-fu said: "What is taking away both the person and the objects." Lin-chi said: "Communication between Shansi and Hopeh is cut off, and each is alone on its side." Every line Lin-chi spoke in reply had such a literary flavor. That was the time of the late Tang and the Five Dynasties. Warlords had divided the country into rival domains: Shansi Province and Hopeh Province were in separate domains, and communication between them was sealed off. No one could go back and forth, and they were totally separated from each other. Each person in isolation lording it over one region represents the realm of the arhat, who just holds to emptiness. As Bodhidharma told the Second Patriarch: "Putting to rest all external entangling objects, and not agitating your inner mind, and making your mind like a wall, you can enter the Path." This is the realm of taking away both the person and the objects.

K'o-fu said: "What is not taking away either the person or the objects?" Lin-chi said: "The king ascends into the jewel palace, and the old peasants sing hallelujah." I am still myself. It is like those of us who have studied Buddhism for several decades: we can work at it all day long, without any experiential realms at all. This is not taking away either the person or the objects. Obviously Zen master Lin-chi's not taking away either the person or the objects is not the realm of the ordinary person: it is buddhahood, great penetrating enlightenment, when we perceive that all sentient beings are fundamentally buddha, and everything appears ready-made, and doesn't have to be cultivated. Lin-chi's everyday teaching method was not outside the scope of these four propositions.

Sometimes a certain person's learning was especially good, but when he came to Lin-chi's place, Lin-chi would nevertheless tell him, "That's not right." By contradicting you without any reason at all, he would make you feel very annoyed. This was taking away the objects but not the person. Sometimes he would say that your learning was very good, but unfortunately your meditation work was not sufficient. Here too you had to put up with a scolding. This too was taking away the objects but not the person. Sometimes he would say that you are wrong either way, and leave you no way out. This was taking away both the person and the objects. Sometimes he would give you a blow of his staff. This was not taking away either the person or the objects. Lin-chi's teaching methods were full of life, not rigid and set.

I especially want to bring to everyone's attention the fact that the Zen school has been abused. Thus, at the same time you are studying Zen, all of you should study the T'ien-t'ai school's methods of cultivating practice, and *The Great Treatise on the Stages of the Path of Enlightenment* by the great teacher Tsongkhapa of the Gelugpa Sect of Tibetan Esoteric Buddhism, and also Zen master Yung-chia's *Yung-chia Zen Collection*.

This Zen master Yung-chia synthesized the best of the T'ien-t'ai school and the Zen school. He clearly pointed out that to go from being an ordinary person to becoming a buddha, you must surely cultivate the "accomplishment of the three bodies." You must fully perfect the *dharmakaya*, the *sambhogakaya*, and the *nirmanakaya*.[3]

When you realize the *dharmakaya*, you will have the quality of cutting off affliction: you will be able to cut off all afflictions and all habit-energies.

The *sambhogakaya* is also called the body you, yourself, receive the use of. It is the body of buddha you, yourself, enjoy and use. For example, we have these bodies here. They are produced by transformations from the ignorance of the *dharmakaya*: they are reward bodies. If we have awakened to enlightenment, and succeeded in our

---

[3] *Dharmakaya buddha*, "the body of reality," "the truth body," represents the ontological basis of all things. It is defined by *The Buddhabhumisutra Shastra* as "the everywhere equal inherent nature of all the Tathagatas." *The Tsung Ching Lu* says: "The oneness of the realm of reality is the everywhere equal *dharmakaya* of the Tathagatas." *The Vijnaptimatrasiddhi Shastra* defines *dharmakaya* as "the true pure reality of all the Tathagatas, which *sambhogakaya* and *nirmanakaya* equally rely on, beyond characteristics, quiescent, beyond all theorizing; possessed of true pure virtues without limit, it is the everywhere equal true nature of all things."

*Sambhogakaya*, "the body of reward," "the body of enjoyment," is buddha as it appears to bodhisattvas who have transcended the dualism between samsara and nirvana, between affliction and enlightenment. According to *The Buddhabhumisutra Shastra, sambhogakaya* "is marked by the perfection of all accomplishments and virtues; formed by the assembling of all factors of enlightenment, it can fulfill all independent functions. . . . It shows all kinds of forms, preaches all kinds of teachings, to enable the great bodhisattvas to enjoy the bliss of reality." The same treatise says: "The buddha's *sambhogakaya* is fully equipped with the true merits of all phenomena of the mind of form, and on behalf of others manifests the accomplished virtues of transformation."

*Nirmanakaya*, the "transformation bodies," are the concrete embodiments which buddha takes on out of compassion to communicate with sentient beings according to their capacities. *The Avatamsaka Sutra* says of *nirmanakaya*: "By means of *nirmanakaya*, all the buddhas in all times perform transformations of infinite differentiation. . . . *Nirmanakaya* teach and transform living beings in all times: sometimes they show clever works, sometimes they appear to be born, sometimes they appear to attain enlightenment, sometimes they show final extinction. Thus they manifest in all sorts of ways great skill in means." The same scripture also says: "All *nirmanakaya* arise from skill in means."

cultivation, these are transformed into buddha-bodies which we ourselves receive the use of. We will be fully equipped with five kinds of spiritual powers, our wisdom will be fully developed, and we will have five kinds of wondrous function.

The *nirmanakaya* is the body for teaching others. Buddha emanates hundreds of millions of transformation bodies, physical manifestations, for the sake of sentient beings, to teach and transform and deliver people. The transformation bodies have the quality of great benevolence, great mercy, and great compassion. Zen master Yung-chia said:

> *Dharmakaya* without ignorance is *prajna*,
> *Prajna* without attachment is liberation,
> Liberation's peaceful extinction is *dharmakaya*.
> *Prajna* without attachment is liberation,
> Liberation's peaceful extinction is *dharmakaya*,
> *Dharmakaya* without ignorance is *prajna*.
> Liberation's peaceful extinction is *dharmakaya*,
> *Dharmakaya* without ignorance is *prajna*,
> *Prajna* without attachment is liberation.

When we are cultivating realization of the *dharmakaya*, we must pay attention, and we must not be ignorant and deluded. Many people cling to the realm of emptiness, and go on concentrating on the emptiness of self and others. They often become fondly attached to this. The great teacher Han-shan said: "To set foot in the forest of thorns is easy, but to transform the body under the curtain in the bright moonlight is hard." People who get stuck in the realm of pure clarity cannot manage to transform their bodies and reenter the world as bodhisattvas. Therefore, to achieve the *dharmakaya* without ignorance is *prajna*, it is great wisdom.

In the *Yung-chia Zen Collection*, Yung-chia sets forth in ten chapters the key issues of seeing truth, meditation work, and carrying out vows. In particular you must make a careful study of two chapters: chapter 8, which gives a simple explanation of the partial and the complete, and chapter 9, which discusses the correct way to cultivate cessation and contemplation.

Volume 6 of *The Record of Pointing at the Moon*, the "Preface on the Source of Zen," by Zen master Tsung-mi of Kuei-feng [d. 840] says this:

> *Dhyana* is a Sanskrit word. In our language it means the cul-
> tivation of contemplation, or in other words, quieting
> thoughts. Both are general terms for concentration and wis-
> dom. The source is the fundamentally enlightened true
> nature of the sentient beings, also called their buddha-nature,
> also called the mind-ground. To awaken to this is called wis-
> dom; to cultivate it is called concentration. Clear mastery of
> both concentration and wisdom is Zen. This nature is the
> fundamental source of Zen, so it is called the Zen-source,
> and it is also called *dhyana*. As for practice of inner truth,
> the fundamental source of this is the inner truth of Zen; for-
> getting sentiments and meshing with this is called Zen prac-
> tice. Thus the term, the practice of inner truth. Yet all the
> present day expositions by the various houses of Zen speak
> too much about the inner truth of Zen, and too little about
> Zen practice. Thus I give [the work to which this is the pref-
> ace] the title "The Source of Zen."

Understanding this principle is called the inner truth of Zen.
"Forgetting sentiments" means not having false thoughts and not
having afflictions, so that the mind is empty. The word "sentiments"
represents emotions, false thinking, false thoughts, and so
on. "Meshing with it" means realizing it, experiencing it, entering
into it.

The situation of the Zen school at the end of the T'ang dynasty
[when Tsung-mi wrote this] had already manifested the tendency of
talking a lot about Zen principles and talking little of Zen practice.
Thus, when people today talk as they please about Zen, this is even
more not Zen. After the T'ang and Sung, this defect had already
appeared. Zen master Kuei-feng could not bear to see it, and so he
composed this work *The Source of Zen*.

Yung-chia said: "There are people these days who call true nature
alone Zen. This is a lack of comprehension of the message of inner
truth and practice, and a failure to differentiate the languages of China
and India. Nevertheless, it is not that there is an essence of Zen apart
from true nature. It's just that sentient beings are deluded about the
real and cleave to the dusts of sensory experience: this is called scattering in confusion. Turning away from the dusts and joining with
the real is called Zen concentration. If we are simply discussing fundamental nature, it is neither real nor false, and there is no turning
away from or joining with, no concentration and no confusion, so

how can anyone speak of Zen?" In other words: Some people only know the principle of illuminating mind and seeing true nature, but they basically do not understand that this principle has to be actually experienced and realized.

In *The Record of Pointing at the Moon*, it is recorded how the Zen worthies of the past generations saw the Path, how they cultivated practice and worked at meditation, and how they carried out their vows. The book explains all of this. The Dharma-jewels that our predecessors left for us are very numerous. It's just that we have not tried to read them, and even more, have not tried to investigate them. We have not developed our own wisdom and so we cannot discern the treasure embedded in the mud wall. Every person who succeeded in the Path was very compassionate, and left something to us, in the hope of helping us attain the fruit of study.

The ancient's route of contemplating mind, the so-called "emptying out past, present, and future," is very simple. When you are sitting in meditation, you don't need to work on anything else: all you need to do is be able to preserve this interval of emptiness after the prior thought has gone and before the succeeding thought arrives. Then it will work. If you can start your cultivation from this, you will spontaneously be able to understand the Zen public case of Shakyamuni holding up the flower, and Kashyapa smiling.

If you cannot do this, then try pretending that you have emptied this thought in between the past thought and the future thought, and that will also do. This bit of pretending will be a seed, and from this seed naturally a flower will grow, and it will set fruit. These few lines are very important, very important indeed.

*The Record of Pointing at the Moon*, Volume 1, says: "The World Honored One was at an assembly on Spirit Peak. He held up a flower and showed it to the assembly. At that moment everyone in the assembly was silent. Only the Venerable Kashyapa changed the expression on his face and gave a slight smile. The World Honored One said, 'I have the treasury of the Correct Dharma Eye, the wondrous mind of nirvana, the absolute reality without form, the subtle wondrous Dharma Gate, the special transmission outside the scriptural teachings that does not set up any words. This I entrust to Mahakashyapa."

In what Buddha said are included seeing truth, cultivating realization, and carrying out vows. For the phrase "the treasury of the Correct Dharma Eye," you can refer to what Zen master Chia-shan said: "There are no phenomena before your eyes. Before your eyes are mental constructs, not the reality that is in front of you. This is not something that the eyes and ears can reach." Seeing truth, cultivating realization, and carrying out vows are all here in this statement too. Thus Chia-shan's disciple Lo-p'u said: "My late teacher's meaning was so simple and direct, but no one knew it."

I previously mentioned that if you can manage to empty out the past, present and future of mind and objects, and maintain this forever, taking away the person but not the objects—that is, with the person empty but not the objects—then you can experience the fruit of enlightenment. You can also generate spiritual powers, and you can also finish with portioned out birth and death. Of course the birth and death of transformation is still not finished: you must pay special attention to this. With Hinayana you can finish with portioned out birth and death, but you cannot finish with the birth and death of transformation. People who advance another step can finish with them both, but they have still not smashed great birth and death, that is, fundamental ignorance.

So how can you finish with birth and death? *The Record of Pointing at the Moon*, Volume 2, contains this passage: "Manjushri asked the maiden Anditya, 'What is the meaning of birth?' The maiden said, 'Birth is born by means of the unborn. This is the meaning of birth.' Manjushri said, 'What does that mean?' The maiden said, 'If you can know clearly that the four causal elements of earth, water, fire, and wind have never been mixed together, and yet they are able to follow what is appropriate to them, this is the meaning of birth.'

"Manjushri asked, 'What is the meaning of death?' The maiden said, 'Death dies by means of the undying. That is the meaning of death.' Manjushri said, 'What does that mean?' The maiden said, 'If you can know clearly that the four causal elements of earth, water, fire, and wind have never been separated, and yet they are able to follow what is appropriate to them, this is the meaning of death.'"

How do our lives come to be? How did the first life come about? It came from the beginningless. Before the beginningless, why did it have to come? Unborn but born, born but unborn: this is the truth of birth.

Our bodies are made up of the four elements gathering together and building a house. Though these four kinds of things have joined together and turned into a body, earth is still earth, water is still water, fire is still fire, and air is still air. None of them infringes on the other:

each rests in its own place. "Yet they are able to follow what is appropriate to them": they still match up and join together, and give form to this phenomenon of life.

The link between the mental and the material is all right here. We see these four elements as joined together, but in reality they have not been joined together at all. To say they have not joined, but they are still able to follow what is appropriate, is the same as the statement in *The Surangama Sutra*: "The pure fundamental state pervades the universe. It follows the minds of sentient beings, and responds to their contents, and becomes manifest according to their karma."

You should not just study Buddhism—you should take its principles and apply them to your own body, to seek realization. If ordinarily you only know to sit in meditation and hold to an experiential realm, this is like a blind cat guarding a dead rat, and you will be a blind cat forever. You should study this: "They have never been mixed together, and yet they are able to follow what is appropriate to them." This is the truth of where birth comes from.

"Death dies by means of the undying. That is the meaning of death." Have you recognized death? Who in the world does not die? They die and yet they do not die. We see how after a person dies, his bones are scattered. But in reality they all still occupy their own places, and "they can follow what is appropriate to them."

The maiden Anditya asked Manjushri: "I clearly know the truth that birth is not birth. Yet why do I still suffer the revolving flow of birth and death?" Manjushri said: "Your power is not yet full."

The maiden is asking Manjushri: I have already awakened to the truth of birth and death, yet I am still dragged along by the power of birth and death. This is the same as when we say, "I clearly know emptiness," but we cannot empty everything out, and we cannot get rid of false thought, so clearly knowing this emptiness is still useless.

Why are we still subject to the revolving flow of birth and death then? Now someone comes forth to comfort us. Manjushri says: Don't feel bad. What you know is correct, but your practice is not yet pure and ripe, and your power has not yet expanded to its full extent, so you are still subject to the revolutions of birth and death. That is, your work in cultivating *samadhi* has not yet been completed. Here he is talking entirely about meditation work: if your meditation work is not perfected it will not work. If you can liberate your body, then if you want to go [die], you can go [die]. In theory it is possible to do this. But we cannot do this because our power is not yet fully developed. This "power" included the power of seeing the truth of the Buddha's teaching, the power of wisdom, as well as the power of the meditation work of cultivating *samadhi*. This point is very important.

When we speak of the gate of practice, the practice of studying Buddhism is most important. This includes both external conduct and all kinds of thinking and concepts in the mind.

Zen master Kuei-shan had this famous saying: "In reality the ground of truth does not admit a single atom of dust, but in the gate of the myriad practices, not a single thing is abandoned." If we give up the moment of thought, so-called good and evil and right and wrong are all absent—good things are not right, and the Buddha Dharma is not right either. This is just what the Sixth Patriarch said:

> *Bodhi* fundamentally has no tree
> Nor does the clear mirror have a stand
> Fundamentally there is not a single thing
> Where then could dust gather?

"In the gate of the myriad practices, not a single thing is abandoned" is the precept of the bodhisattvas. In the myriad practices in which bodhisattvas arouse their minds and let their thoughts move, as soon as their minds and thoughts move, they speak of good and then act for good, and they do not abandon anything.

In years gone by I went to see Master Ch'uan-po. In those years he and Hsu-yun and Neng-yuan were the three great teachers of the Zen school in mainland China. As soon as I arrived, the old master hastened to fan the fire in the stove and brew tea. I said, "Master, I am not worthy. Please do not boil water for me." The old master said, "You do not understand. You are the guest and I am the host. In the gate of the myriad practice not a single thing is abandoned. By rights I must boil water for you." This was the road traveled by the older generation. You must pay attention to every detail.

Within the Zen school there is carrying out vows, seeing truth, and the work of cultivating realization: not one of these three can be lacking. In terms of the principles of the teaching, carrying out vows is a form of merit, and as long as accomplished merit is not complete, wisdom cannot be achieved. In other words, failure to achieve wisdom means the accomplished merits are not complete.

*The Record of Pointing at the Moon,* Volume 12, gives this: "Kuei-shan said to Yang-shan: 'When you are alone you must turn the light around and reflect back. No one will know what you have understood. Try to take your real understanding and offer it to me so I can see.'"

Here Kuei-shan is talking about meditation work, and he is also talking about seeing truth. This is connected with the treasury of the Correct Dharma Eye, and it is also connected with the patriarch Bodhidharma's "reversing the workings of a moment of mindfulness."

When we sit down and start to meditate, as soon as we close our eyes, our vision follows and falls into a deep pit. It is almost like being dead. What does it mean, to turn the light around and reflect back? This is similar to the Taoist path of looking within, of extending life and looking for a long time. If you cannot turn the light around and reflect back, you will not be able to get started on the road of meditation work. Thus Kuei-shan had Yang-shan tell him something about the level he had attained by his most recent efforts.

Yang-shan replied: "If you tell me to observe myself, in here there is a state of complete nothingness, and there is not a single thing or a single understanding that I can offer to you, Master." Kuei-shan said, "Where there is a state of complete nothingness, actually this is you constructing an understanding. You have not yet detached from mental states." In other words, if you have really reached a state where there is complete nothingness, and you are nowhere and everywhere, this is an understanding, a view.

Not yet detached from mental states means you are still in the realm of the mind's consciousness, and you have not yet completely emptied out all the way through. Pay attention to this line! Even if you reach the level where this mind is empty all the way through, and is not inside the body or outside the body, and abides nowhere, you still have not detached from mental states.

Yang-shan said: "Since it is a state of complete nothingness, where are there any phenomena, and what can be taken as a mental state?" In other words, given that it is a state of complete nothingness, how could there still be any experiential realms then?

Kuei-shan said: "Just now, is this how you understood?" Yang-shan said: "That's right." Kuei-shan said: "If so, then you are full of the phenomena of mental states, and you have not yet escaped from the mind of self and objects. Actually then, you do have an understanding that you are offering to me. I grant that your station of belief is evident, but your station of humanity is still hidden."

In other words, Kuei-shan is telling Yang-shan: since you have this interpretive understanding, you have still not yet been liberated from [dualistic perception in terms of] subject and object. Still, Kuei-shan encourages Yang-shan by telling him that it is not at all easy to reach this state. In terms of the principles of the teaching, and in terms of the ten kinds of faith and the ten kinds of abiding and the ten kinds of dedication, and in the fifty-five stations of bodhisattvas, and in the stations of the ten kinds of faith of bodhisattvas before the stages, in being able to believe in himself, it can be said that Yang-shan has gone beyond the level of ordinary people. But he had still not entered enlightenment.

In *The Record of Pointing at the Moon*, Volume 12, is the story of the circumstances of Chia-shan's enlightenment. At that time Tao-wu, Yun-yen, and the boatman Teh-ch'eng left their teacher Yao-shan. The first two opened teaching centers and became teaching masters. As for the boatman Teh-Ch'eng, he helped people by operating a ferry boat, and he did not become a public Zen teacher. Nevertheless, he said to the other two men, "You know where I am staying. Later on, if you encounter any spiritually sharp advanced monks, direct them to me, and I may be able to polish them, and bequeath to them what I have attained through my life. I will do this in order to repay the benevolence of our teacher."

At that time Chia-shan was already a great Dharma teacher. Tao-wu went to Chia-shan's place to take him on and teach him. Tao-wu deliberately did not reveal himself, but simply sat in the audience listening to Chia-shan expound the Dharma.

There was a monk who posed a question to Chia-shan, asking him: "What is the *dharmakaya*?" Chia-shan answered, "The *dharmakaya* is formless." The monk asked: "What is the Dharma-eye?" Chia-shan answered: "The Dharma-eye is flawless."

Chia-shan had answered very well, but after he did, there was a monk who burst out laughing—this was Tao-wu. Chia-shan very humbly got down from the teacher's seat and asked this monk: "Just now when I replied to this monk's question, I must have been wrong to make an advanced monk like you laugh. I hope you will not spare me your compassion and tell me where I erred." Master Tao-wu said: "You have appeared in the world well enough, Master, but you have not had a teacher yet." That is to say, you were not wrong, it's just that you have not been taught by a good teacher. Chia-shan then said: "I hope you will explain to me where I was wrong." Tao-wu said: "I never explain. Instead, please go to the boatman's place at Hua-t'ing." That is to say, I will not explain: you should go yourself and find Master Teh-ch'eng the boatman. Chia-shan was right in theory, but he had not really experienced it himself.

At this point Chia-shan asked for Tao-wu's advice, saying: "What kind of a man is he?" Tao-wu said: "This man has no tile over his head and not enough ground to stick an awl into under his feet. If you go see him, you should change your attire." At this time Chia-shan was putting on airs, and his reputation was very lofty, and he made a grand show of himself. Therefore Tao-wu told him, if you go like this, it won't work. Behave properly when you go to him, and put aside your reputation and your status, and above all do not put on the airs of a great Dharma teacher.

Pay attention to this! In this passage there is seeing truth, cultivating realization, and carrying out vows.

The account continues: "So then Chia-shan dismissed his congregation, put on traveler's garb, and went directly to Hua-t'ing." As soon as the boatman Teh-ch'eng saw him, he asked: "What temple do you dwell in, O virtuous one?" Chia-shan said: "I do not dwell in a temple. Dwelling is not like it." The Buddha Dharma fundamentally abides nowhere, and has no form. If you dwell in any given realm, naturally this is not the Path.

The boatman said: "Not like what?" Chia-shan said: "It is not the phenomena before our eyes." The boatman said: "Where did you learn this?" In other words, where did you learn these slippery words?

Chia-shan said: "It is not something that ears and eyes can reach." It was like counterattacking the old master, saying in effect: if you do not recognize me as brilliant, perhaps you do not understand me.

The boatman said: "A fitting sentence can be a stake to tether a donkey to for ten thousand eons." This line later became a famous saying. The meaning is, if a person keeps on saying such a definitive sentence, this is stupid. It is like pounding a stake into the ground, and then tying an animal's halter to it. In other words, there you are clinging to the Dharma: you shouldn't be playing verbal tricks. When the boatman said this, Chia-shan was dumbfounded.

The boatman then said: "The line is hanging down a thousand feet, the intent is deep in the pond. You are three inches away from the hook. Why don't you say something?"

The language here is very beautiful. It was not composed by people who came later and wrote down this story. The learning of Chia-shan and the boatman was very good. In this statement, the boatman is talking about meditation work. When we are doing this work, and we have emptied out those thoughts of ours a little bit, if we say they have been emptied, they are still there, and if we say they are there, we still feel that we have done our sitting meditation well enough.

> It wondrously connects you, me, and him.
> So many floating gossamer threads cannot tie him down
> Rolling up the curtain, the people are in a painting.

Chia-shan had been prodded on all sides by the boatman, and he had reached this realm, and he stood there without moving. The boatman Teh-ch'eng said, it is like fishing; I have let down such a long line, and now it is just a little ways from you. That is, you have done so much meditation work and you want to awaken to enlightenment; now you are not very far away, so why don't you say something?

The story continues: "Chia-shan was about to open his mouth, when the boatman hit him with an oar and knocked him into the water." Chia-shan was getting ready to open his mouth and wanted to say what it says in the scriptures, but before he could say anything, there was a thump, and he had been knocked into the water by a blow from the boatman's oar.

When people fall into the water, they will risk their lives to go toward where the light is. Perhaps Chia-shan understood the nature of water—he did not sink toward the bottom. He lifted his head up, and as soon as he emerged above the surface: "The boatman again said, 'Speak! Speak!' As Chia-shan was about to open his mouth, the boatman hit him again. Chia-shan opened up in great enlightenment, and he nodded his head three times."

Try to imagine a man with a bellyful of learning, standing next to the boatman, having a conversation with him. Suddenly, blam, he knocks him into the water. When he has been struggling for quite a while to get his head above water, where has this learning gone to? It has already gone beyond the clouds, all false thoughts have been cleared away. This is the method Zen master Teh-ch'eng the boatman used to deal with Chia-shan.

Chia-shan understood everything in the entire Buddhist canon: consciousness-only, true thusness, transcendent wisdom. He clearly understood it all. The only thing to do was to make him get rid of all this, to knock him into the water so he didn't even have time to draw a breath or to think, and when he stuck his head up from the water, to tell him "Speak! Speak!" Chia-shan still wanted to talk about transcendent wisdom! So Zen master Teh-ch'eng the boatman hit him again. When Chia-shan stuck his head out of the water again, he couldn't say anything anymore: this time he was enlightened. After he was enlightened, he was afraid the boatman would hit him again and there was not time to speak, so he quickly nodded his head three times, to convey the message "I understand, don't hit me again." The boatman said:

I will let you play with the line on the end of the pole
Without disturbing the clear waves, the intent is spontaneously
    distinct.

The situation of the teacher is like fishing, and letting down a line. He lets you play with this line. It is like when we are sitting and doing meditation work: refining the breath is fine, and reciting the buddha-name is fine, and being empty is fine, too.

"Without disturbing the clear waves, the intent is spontaneously distinct." What false thoughts are you afraid of: when false thoughts come they do not interfere! If you do not pay attention to them, isn't this very good? When I am reciting the buddha-name, I am aware that false thoughts persist. But those false thoughts cannot touch Buddha, so don't be afraid. If you are afraid, this is what is called being upside down. Since you are an ordinary person, naturally there will be false thoughts. But you don't have to be afraid of them or pay attention to them! False thoughts will slowly subside and habit-energy will slowly disappear.

At this point in the story Chia-shan asked: "If you throw away the hook and the line, what is your intent, Teacher?" In other words, if you don't have the fishing pole and line, if you throw them away, then what? As soon as Zen master Teh-ch'eng the boatman tells him methods for making effort, there is still a hook and line there.

The boatman said: "The line is hanging down in the green water, floating to set the meaning of existence and non-existence."

Throwing away the hook and line is all well and good. If you speak of emptiness it is not right, and if you speak of existence it is not right, either. Neither empty nor existent, you go where you please independently. The line is floating on the surface of the water. The power of karma and habit-energy are becoming weaker and weaker.

Zen master Chia-shan understood this. He said: "Words carry the mystery, but there is no road for them. The tongue speaks without speaking." In other words, your speaking is the same as not speaking. Emptiness equals existence and existence equals emptiness.

Teh-ch'eng the boatman was very happy and said to Chia-shan: "After having fished through all the river waves, I finally encounter a golden carp." [A golden carp represents an enlightened person.] Chia-shan covered his ears.

The boatman was saying in effect: I have been here for many decades, piloting a ferry boat day after day, wanting to carry someone across. But all along no one let me take them across. Today by all accounts I have caught a big fish. Chia-shan would not listen to his teacher's words of acclaim, so he covered his ears.

The boatman said: "Just so, just so." Then he gave Chia-shan some instructions: "From now on you must leave no tracks where you hide yourself. But you must not hide yourself where there are no tracks."

What a subtle set of linked words! Because Chia-shan was too famous, the boatman instructed him to conceal his name and fame after leaving him, and go into hiding, and not let anyone know of his whereabouts. But right after that the boatman told Chia-shan that it would also not be right to have his mental state dwell entirely in emptiness.

The story continues: "Then the boatman said: 'I was with Yao-shan for thirty years and I only understood this. You have already attained it. In the future you should not live in towns or villages. Go deep into the mountains with your hoe, and find one or two people to continue the teaching, and do not let it be cut off.' Chia-shan then bade the boatmen farewell and went off, looking back at him again and again."

When Zen master Chia-shan hoisted his bundle onto his back, he was probably not even dry yet. He took a few steps and then turned around and looked back at the boatman. On one hand, he couldn't bear to leave his teacher. On the other hand, he was thinking: "Don't tell me the Buddha Dharma is just like this?" Greed, anger, ignorance, pride, doubt—obviously!

As soon as Zen master Teh-ch'eng the boatman saw this, he shouted to him in a loud voice, "You, monk!" When Chia-shan turned around, "The boatman held up an oar and said, 'Did you think there was something else?' Then he capsized the boat and disappeared into the water."

He was saying: did you think I have some secret that I did not give to you? Look! Then he capsized his boat, and disappeared under the water to show there was nothing else. The Buddha Dharma is just like this. The boatmen showed Chia-shan his own death, to solidify and settle his disciple's faith. In reality, the boatman did not die, but no one knows where he went.

This story talks about seeing truth, about how to cultivate practice, and about how to carry out a bodhisattva's vows.

# 13

# STORIES OF
# ZEN ENLIGHTENMENT

We will now discuss the Chinese Zen school, the heart of Zen, and the Five Houses of Zen. The point is not that we take our own thoughts and ideas and go look at the Zen school. The situations we discuss must be related back to the cultivation of our own mind-ground. We must do the work of cultivating practice and try to understand this work through direct experience. If all you do is listen and get enthusiastic, it will be the same as the kind of Zen that is popular here and abroad: the kind that does not talk about cultivating practice or seeking realization, but just takes a collection of theories and stories and performs a supposedly objective critique. This is a description of ordinary Zen studies, but our emphasis is placed on seeking realization.

When I previously mentioned the Zen school, I said that we might as well follow the path of the ancients and use the method of contemplating mind—and observe ourselves. In terms of present day concepts, this amounts to investigating our own psychological state. Our psychological state—all our thoughts and feelings—can be summed up into three stages. They are divided according to three phrases of time—past, present, and future.

To use this method of contemplating mind, is not necessarily to sit cross-legged. When you get quiet, and observe your own thoughts, you will discover a mass of confusion. One portion of your psychological state belongs to the category of thoughts. Another portion belongs to the category of feelings—like backaches, pains in the legs, etc. There is another portion that belongs to the category of emotions, like when you feel depressed or annoyed. In sum, these are all psychological states. In Buddhist terms, this is called "a moment of thought," "a mind-moment."

Then you observe your own thoughts. After the previous thought has passed away, it is not there anymore. It is like when something is said and you have already heard it: every sentence, every word, becomes something that belongs to the past. It cannot stop for a minute or a second. You should not burden your mind: thoughts cannot be kept forever in your mind. Thoughts, in themselves, cannot be stopped; they are always flowing and moving like a stream of water that flows on uninterruptedly forever. Thoughts follow each other like wave upon wave, closely connected to each other. If you analyze them even more minutely, they are like molecule after molecule of water, tightly joined together to form a flowing stream.

In fact, when the previous wave has passed, and it has already flowed away, the next one has not yet joined it. At this point, if you take it and cut it off in the middle and do not let the next wave arise, there would be no more water in between. Psychological states are also like this.

To consider another example: when you look at an electric light, it seems to be always shining. But in reality, after you turn on the switch, the first electron begins to function and immediately emits light, and then very quickly disappears; and the functioning of the later electrons continues after it without interruption. You see light continuously, but in reality the light is being born and disappearing instant after instant. This is why you can see fluorescent lights flickering.

Your own psychological states are also continuously in the process of being born and disappearing like an electric light. You are not aware of this, and may think that you are continuously thinking without a break. Let's conduct an investigation of this idea. As soon as you wake up in the morning, the first thought is ... what are you thinking? Has that first thought in the morning lasted up till now? Of course it has not. It cannot possibly remain in your mind all along; it has long since departed. Therefore, it is useless to get rid of thoughts: it is too much wasted effort, they are originally empty. When the average person hears of Buddhism, as soon as he or she sits down to meditate, he or she seeks emptiness using his or her own consciousness to imagine emptiness. This is adding a head on top of a head: it is too much.

Nevertheless, the question now is: the way thoughts flow off is easy to understand, but how is it that the second thought, the succeeding thought, comes along? We cannot find its source. This is a question well worth investigating. Why is it that thought comes along by itself, totally unwanted by us? This is especially true for people who do sitting meditation. Originally what they want is purity, but despite that, thoughts come along. There are thoughts that their ordinary basic thinking would never think of: all they have to do is start sitting in meditation and they start to think of all sorts of things from years ago.

For instance, here is a joke. An old lady does some sitting meditation. After she is finished, she tells people: "Hey! Sitting meditation really works. More than ten years ago, someone borrowed a dollar from me, and has still not returned it. When I sat in meditation, I unexpectedly began to think of it." This is really not a joke, because it explains a real fact. The more peaceful and quiet the mind becomes, the more all sorts of things spontaneously float up and appear in the mind. How does this come about? This is a very important question.

If the previous thought has gone, and the next thought has not yet joined it, in between, is it not empty? How does this next thought come along? The one that goes to try and find out is also a thought. You should not try to bring it on, nor should you go searching for it, nor should you fear it. Although the next thought comes along, it, too, is sure to pass. It's just that in this there is something that knows your own thoughts have passed by, and knows that another thought has come. This thing does not move: what you have to find is this one. This one is the "awareness" that *The Heart Sutra* talks about: the awareness "that is aware that the five skandhas are all empty as the Bodhisattva Kuan-yin practices the perfection of profound wisdom"; the awareness that is always shining. This word "shining awareness" is used very well. It is like when you turn on an electric light, and the light shines on you.

Because you do not clearly understand this principle, you concentrate on thinking of some way to cope with thoughts running around in confusion, and want to cut them off. In reality, the one that observes thoughts and is aware of thoughts never moves at all, and does not have to cut off thoughts. You must understand that there is a host who sees these miscellaneous, chaotic thoughts. This is an inherent capability of yours. This capability is always quietly there. After a long long time, this continuous thread of false thoughts will not come anymore.

False thoughts are like guests who come to the house. The host certainly does not tell them, "Get out!", nor does he tell them, "Please come in." He neither rejects them nor welcomes them, and the false thoughts spontaneously run off. This is the very first step. If you can be in this state at all times, you will gradually contemplate mind, and observe the habit-energy of affliction. All you have to do is observe it, and the habit-energy of affliction will not be there anymore. All you have to do is shine awareness on it, and it will empty out. You must pay particular attention to this principle.

Someone asked: "After maintaining a peaceful and quiet mental state for two or three days, without experiencing any transformation of my body and mind, a question came to me. My mind felt very bored and dejected. Sometimes I think: isn't this 'dead-tree Zen'? What's this difference between my present state of mind and a dead tree? Both are indifferent, without thoughts. What's the difference?"

This question in itself raises some questions. First: you feel that you have emptied out past, present, and future, but your mental state is one of boredom. Isn't this still a thought? Obviously you have not emptied out past, present, and future. Second: you feel this is a state without thought, but in reality your thoughts are very numerous: not only do you have past, present, and future, but at least several other frames of reference. What has happened is that you have exerted yourself too intensely, and your body and mind have produced a feeling of boredom.

This is why Buddha said that cultivating practice should be like tuning a stringed instrument. If you try too hard, and get too tense, this is like making the strings of the instrument too tight, and you will feel bad. In other words, some people who study Buddhism and study the Path, start out boldly and energetically, wanting to have immediate success. If we measured their blood pressure at this point, it would certainly be too high because of nervous tension.

Take note! The question is not a reflection of emptying out past, present, and future. If you really manage to empty out past, present, and future, after the previous thought has gone, the next thought does not come, and the intervening interval is in itself empty: in reality, fundamentally, there is no thought in between. Thus, *The Diamond Sutra* says: "Past mind is ungraspable, present mind is ungraspable, future mind is ungraspable." Past, present, and future are all ungraspable: this does not mean that they don't exist, but that they cannot be grasped and held fast. The future has not come yet: can you get a grasp on what thoughts will be in your mind tomorrow? Future mind is ungraspable. The present mind is ungraspable: the present I just now spoke of has already become the past.

When *The Diamond Sutra* tells us these are ungraspable, it is not telling us that past, present, and future mind are empty, nor is it telling us that past, present, and future mind do not exist. The Buddhist translations made by the ancients were very careful. Even if there really is such a thing as emptying out past, present, and future, there would be no way to get hold of this either. Why? If you could get hold of the realm of emptying out past, present, and future, this would be the present mind. If you understand that the present mind is ungraspable, it doesn't matter. This is the first point.

The second point is this. If you really manage to empty out past, present, and future, the body no longer exists, and is merged with emptiness. This is true untrammeled freedom—utter freedom. The purpose of studying Buddhism is to learn the freedom of liberation. Too bad that what present day people who study the Buddhist Path accomplish is not freedom or independence, and even less is it liberation. How painful! Instead of freedom the result is that they tie themselves up with those things. You must pay attention to this principle, and understand it clearly.

I have mentioned Zen master Lin-chi's four selections, and discussed matching up the person and the objects. In general whenever people do meditation work, whether in Taoism or Esoteric Buddhism or any school of Buddhism, there is one thing none of them can get away from. That is some way of constructing the physiological and the psychological. When doing meditation work, it is a question either of the physiology generating feelings, or the psychology producing thoughts. In either case, these are false thoughts. Because these are only there when doing meditation work, and absent otherwise, in terms of the four selections they are all "the object." But who is doing the meditation work? It is me doing the meditation work. In terms of the four selections I am "the person." In terms of the principles of the teaching, both the objects and the person are termed forms, that is, appearances. So what is causing me, this person, to sit here? True nature. True nature and apparent forms are the two gates. That is, I myself know I am sitting here, and I know I am making an effort. Therefore, both aspects (the person and the objects) are revolving back and forth.

Because of this, Lin-chi proposed the four selections. On one hand he was teaching people, and on the other hand, he was telling us that when we do meditation work we must pay attention: sometimes he takes away the person but not the objects, sometimes he takes away the objects but not the person, sometimes he takes away both, and sometimes he takes away neither. These four modes must be appropriately coordinated and selected. In Taoism they call this the temperature. It is like boiling rice. If the heat is too high, you turn it down a bit, otherwise you will burn the rice. If the heat is too low, the rice will not cook thoroughly. You must always make the proper adjustment yourself. Thus this teaching device of Lin-chi's is called "selection."

No one else can help you with all of this, no enlightened teacher can help you at all. Even if Buddha were sitting right in front of you, it would be to no avail. Otherwise Buddha's sons and his brother Ananda would not have had to cultivate practice because Buddha would have saved them. You can only save yourself. No one else can save you. So "selection" means that we must make the proper adjustment ourselves.

This method of the Zen school is most amazing. It includes the methods of both the exoteric and the esoteric teachings.

There are three kinds of things that are inseparable from Zen. The first is military affairs. All the famous generals of olden times had a bit of a taste for Zen. Famous generals were born with natural talent. But when you are in a battle, surrounded on all sides by the enemy, with death the only way out, how do you make your mind work and remain lucid and transform defeat into victory? This is Zen. If you say that at such a time you could ponder the strategies of all the famous military thinkers, none of them would work, no strategy could save you. The second thing that is inseparable from Zen is true poetry. When you write a good line, even you, yourself, do not know how you wrote it. The third is the best products of technologists. This, too, is close to Zen.

Therefore, in the period of the late T'ang and the Five Dynasties, the Zen school was very important in Chinese culture. This is especially true of its literary quality, which was apt to be expressed in poetry. In reality, those Zen masters were not composing poems: instead, it was a spontaneous outflow from their inherent nature. When the fundamental nature attains its most empty and aware, perfectly good and perfectly beautiful state, beautiful feelings naturally flow forth. Thus the realm of literature was elevated by the Zen influx. This literary excellence was by no means deliberately learned; rather, it was spontaneous. Thus the Zen masters wrote essays without using the standard essay form. Instead, every passage is meditation work, and they are really hard to read and understand.

Now let's return to Chia-shan. After he was enlightened there with Zen master Teh-ch'eng, the boatman, where did he go? Teh-ch'eng told him: "You must leave no tracks where you hide yourself. But you must not hide yourself where there are no tracks." There is much contained in these two lines. In relation to meditation work, "Leave no tracks where you hide yourself," means that there should be no bodily sensations and no miscellaneous thoughts in the mind; past, present, and future have been emptied, and there are no shadows at all.

But you cannot stay in the realm of emptiness for too long; if you stay too long, you can get lazy. Therefore, abiding in emptiness is permissible in connection with cultivating realization, but not in connection with carrying out the bodhisattva vows. In terms of the precepts for bodhisattvas, this is a violation of the precepts. To sink down into *dhyana* and not arouse compassion, and fail to perform the tasks of saving others and saving the world, is a violation of the precepts for bodhisattvas. Therefore Teh-ch'eng said to Chia-shan: "You must not hide yourself where there are no tracks." In other words: you should not stay too long and not set to work; you cannot stay forever in the mountains as a man who understands himself. You must go forth and do meritorious deeds. You must undertake the mission of rescuing others from their suffering and difficulty. Thus Teh-ch'eng the boatman called upon Chia-shan: "You must not hide yourself where there are no tracks." First go and dwell in a hermitage, and hide away, and do not let anyone know about you. After your meditation work reaches the ultimate goal, "You must not hide yourself where there are no tracks."

Zen master Chia-shan had a disciple called Lo-p'u. Originally Lo-p'u was Lin-chi's disciple: he was intelligent and capable, and his learning was good. He had mastered all the Buddhist scriptures and he kept the precepts of discipline very strictly. At first he was Lin-chi's attendant. Lin-chi was very pleased with this disciple of his, and often praised him saying: "This is the arrow in the gate of Lin-chi. Who will dare to oppose him?"

Given this encouragement, Lo-p'u thought that he was already enlightened. Later on, whenever Lin-chi discussed things with him, he was not at all submissive toward his teacher, so there was no way for Lin-chi to instruct him further. Subsequently Lo-p'u asked Lin-chi for permission to leave and went away. Lin-chi said: "In the gate of Lin-chi there is a red-tipped carp: wagging his head and shaking his tail, he is going off to the south. I wonder whose jar of minced pickles he will drown in?" In the Zen metaphor, when the carp leaps through the Dragon Gate he changes into a dragon. In this statement, Lin-chi was saying of Lo-p'u: This carp had still not turned into a dragon. Originally he had wanted to be transformed, but he has not yet been transformed. Now he has gone south: I wonder who will be able to take him in and subdue him? (Lin-chi, the place after which the Zen master Lin-chi was named, was in Shantung Province in the northern part of China.)

The story continues: "When Lo-p'u had finished with his travels, he went to Chia-shan Mountain and built a hut there. For a year he did not pay a visit to Zen master Chia-shan. At that point Chia-shan wrote him a letter and had a monk deliver it to him. Lo-p'u took it and put it under his seat, then extended his hand again as if asking for something. The monk had no reply, so Lo-p'u hit him and said: 'Go back and describe to your master what happened here.' The monk returned to Chia-shan and told him what had happened. Chia-shan said: 'If that monk opens the letter, he is sure to come within three days. If he does not open the letter, this man cannot be saved.' Chia-shan then sent someone to watch for Lo-p'u to leave his hut, and then when he had left, to burn it down. After three days, sure enough, Lo-p'u did leave his hut. The man who had been sent reported back saying: 'When the fire rose up inside the hut, Lo-p'u paid no attention.'"

At that time the Zen school was in full flower. A proverb describes it well: "Do not fear that the whole country will go to ruin, just fear that your head will not be illuminated." You could live anywhere in China and study Buddhism: there were great teachers everywhere. Lo-p'u traveled all over visiting them, but he looked down on them all. He went straight to the mountain that was the abode of Zen master Chia-shan, built a thatched hut in the vicinity of his temple, and practiced sitting meditation. Such a young monk he was, but when he went to Chia-shan's place, for a whole year he did not go to pay his respects.

Chia-shan wrote a letter, and had someone deliver it to Lo-p'u. What the contents of the letter were is not recorded. No doubt he was enticing him, inviting him to come to his temple. But as it turned out, Lo-p'u took the letter and put it under his seat and paid no attention to it at all, and went on sitting in meditation as before. Chia-shan said to his disciples: if he opens my letter, he is sure to come within three days; if he does not open my letter, this man will not be saved.

Chia-shan dispatched a man to keep watch outside Lo-p'u's hut. If within three days he saw Lo-p'u leave the hut, he was to take a torch and burn his hut down. As things turned out, on the third day, sure enough, Lo-p'u left the hut. Here there is a question. Lo-p'u thought that he had already penetrated through to great enlightenment. After being examined by Chia-shan in his letter, there was nothing else he could do but question this. The Second Patriarch called it pacifying mind: Lo-p'u had not pacified his mind, so he had to come to see Chia-shan. Once Lo-p'u left the hut, it started to burn—Chia-shan's disciple had set it on fire. He shouted to Lo-p'u from behind: Your house is on fire! But Lo-p'u didn't even turn around. He wasn't pretending to be aloof: the doubt in his mind had really been grabbed by Chia-shan and he was in a great hurry to seek him out.

The story continues: "He went straight to Chia-shan, and without bowing, stood there in front of him with his hands on his hips." When Lo-p'u got to Chia-shan's place, he was very arrogant. At that time Chia-shan was very famous and also very advanced in years. When Lo-p'u saw Chia-shan, he did not kneel down: he stood there with his hands on his hips. Chia-shan said to him: "A chicken's roost and a phoenix nest are not the same. Get out!" He was giving Lo-p'u a dose of his authority. Lo-p'u said: "I have come from afar hastening toward your enlightening influence. Please receive me, Teacher." In other words: I came all the way from the north to study here, please accept me. Do I have the great affair of enlightenment or not?

Chia-shan said: "You are not there in front of me, and I am not here either." Lo-p'u then gave a shout. In other words: Chia-shan said, you are not here and neither am I. The Buddha Dharma here at my place is like this: here before us there is no you and no me. At this point Lo-p'u imitated a method of Lin-chi's, and directed a shocking shout at Chia-shan! Chia-shan's style was not the same as Lin-chi's. Lin-chi had the air of a king: when he fixed his eyes on someone, that person was always scared to death. Chia-shan on the other hand was very gentle and refined. When Lo-p'u shouted, Chia-shan said: "Stop! Stop! Don't be so crude. The clouds and the moon are the same, the streams and the mountains are different." In other words, Chia-shan told him: The same moon and the same clouds look down on different places where the scenery is not the same. There at your teacher's place you make noise and shout: this practice will get you nowhere here at my place.

Then Chia-shan said to him: "Though you are not lacking in cutting off the tongues of everyone in the world, how can you tell a man without a tongue to know how to speak?" When Lo-p'u heard this, "he paused to ponder," he was absorbed in thought. "Then Chia-shan hit him. From this point on, Lo-p'u submitted." This time he submitted: he did not go back to live in a hut, but followed Chia-shan.

One day Lo-p'u asked Chia-shan: How can we understand the place that neither the buddhas nor the demons of delusion get to? The experiential realm of his meditation work had reached this level. He had totally emptied out; past, present, and future were all emptied out; there were no buddhas and no demons of delusion. He was asking Chia-shan: how can this be understood?

Chia-shan answered him: "The candle lights up images for a thousand miles, but in the dark room the old monk is lost." Once the candle is lit, it shines forth on all the far off places. But the old monk in the dark room cannot see. What does this mean? Naturally when the lamp is lit you can see, and if the lamp is not lit you cannot see. But people who study Buddhism think there is a secret teaching in this: why is this kind of realm a place that neither buddhas nor demons of delusions can reach. Neither buddhas nor demons of delusion have a way to get hold of you. What is the reason for this? Seeing truth and cultivating realization are both in this.

Lo-p'u also asked: "How is it when the morning sun has already risen but the night moon has not yet appeared?" This describes a realm of meditative accomplishment. You sit in meditation and forget both body and mind, and there is just a single expanse of light. It is as if the sun has already come out. "The night moon has not yet appeared." At night it is not the same. The light of inherent nature is pure and cool.

This is what the Taoist classic *The Triplex Unity* [*Ts'an-t'ung-chi*, c. A.D. 200] speaks of like this: "Perfect *yang* is brilliant, perfect *yin* is reverent." When you reach the realm of emptiness where nothing at all is present, you must pay attention: this still is in the category of "perfect *yin* is reverent." After *yin* culminates and *yang* is born, when body and mind share the same root with heaven and earth inside and outside, and it's a single light, this is the realm of "perfect *yang* is brilliant."

At this point you have already gone beyond the issue of whether the *ch'i* channels are open or not. When you talk of the three channels and seven chakras, you have not even reached the first stage of *samadhi*. At this point Lo-p'u had already transcended this state of *samadhi*. That is "when the sun has already risen but the night moon has not yet appeared."

Chia-shan said: "The dragon carries the ocean pearl in his mouth, paying no attention to the fish swimming by." At these words Lo-p'u experienced great enlightenment. There is something here. In the single expanse of light that is both inside and outside, it seems that a dragon is swimming through the ocean, and in his mouth he is holding a bright pearl. This bright pearl is the dragon's root of life. Fish are swimming by on all sides of him, but the dragon does not even glance at them or look their way.

If you cultivate your *ch'i* channels properly, and recite the buddha-name properly, and your cultivation reaches the point that there is just this moment of mindfulness, you, too, will be the same as the dragon carrying the ocean pearl in his mouth, paying no attention to the fish swimming by. You will fundamentally pay no attention to those false thoughts all around you. Why get rid of false thoughts? The highest truth can be put to use at the most elementary stage. When you do meditation work, no matter whether it is by refining the breath or reciting the buddha-name or any other method, all you have to do is hold onto that moment of mindfulness, and focus your mind on one object without letting it move, and remember "The dragon carries the ocean pearl in his mouth, paying no attention to the fish swimming by." Slowly you, too, will be able to really reach this realm. This is not only a theoretical statement. It also has the characteristics of the work of genuinely cultivating realization. It is an actual realm of meditation work. Before I mentioned the Naga maiden offering a pearl to Buddha. Both stories are true phenomena, things that really happened, actual realms of meditation work.

When people talk of becoming enlightened, ultimately what is this thing they call becoming enlightened? What are the criteria for it? The truest explanation is put forward by Zen master Yen-shou of Yung-ming in *The Source Mirror*. This includes the Zen school's perspective on seeing truth, cultivating realization, and carrying out vows.

In the Sung dynasty [960-1279], two great books were written. One was Ssu-ma Kuang's *Comprehensive Mirror for Aid in Governing* [the *Tzu Chih T'ung Chien*] and the other was Zen master Yen-shou's *Source Mirror* [the *Tsung Chin Lu*]. The two works appeared at almost the same time. Unfortunately, many people in China studied *The Comprehensive Mirror for Aid in Governing*, which discusses worldly learning, but *The Source Mirror* was virtually consigned to the trash. This went on until the Ch'ing Dynasty, when early in the 18th century it was brought forth again by Emperor Yung-cheng, who issued several edicts especially emphasizing that everyone must study this book.

*The Source Mirror* tells us what enlightenment means. In the book, ten questions about enlightenment are raised. There are no enlightened people who have not mastered the scriptural teachings. They know all the principles of the Buddhist scriptures at one glance. For them reading the scriptures is like reading a novel: they understand everything as soon as they read it, and they do not have to study them in depth. Zen master Yen-shou's *Source Mirror* says this in Volume 1:

Suppose there are people who stubbornly cling to their own views, who do not believe the words of the Buddha, who create attitudes that block them, and who cut off other routes of study. For their sake I will now discuss ten questions in order to firmly establish the guiding principles.

First question: when we completely see true nature as plainly as we see colors in broad daylight, are we the same as bodhisattvas like Manjushri?

Second question: when we can clearly understand the source in everything, as we encounter situations and face objects, as we see form and hear sound, as we raise and lower our feet, as we open and close our eyes, are we in accord with the Path?

Third question: when we read through the teachings of Buddha for our era contained in the Buddhist canon, and the sayings of all the Zen masters since antiquity, and we hear their profundities without becoming afraid, do we always get accurate understanding and have no doubts?

Fourth question: when people pose difficult differentiating questions to us, and press us with all sorts of probing inquiries, are we able to respond with the four forms of eloquence, and resolve all their doubts?

Fifth question: does your wisdom shine unhindered at all times in all places, with perfect penetration from moment to moment, not encountering any phenomenon that can obstruct it, and never being interrupted for even an instant?

Sixth question: when all kinds of adverse and favorable and good and evil realms appear before us, are we unobstructed by them, and can we see through them all?

Seventh question: in all the mental states in *Treatise on the Gate for Illuminating the Hundred Phenomena*, can we see for each and every one of them, their fine details, the essential nature, and their fundamental source and point of origin, and not be confused by birth and death and the sense faculties and sense organs?

Eighth question: can we discern reality in the midst of all forms of conduct and activity, whether walking, standing, sitting, or lying down, whether receiving instructions or responding, whether dressing or eating?

Ninth question: can we be singleminded and unmoved whether we hear there is a buddha or we hear there is no buddha, whether we hear there are sentient beings or we hear there are no sentient beings, whether we are praised or slandered or affirmed or denied?

Tenth question: can we clearly comprehend all the differentiating knowledge we hear, and comprehend both true nature and apparent form, inner truth and phenomena, without hindrance, and discern the source of all phenomena, even including the appearance of the thousand sages in the world, without any doubts?

The preceding ten questions can provide definitive criteria for deciding whether or not a person is really enlightened.

The first question deals with the realm of illuminating mind and seeing true nature, being totally clear at all times in all places about all things, just as you would be when seeing the colors of a painting in broad daylight, and being in the same realm as such exemplars of wisdom as the Bodhisattva Manjushri. Can you be this way?

The second question asks whether you can be in accord with the Path when you encounter people and situations, or when other people get in your way. The expression "encounter situations and face objects" is very broad. Can you see forms and hear sounds without your mind moving? In your daily life, even at night when you fall asleep, can you be in accord with the Path in all things? Can you do that?

The third question is about the Buddhist scriptures. Can you take *The Lotus Sutra* and *The Surangama Sutra* and read them and fully understand them? Can you hear the loftiest explanations of the Dharma without becoming afraid? Can you thoroughly understand them, without having any doubts? Can you do that?

The fourth question asks, when students bring to bear all sorts of learning to ask you questions, are you able to answer them with unobstructed eloquence? All of you can investigate the last six questions for yourselves. The final passage of *The Source Mirror* presents the following information.

If you cannot really do these things, you should not assume a proud, deceptive, lying attitude, or take a self-satisfied attitude. What you must do is make a wide-ranging study of the ultimate teaching, and broaden your learning of previous people of knowledge. Penetrate to the inherent nature that is the source of the enlightened teachers and buddhas, and reach the stage of freedom from doubt that is beyond study. Only at this point can you stop your studies and give your wandering mind a rest. Then you will handle yourself with concentration and contemplation in harmony, and act on behalf of others by teaching with skill in means.

If you cannot go everywhere in the universe to study, or make a broad study of the multitude of scriptures, just make a careful reading of *The Source Mirror*, and you will naturally gain entry. This is the most important of all the teachings, the gate for moving toward the Path of enlightenment. It is like watching the mother to know the child, like finding the root to know the branches. When you pull the main cord, all the meshes of the net are straight. When you pull the cloth, all the threads from which it is woven come along, too.

If you cannot accomplish even one of the items mentioned in these ten questions, then you should not deceive yourself or others and think you are right. If you have any doubts at all, you must ask for instruction from enlightened teachers everywhere. You must certainly reach the realm of the buddhas and the enlightened teachers. Only when you have accomplished all that the enlightened teachers awakened to, can you reach the level of freedom from doubt beyond study, where you no longer have to study. When you "give your wandering mind a rest," the mind of false thought totally stops. "Then you will handle yourself with concentration and contemplation in harmony and act on behalf of others by teaching with skill in means." After you have attained great penetrating enlightenment, you either travel the Hinayana road, and further cultivate the four *dhyanas* and the eight *samadhis* and realize their fruit, and become fully equipped with the six spiritual powers and the three buddha-bodies and all the wondrous functions of the spiritual powers; or else you travel the Mahayana road, and sacrifice your own cultivation to help others, and appear in the world to propagate the Dharma.

"If you cannot go everywhere in the universe to study, or make a broad study of the multitude of scriptures," that is, if you think there are too many works in the Buddhist canon for you to be able to read them all, "just make a careful reading of *The Source Mirror* and you will naturally gain entry. This is the most important of all the teachings, the gate for moving toward the Path of enlightenment." Zen master Yen-shou urges you to make a careful study of his *The Source Mirror*, because he has collected together in this book all the essential points of all the scriptures. "It is like watching the mother to know the child, like finding the root to know the branches. When you pull the main cord, all the meshes of the net are straight. When you pull the cloth, all the threads from which it is woven come along, too." How beautiful the language is here. This is the importance of this book as Zen master Yen-shou explains it.

Now let us continue telling the story of Lo-p'u after his enlightenment. When he inherited Chia-shan's Dharma lineage, his teaching methods were very strict. This was because he combined the advantages of several schools of Zen, because his meditative accomplishments and perception of truth were lofty, and because his *ch'i* channels were greatly developed.

Lo-p'u had this famous saying: "Only at the last word do you reach the locked barrier. It cuts off the essential crossing place, and does not let ordinary people or sages pass through."

This saying pertains to the realm of meditative effort. Lo-p'u says that only at the last word can you reach the one road of transcendence; only then can your cultivation reach the point of achieving the three buddha-bodies. The Zen school distinguishes three barriers: the first barrier, the double barrier, and the final locked barrier. What is the locked barrier? This body of ours is the locked barrier. If we cannot break through it, we cannot fly free. When we reach the point of death, this locked barrier is finally broken, but this is a false breaking, and we are transformed into the immediate *yin* body (of the after-death, pre-birth state), and enter back into the cycle of birth and death. "Only at the last word do you reach the locked barrier." At this point, "It cuts off the essential crossing place, and does not let ordinary people or sages pass through." At this point you are not an ordinary person, nor are you a sage: this is the place that neither buddhas nor demons of delusion get to. Only this counts as success.

When Zen master Lo-p'u was about to depart from this life, he earnestly instructed his disciples saying: "The Dharma of leaving home does not let us hold onto anything forever." He was telling them: you must not covet anything; leaving home basically means throwing away everything, abandoning the myriad entangling objects.

238 / Master Nan Huai-Chin

He also told his disciples: "When you are sowing seed, you must be economical." In ancient times the Zen communities all did their own farming, so he was admonishing his disciples not to be wasteful in their sowing. These two sayings are double barrier sayings that apply alike to doing meditation work and to doing ordinary things.

Lo-p'u also told them: "From now on stop all your building activities." In effect he was saying: all you are doing are activities related to constructing buildings. You must stop all of this and do your best at your meditation efforts. Only this will do. He also told them: "Time flows by swiftly, and the Great Path is profound." In other words: time passes very quickly, but the work of the Path is very profound and far-reaching. He said to them: "If you follow routines, how will you experience enlightenment?" That is, if you go on passing your days in this muddled way following routines, and do not exert yourselves and work diligently on the Path, then when will you ever succeed?

The story continues: "Though Lo-p'u earnestly urged them on, the assembly took it as a commonplace event, and it did not wake them up at all." Even though Lo-p'u had instructed his disciples in the most earnest of tones, the disciples were used to hearing their teacher's scolding admonitions all the time, and so no one took these words to heart.

The account goes on: "When winter came, Lo-p'u showed signs of a slight illness, but he tirelessly kept seeing those who came to him for instruction. On the first day of the twelfth month he told the assembly: 'I will die either tomorrow or the day after. Now I have something to ask you. If you can say something right, this is putting a head on top of a head. If you say something wrong, this is cutting off the head to seek life.' The head monk replied: "The green mountain does not raise its foot, the sun goes down without pushing up the stirrup.' Lo-p'u said: 'What time is it that you make such a statement?'

"Then the advanced monk Yen-ts'ung said, 'Apart from these two roads, please Master, do not ask anything.' Lo-p'u said to him: 'You're not there yet. Say some more.' Yen-ts'ung said: 'I cannot say it all.' Lo-p'u said: 'I don't care if you can say it all or not.' Yen-ts'ung said: 'I have no attendant to answer you, Master.' Lo-p'u stopped at that.

"That night Lo-p'u sent his attendant to summon Yen-ts'ung. He asked him: 'What reason was there for your reply today? You should experience directly my late teacher's intent. My late teacher said: "Before your eyes there are no actual phenomena, only conceptual constructs. These are not the reality that is before you: it is not something that the ears and eyes can reach." Tell me, which sentence is the guest, and which is the host? If you can pick them out, I will give you the robe and bowl and recognize you as my successor.' Yen-ts'ung said: 'I do not understand.' Lo-p'u sad: 'You must understand.' Yen-ts'ung said: 'I really do not understand.' Lo-p'u drove him out with a shout. Then he said: 'How painful! How painful!'"

In the line of Zen master Lo-p'u, the method of teaching was very strict. Not only did his students have to master the principles of the teaching, their learning also had to be good, and they had to strive for a very high level in their perception of truth and their meditation work. Therefore, when Lo-p'u reached the end and was about to die, he couldn't find anyone who was qualified to be his successor. When Zen master Lo-p'u asked his disciples which one of them could receive his Dharma, no one answered except Yen-ts'ung. But Yen-ts'ung was not willing to be a teaching master, so when Lo-p'u questioned him, he said he didn't know.

The story continues: "At noon on the second day of the twelfth month, another monk asked Lo-p'u about what had been said the day before. Lo-p'u said: 'You don't row the boat of compassion over the clear waves. Here at Sword Narrows I have set up my *mu-o*, my covered portable bridge[1] in vain.' Then he died."

"You don't row the boat of compassion over the clear waves" refers to how a Mahayana Bodhisattva carries out his or her vows. For the boat of compassion to save people, it must go into the muddy streams. The next line is a lament for not having managed to save a single person in several decades. "Here at Sword Narrows I have set up my covered portable bridge in vain." The meaning is this: Where Lo-p'u lived there was a mountain defile named Sword Narrows. Even though Lo-p'u had built a bridge to draw people across, no one was willing to get up on it. This is the same as what is expressed in a famous saying by an ancient worthy:

---

[1] The *mu-o* was a kind of medieval siege engine. It consisted of a scaling ladder and behind it a rolling portable shelter on wheels with a peaked, rawhide covered roof to ward off the defender's missiles, that protected the attacking soldiers while they closed in on the city walls and attempted to storm them.

The ship of compassion is basically something to carry people
  across in
But what can we do if sentient beings will not come on board?

What can be done? What Lo-p'u said was this kind of lament!

The explanatory notes in small characters in *The Record of Pointing
at the Moon* are notes added by several great teachers who lived after
the T'ang dynasty and before the Ch'ing dynasty, after they had
attained the Path. These notes are also very important.

Now I will discuss the three mysterious gates spoken of by
Lin-chi. With effort we can explain these by matching them up with
the T'ien-t'ai school's three forms of cessation and contemplation.
But for their ultimate truth, you will have to investigate them for
yourself. It will only work if you do the meditation work.

*The Record of Pointing at the Moon* says in Volume 14: "Lin-chi
said: 'Sometimes a shout is like the Diamond King's precious sword.'"
The shout gets rid of all the false thoughts and afflictions in your
mind. "'Sometimes a shout is like a lion crouching on the ground.
Sometimes a shout is like a probing pole or a shade that lets you see
beneath the surface of the water.'" Sometimes he bawls you out, deliberately provoking you to get mad, to see how much power of stable
concentration your meditation work has brought you. This is like a
probing pole, or a shade that lets him see beneath the surface of the
water. Perhaps there is a poisonous snake in the grass: you take a
stick and poke around in the grass a few times. "Lin-chi said:
'Sometimes a shout does not function as a shout: how will you understand this?'" This is Lin-chi saying something polite. The story continues: "The monk to whom Lin-chi was saying this hesitated,
thinking, so Lin-chi shouted." This is a shout of rebuke.

Lin-chi regularly said: "If for a moment causal origination is not
born, you transcend the provisional learning of the three vehicles." Is
this statement the same or different from, "You must activate your
mind without dwelling anywhere?" All of you should study this
and see.

The story I am now going to discuss has a very important connection to how people who study Zen see the truth of the Buddha's
teaching and cultivate practice. Lin-chi brought up this story: "The
titans did battle with Indra, king of the gods. When the titans lost the
battle, their king led his whole host of eighty-four thousand titans
into a tiny hole in a lotus-root fiber to hide."

This story is recorded in the Buddhist scriptures. Look and see: aren't the supernatural powers of the king of the demons of delusion limitless? Lin-chi asked: "Was this evidence of the powers of a sage?" In other words: was this not the same as the spiritual powers of the sages?

Lin-chi said: "In the story I have told you, these were nothing but powers due to karma, dependent powers." What are powers due to karma? The development of science in the modern world, which can even fly into space—this is power due to karma, produced by the joint karma of sentient beings. It is also spiritual power and wisdom. As for dependent powers, telling fortunes, reading people's futures from their physiognomy, divining with the *I Ching*, studies of the soul and of spiritual secrets are all examples of dependent powers that come about by depending on something. They are not true spiritual powers.

The Buddhist scriptures speak of "putting Mount Sumeru[2] into a mustard seed." We know that hiding a mustard seed in Mount Sumeru would be a matter of course. But what would it be to put Mount Sumeru into a mustard seed? "For the six spiritual powers of the buddhas, it would not be so [impossible]." That is, when you reach the realm of the buddhas, it is not this way. "You enter the realm of form without being deluded by form, and you enter the realm of sound without being deluded by sound, and you enter the realm of scent without being deluded by scent, and you enter the realm of taste without being deluded by taste, and you enter the realm of touch without being deluded by touch, and you enter the realm of phenomena without being deluded by phenomena. Thus you comprehend that form, sound, scent, taste, touch, and phenomena are all empty. They cannot bind this independent person of the Path. Even the gross physical body of the five skandhas cannot bind the independent person of the Path: this is the spiritual power to go anywhere."

Lin-chi continues: "The true Buddha has no shape, the true Dharma has no form." Pay attention to this! "If you go on like this concocting set patterns and models on top of illusory transformations, even if you find something, it will only be an apparition of your

---

[2] In Indian Buddhist cosmology, Mount Sumeru is the colossal polar mountain in the center of the world.

wild fox spirit." In other words, if you really think you have accomplished something by your meditation work, and have found some experiential realm, and you assume that this is enlightenment, you are wrong! This is an apparition: it is not by any means the real buddha, but the view of someone outside the Path.

Lin-chi goes on: "A person who really studies the Path does not cling to being a buddha or a bodhisattva or an arhat. He does not cling to any of the special forms of excellence of these three fruits. He is far beyond them, independent and free. He is not bound by anything. Heaven and earth may switch places, but he has no more doubts."

When Lin-chi was about to depart from the world, he spoke this verse:

> Going along with the flow
>> without stopping to ask how
> True awareness shining boundlessly,
>> describing it to them
> Detached from forms,
>> detached from names,
>> people don't accept it
> After the sword of wisdom has been used,
>> we must hurry to hone it.

When Zen master Lin-chi was alive, his methods of teaching were eccentric and out of the ordinary. When he was about to die, he punctiliously told us: "Go along with the flow without stopping to ask how." Thoughts and thinking cannot be stopped: they are like a flowing stream running along with us. What can we do about it? "True awareness shining boundlessly, describing it to them." Don't pay attention to those false thoughts. The one that knows your own false thoughts are going back and forth does not, itself, move. You must hold firmly to that one.

The pure clarity of true awareness shining boundlessly is very close to true thusness and buddha-nature. All we have to do is hold firmly to it. But when we fall into this world, it is easy to make a mistake: we add another level of awareness to this true awareness, and that becomes false thought. Don't make any special effort, and it will clarify very spontaneously and naturally. And don't hold onto the clarity either.

"Detached from forms, detached from names, people don't accept it." With this thing, it is fine to call it "mind" or call it "true nature" or call it "the Path." We must not pay any attention to anything at all. This is also what Lin-chi meant when he said: "If for a moment causal origination is not born, you transcend the provisional learning of the three vehicles." But can you really pay attention to nothing at all?

"After the sword of wisdom has been used, we must hurry to hone it." The precious sword of wisdom is called the sword so sharp it cuts a hair blown across it. How can the sharpness of a blade be tested? Take a hair and put it on the sword, then blow on it; if the hair is cut through, it is called a sword so sharp it cuts a hair blown across it. But such a sharp blade must be taken care of after it has been used. In other words, Zen master Lin-chi is instructing us that before we have illuminated mind and seen true nature, we must reflect back and examine ourselves at all times, to reverse the workings of thought and cultivate *samadhi*, and not let false thoughts arise. For a person who has already been enlightened, after using his meditative accomplishments, he must immediately take them back and hone them further.

In terms of worldly things, the Confucian philosopher Tseng-tzu enunciated the same principle in *The Analects* [1.4]: "Every day I examine myself on three points: Have I been unfaithful in making plans with others? Have I been untrustworthy in my dealing with friends? Have I failed to practice the precepts my teacher has taught me?"

One basic principle of the Buddha Dharma is this: at all times, wherever you happen to be, always reflect back and examine yourself. "After the sword of wisdom has been used, you must be quick to hone it." This is an outline of the message of the Lin-chi school. The rest you should go investigate for yourselves.

Now let's discuss the Ts'ao-Tung school of Zen. Most of the Japanese Zen schools that are popular nowadays are offshoots of the Ts'ao-Tung school. The Ts'ao-Tung school was one of the great Zen schools of the late T'ang and Five dynasties periods. Tung-shan was the master, and Ts'ao-shan was his disciple. [Their names are listed in reverse order in the name of the school because it is more euphonious that way in Chinese.]

The great Sung dynasty Neo-Confucian philosopher Chou Tun-i put forward as an epitome of his philosophy the "Diagram of the Great Ultimate." This "Diagram of the Great Ultimate" was given to him by a Buddhist monk, but the origin of this monk is not related in the historical sources. This is point one. The diagrams of the *I Ching* and the River Diagram and the Lo Writing and the Eight Trigrams used by the eminent Sung dynasty Neo-Confucian philosopher Shao Yung were derived from the Ts'ao-Tung school of Zen. Most of the Chinese Taoist works on cultivating spiritual alchemy are also derived from the Ts'ao-Tung school. Thus, there is an inescapable connection between Ts'ao-Tung Zen and the later generations of Chinese Taoist spiritual alchemy. But it is the spiritual alchemy tradition that uses Ts'ao-Tung materials, not the other way around. The Ts'ao-Tung school used the trigrams by which the *I Ching* fathoms the true pattern, and constructed the theory of the "Diagram of the Great Ultimate," and this developed into the Chou Tun-i line of Neo-Confucianism. The explanations of the images and numbers in the *I Ching* turned into Shao Yung's line of Neo-Confucianism. Both these lines of Neo-Confucianism came from Zen. This is the first time I have publicly discussed this secret.

Zen master Tung-shan's personal name was Liang-chieh and his sobriquet was Wu-pen. He went to Kuei-shan's place to study, but Kuei-shan could do nothing with him, so he directed him to go to Yun-yen's place. There at Yun-yen's, Tung-shan awakened a little bit, but his awakening did not penetrate all the way through. At that point, Tung-shan was about to leave.

*The Record of Pointing at the Moon*, Volume 16 says: "When Tung-shan was saying good-bye to Yun-yen, Yun-yen said to him, 'Where are you going?' Tung-shan said, 'Though I am leaving you, Master, I have not yet determined where I will stay.' Yun-yen said, 'Aren't you going to Hunan?' Tung-shan said, 'No.' Yun-yen said, 'Aren't you returning to your home village?' Tung-shan said, 'No.' Yun-yen said, 'So will you return here sooner or later?' Tung-shan said, 'When you have a place to stay, Master, I will come.' Yun-yen said, 'After this parting, it will be hard to meet again.' Tung-shan said, 'It will be hard not to meet again.'" Inherent nature is basically formless, and the same for everyone, so it will be hard to not meet again in it.

"As Tung-shan was about to go, he asked, 'After you are dead, if someone suddenly asks me, "Can you describe what your teacher looked like?" how should I answer?' Yun-yen kept silent for a long time and then said, 'Just like this.' At that point Tung-shan gave an appreciative, reflective, 'Hmmm.' Yun-yen said, 'Liang-chieh, to take on this thing, you must give it careful consideration.'"

At that moment Tung-shan felt very sad. He felt great compassion for his teacher. Yun-yen rebuked him: Do you think it will work if you are like this? To learn Zen you must have the mettle of a great man. If you still have these commonplace vulgar feelings, and you are worrying about me, and can't let me go, then how will you be after I am dead and gone?

The account continues: "Tung-shan was still in doubt." At this point, Tung-shan finally began to have his doubts, and he felt more and more doubtful.

"Later on, when he happened to look at his reflection as he was crossing a stream, Tung-shan had a great awakening toward what Yun-yen had meant before. He made a verse.

> Do not seek from others
> They are far distant from me
> Now I will go on alone
> Everywhere I encounter *him*
> Right now *he* is me
> Right now I am not *him*
> One must understand this way
> Only then does one merge with Thusness.

Afterward, Tung-shan left his teacher Yun-yen. As he was crossing a stream, he looked at his own reflection in the water. This time he experienced great awakening, and immediately he composed an enlightenment verse.

"Do not seek from others." What does "others" mean? When we seek *ch'i* channels, when we seek thoughts, these are all "others." The more we seek, the farther away we are. It won't work.

"Now I will go on alone." When the spiritual light is shining alone, far removed from the sense faculties and sense objects, then you can find *him* everywhere. "Everywhere I encounter *him*." This *him* is the true self.

"Right now *he* is me." When we see our bodies right now, these are "others," they are not our true selves. But now with enlightenment, the true self comes alive: "Right now *he* is me."

Where is the true self? "Now I am not *him*." The true self is not that one: he can change, he is not the same at age 10 as at age 20. Now my hair is white, and I am no longer the same as when I was young. This thing that can change is not the true self.

> One must understand this way
> Only then does one merge with Thusness.

This is where you must search. Only when you have found it will you understand the truth of the inherent nature of thusness.

In Chuang-tzu's essay on "Equalizing Things," there is a tale called "The penumbra asks the shadow." When we are walking in the sun, how many shadows are there? Outside the shadow itself is another circle called the penumbra. It asks the shadow: "Why do you act so disorderly, sometimes sitting, sometimes lying down?" The shadow tells the penumbra: "Don't you know I have a boss? When he sits down I sit down with him, and when he lies down all I can do is lie down with him and sleep." He also said, "My boss himself is not the master. Behind his back is another big boss." This illustrates what Tung-shan said in his verse:

> Now *he* is me
> Now I am not *him*.

The Zen school just took methods of Buddhist cultivation and summed them up in the literary realm. But its principles were the same as the principles in the Buddhist scriptures.

# 14

# TRUE AND
# FALSE EMPTINESS

Several years ago, a Belgian student of mine was studying with a Dutch teacher. He, himself, had been cultivating realization for several years, when this teacher taught him the "Dharma Gate of Nonduality." This method involved recognizing that all things have no self, that all things are mind-only. He was taught to observe all the selfless things clearly and do his best to understand them by direct experience. Thus he was not to try to understand anything rationally.

This Dutch teacher taught the student that when problems arise, whether they are physical or psychological problems, he should always observe them impartially. He should not try to resist them, but rather observe them spontaneously being born and spontaneously disappearing. This is what he called "the Dharma Gate of Nonduality."

The method of cultivating practice in this "Dharma Gate of Nonduality" was not to do any meditation work at all, but to preserve a sense of quiet equanimity, and slowly open up the mind. After a few years of doing this, emotions and thoughts will not run on, and nothing will be there anymore. All that will be left will be that thing that is fundamentally there observing, that thing which does not change. At that point, everything will be like a flash of lightning, and the student will suddenly awaken. This is the road taught by the Dutch teacher.

The student recognized that the great majority of those who cultivate practice achieve nothing at all precisely because they do not manage to reach this point where they suddenly awaken. His question is this: it seems that not caring at all is not right, and trying to escape from emotions and thoughts is not right, either. Isn't the work of tempering the breath a form of escape? Is the method taught by this teacher cessation followed by contemplation, or is it contemplation followed by cessation? If the method is not correct, the student is willing to abandon a wrong road.

What this Dutch teacher says does not deviate from tradition, but it still has problems. Later on this teacher got sick and had to enter the hospital for surgery. It must have felt very painful, but he said nothing. In other words, he did not look upon his body as his true self, and because of this he was very calm. The doctors were quite surprised. He did not advocate sitting meditation because he thought that sitting meditation was a creation of consciousness, and violated the principle of the "Dharma Gate of Nonduality."

This type of teacher is found all over the world. There is a teacher in Germany who has made a great stir: among his disciples are scientists and university professors and the like. This teacher's parents were awakened, and had spiritual powers. When he was 3 years old he became aware of his past life, and he, too, awakened. When he was 20 he became a teacher. At present, he is still not yet 35, and he has grown up to look like a buddha.

These teachers all have appropriately cultivated their meditation work. We Chinese, on the other hand, do not equal them either in Buddhism or in meditation work or in the cultivation of Confucianism, Buddhism, or Taoism. So we definitely must not "close our doors and proclaim ourselves kings."

There is nothing wrong with the method used by that Dutch teacher, but perhaps what he said is not detailed enough, or perhaps the people who study the method have not understood it very clearly. They are missing one point. All things are mind-only, true enough, but this body and mind are also mind-only. If you only recognize psychological states as belonging to the realm of "all things are mind-only," you will not be able to transform this body. This is the first point. If the principle that "all things are mind only" is properly understood to include body and mind, there is no reason that this body cannot be transformed.

The second point is this. In Tibetan Esoteric Buddhism after the T'ang dynasty, there was the method of *Mahamudra*, and this was also transmitted to the Zen school. Another tradition says that the Dharma Gate of *Mahamudra* was transmitted to Tibet by the Zen patriarch Bodhidharma after he left China. One essential point in the cultivation of *Mahamudra* is this: "First let the mind calmly abide, detaching from false thoughts without grasping them and without indulging in them." When you first set to work at this, it is calmly abiding, without doing meditation work, without cultivating *samadhi*, just sitting there very calmly. When false thoughts come, "without grasping them," you observe them steadily, but without indulging in them either. They are empty in themselves, and you detach from false thoughts. This is the very first step of the method of *Mahamudra*: it does not require cessation and contemplation, or studying meditation sayings, or doing meditation work. This is one of the highest techniques of Esoteric Buddhism's *Mahamudra*.

The Sung dynasty Neo-Confucian Cheng Hao wrote a letter on stabilizing true nature. Discussing how to cultivate concentration, he wrote: "Not sending away and not welcoming, there is no inside or outside." Here "sending away" means "repelling." He meant that when a thought comes, do not welcome it, and do not block it; it is not on the inside or on the outside. This is a high level Buddhist method of cultivating mind. But if we say this is the "Dharma Gate of Nonduality," this is incorrect. This is because the Dharma Gate of Nonduality means that the real and the false are not two: the real is the false and the false is the real. What Cheng Hao said can only be counted as one of the methods for entering the Dharma Gate of Nonduality. That Dutch teacher's method is also like this: it is close to Zen, and it is also close to *Mahamudra*.

But there is one question. This body of yours is also an important matter in the practical philosophy of mind-only. If it cannot transform this body, in the end this kind of cultivation is unreliable. No matter how lofty the experiential realm you attain through this method may be, it still falls into the naturalistic heresy because it goes along with nature in everything. People who follow what is natural cannot be said to have completely finished with birth and death, because they let birth come by itself and they let death go by itself. Their attitude is: what need is there to ask how birth comes about? It has already come, hasn't it? What need is there to ask how we will die? When the time comes we will die, won't we? This attitude by no means counts as thoroughly illuminating mind and seeing true nature.

It really is necessary to sit in meditation and cultivate *samadhi*. Sitting cross-legged in meditation and cultivating *samadhi* does not have that great a connection with illuminating mind and seeing true nature. Truly illuminating mind and seeing true nature does not necessarily depend on sitting meditation, but there is still a positive connection. If you want to return to the pure original face, and take a step further and transform this physical body, it will be impossible to do unless you rely on sitting meditation. Apart from this, there is no other road to take. Moreover, it is impossible without going through the work of cultivating practice. Why? Clearly that original face is something natural, but this natural thing has been dirtied and darkened so much by dust and dirt since time without beginning, that it must be given a cleaning. Thus, the goal of all the various kinds of meditation work is just to clean this first; only then can you see what was originally there.

The Zen school, the method of *Mahamudra*, and also what the Dutch teacher taught are all correct: first we see the original face, and then slowly we talk of cleaning it. But such people can create a problem: they often fall into the naturalist heresy, and only seek the natural, without doing meditation work.

On this question we can consult *The Surangama Sutra*, Volume 6, the verse spoken by Manjushri about the twenty-five forms of perfect penetration:

> The ocean of awakening, by nature
>      clear and perfect
> Perfectly clear,
> the original wonder of awakening
> The awareness of original illumination
>      produces objects
> When objects are established,
>      the true nature of awareness is lost
> With delusion and falsity,
>      there is space
> In space worlds are established
> Thought clarifies, forming lands
> With knowledge and feeling
>      there are sentient beings.

The first line, "The ocean of awakening, by nature clear and perfect," proceeds from the metaphysical basic essence to explain that the basic nature of the ocean of awakening of our present human lives and all sentient beings is fundamentally pure and perfectly illuminated. This is the Dharma Gate of Nonduality. But how can we find the ocean of awakening? "Perfectly clear, the original wonder of awakening." Going the other way, first we must do our meditation work until it is complete and pure. After that we can awaken to this fundamentally enlightened true nature, and understand that it actually is originally illuminated and wondrous.

How can we reach the realm of "perfect clarity?" The Dutch teacher's method is an approximation, but we must revise and enlarge it. When all the false thoughts come, we should not concern ourselves with them. We should be like adults observing children. We do not pay any particular attention to them: when they have gotten tired of running around, they will stop. But you cannot make them stop. The more you try to stop false thoughts by observing them, the more they will come. What is the reason for this? The basic reason is because "the awareness of original illumination produces objects."

Our capability of original illumination has the power of awareness. It is aware of false thoughts, but after being aware of them for a long time, it turns into false thought itself. This is the principle of "when *yang* reaches its extreme, *yin* is born." This electric power is too strong, and it shines very fiercely; after its capability is used up, then we can't see anything anymore. There is awareness and there is functioning. False thoughts are produced like this. Thus "the awareness of original illumination produces objects." What observes them is awareness. Awareness produces objects: that is, the capacity of awareness itself produces false thoughts.

When false thoughts arise, objects are established, and the true nature of awareness is lost. After big false thoughts arise and take shape, this capacity for awareness is covered over: they turn around and cover over fundamental enlightenment. Therefore emotions and afflictions sometimes come to us, or else we exert ourselves too much, and false thoughts increase even more. The reason for all of this is that "The awareness of original illumination produces objects / When objects are established, the true nature of awareness is lost." Based on this, worlds, the second layer, take shape:

With delusion and falsity, there is space
In space worlds are established
Thought clarifies, forming lands
With knowledge and feeling
there are sentient beings.

I have used this passage from *The Surangama Sutra* so my student will take note that if he follows his original line, he will always produce a deviation: namely, "The awareness of original illumination produces objects / When objects are established, the true nature of awareness is lost." Let us look again at *The Surangama Sutra*, Volume 5.

True nature, contrived emptiness
Because it is born from causal circumstances,
        it is like an illusion
Uncreated, neither born nor destroyed
Unreal, like an optical illusion
Words are false, but they reveal the real
The false and the real are both false
Still neither real nor false
How can seeing and objects of seeing be?
In between there is no real identity
Thus they are like hollow reeds joined together.

Inherent nature is fundamentally empty. Since it is fundamentally empty, why does the sutra call it contrived emptiness? Causal origination is inherently empty: only because it is empty can it produce from causal conditions the myriad forms of being. If emptiness could not produce from causal conditions the myriad forms of being, it would be inert emptiness. But the myriad contrived forms of being arise from causal conditions and are inherently empty. (We impose a name and call this true thusness.)

"Birth from causal conditions" means that when all the myriad forms of being arise, they are produced from causal conditions, like dreams or illusions. In the Buddhist scriptures it says that they are like dreams and like illusions: this does in no sense mean that they are absolutely nonexistent. They do exist! But this existence is a chance existence, a temporary existence, a provisional state of being. All "beings" are in the process of passing through this phase of "existence" and going on to become empty. "Because it is born from causal circumstances, it is like an illusion." Once we see they are like dreams or illusions, we immediately take our thoughts and put them in the emptiness. "Like dreams, like illusions," means a provisional state of being—wondrous being. Hinayana recognizes it as a provisional state of being. Mahayana bodhisattvas recognize it as wondrous being: "being" is very wondrous.

False thoughts arise, emotions come into being: this is causal origination, and hence illusory being. For this reason we must not pay attention to them. They are just "Uncreated, neither born nor destroyed / Unreal, like an optical illusion." The inherent nature of the basic essence is fundamentally without contrived activity: it acts without acting. Though it gives rise to a false thought, it cannot be stopped because the second false thought has already arisen. So in an ultimate sense, false thoughts are neither born nor destroyed. Our thoughts are eternally like the waves in the ocean: one wave follows another. False thoughts are not really there: they are like the lights we see in front of our eyes when we rub them. We cannot say they are not there, but after they pass, they are naturally not there anymore.

"Words are false, but they reveal the real." Right now we are calling all mental states and emotions false thoughts. Why do we call them false thoughts? This is a relative term, a teaching method. It makes us recognize clearly that the one which is not false thoughts is true thusness. In fact, what Buddha says in the sutra is very clear: "The false and the real are both false." Those false thoughts and emotions are certainly false, but the pure, peaceful, empty realm of true thusness is also false. Therefore, fixing our awareness on it, and observing it, is also a big false thought. If we depend on the big false thought to take care of the little false thoughts, when the little false thoughts have gone to sleep, that big false thought is still sitting there. The big false thought is what this passage describes: The awareness of original illumination produces objects / When objects are established, the true nature of awareness is lost. Therefore, it will only work if we neither grasp the false nor establish the real.

"Still neither real nor false." When you reach emptiness in your meditation work, you feel that this is inherent nature, that this is enlightenment. But this is definitely not the real inherent nature or the real enlightenment.

"How can seeing and objects of seeing be?" With real illuminating mind and seeing true nature, it is wrong to think that we can use our eyes to see it, or use our mind's consciousness to understand it. That seeing is not the eye or the consciousness seeing. That's why Zen master Chia-shan said: "Before your eyes there are no phenomena, just conceptual constructs. It is not the actual reality in front of you: that is not something that the ears and eyes can reach." *The Surangama Sutra* also tells us: "When seeing sight, this seeing is not [ordinary] sight. This seeing is apart from [ordinary] sight: [ordinary] sight cannot reach it."

Thus, the method of cultivating practice taught by the Dutch teacher is not wrong: if it is extended to the immeasurable and the boundless, it will be correct. Right now when you observe your own false thoughts steadily according to his method, the one that is doing the observing is itself a big false thought. Do you understand? If you clearly understand this principle, you will have to revise your method of cultivating practice from the foundation up, and first do the work of stopping the breath. Stopping the breath is something our minds create: this deliberate action is for the sake of transforming this body. Only after the physical body of the four elements has been entirely transformed, will you be able to see the real one: "The ocean of awakening, by nature clear and perfect / Perfectly clear, the original wonder of awakening."

Thus, as I have just explained, in general, the later generations of people in the Zen school have used this method of letting nature take its course, as well as the Esoteric Buddhism method of *Mahamudra*, and in the end they have only transformed their psychological states. When they actually reach the point when they are about to die, their bodies hurt so much they cry out in pain over and over again. When the oxygen mask is put over their noses, they cannot empty out. That thing capable of awareness, that thing which consciousness has created, is not there anymore, and they pass away in boundless darkness.

In the Zen school there was a Zen master called T'ien-wang Wu. He was a disciple of Ma-tsu. Before he was enlightened, he cultivated practice until his meditative accomplishments and his power of *samadhi* were excellent. Once a provincial military governor saw how great his power to attract people was, and thought that he might incite the masses with seditious talk, so he had him thrown in a river. As it turned out, a lotus flower popped up on the surface of the water, and T'ien-wang Wu was in the lotus flower sitting in meditation. As soon as the military governor saw this, he thought he was enlightened, so he had him pulled out of the water and became his disciple. At this time T'ien-wang Wu was not yet enlightened, but still his abilities were great.

Later on, after T'ien-wang Wu was enlightened, no more lotuses came. Subsequently, when he was on the brink of death, he was in so much pain he lay there crying and moaning. One of the monks in the house asked him, "Master, could you make a little less noise? Before you were enlightened, you were thrown into a river, and you floated up on a lotus. That was such a famous event that now everyone says you are enlightened. If the news gets out that you are crying in pain so much now that you are about to die, we will be very embarrassed. Please try to be a little quieter."

When T'ien-wang Wu heard this, he knew the monk was right. He asked him, "You know that right now I am in great pain. But do you realize that in the midst of the pain there is one who is not in pain?" The disciple said he did not know this. So T'ien-wang Wu said to him, "These cries of pain are the one that is not in pain. Do you understand?" The disciple said he did not understand. He didn't understand, and that did it. T'ien-wang Wu drew his legs up so he was sitting cross-legged, and died.

If you say T'ien-wang Wu had ability, then why was he in so much pain that he was crying nonstop? If you say he had no ability, then how was it that when someone asked him not to cry, he did not cry? This is another meditation case.

Strictly speaking, Zen master T'ien-wang Wu had only transformed his sixth and seventh consciousnesses; he had not transformed the first five consciousnesses and the eighth consciousness. At most he had attained the *dharmakaya*, but he had not yet transformed the *sambhogakaya* and *nirmanakaya*. Therefore those who study consciousness-only must realize, as the Sixth Patriarch said, "The sixth and seventh consciousnesses are transformed at the level of cause. The first five consciousnesses and the eighth consciousness are transformed at the level of effect."

The sixth and seventh consciousnesses are easy to transform. Once thoughts are empty, and past, present, and future are emptied out, the sixth consciousness is transformed into a pure illuminated realm of immediate awareness. If your meditation work advances further, the seventh consciousness can also be emptied out. This is easy: it is a transformation at the level of the causal basis. Many people who cultivate practice reach at most to the station of bodhisattvas at the level of the causal basis.

Transformation at the level of effect is difficult. The first five consciousnesses, the consciousnesses associated with the eyes, ears, nose, tongue, and body, encompass this physical body. The eighth consciousness, the *alaya* consciousness, encompasses not only the physical body, but the whole material world. The first five and the eighth consciousnesses can be transformed only when the level of effect is complete, only when you have realized the level of the fruit of enlightenment. How can this be called easy?

So if you want cultivation, cultivate the whole thing. If you only cultivate half, all you can do is come again in future births. If you have enough time, the best thing to do is complete the whole project in this lifetime.

I have previously discussed Zen master Tung-shan's enlightenment verse. Here it is again.

Do not seek from others
They are far removed from me
Today I go on alone
Everywhere I meet *him*
Today *he* is me
Today I am not *him*
We must understand this way
Only then do we accord with Thusness.

In general, people who cultivate the Path are always seeking from "others." Here the meaning of "others" includes both psychological and physical states. In particular, the *jen-mai* and *tu-mai* channels are "others," the lights of experiential realms are "others," and realms of purity are "others." If you continue doing your meditation work oriented toward these "others," if you continue to seek from the mind of falsity, then the more you cultivate it, the farther away from the Path you will get.

When we study Zen master Tung-shan's enlightenment verse, we must not forget one thing. At the time, he was enlightened as he was crossing a stream, when the sun was out and the water was reflecting his image, and he looked at his own reflection. He had to get a firm grasp on this realm: at this point in time "Today I go on alone / Everywhere I meet *him*." In other words, everywhere I go I encounter him. "Now *he* is me." Right now he is me. This body of ours is him, and he has become us. "Now I am not *him*." In reality, though this fundamental true nature of ours is not this body and mind, it is certainly not apart from this body and mind. We must take guest and host and join them together. "We must understand this way / Only then do we accord with thusness." He is not saying that he has already seen the Path of enlightenment, but that he is near to the Path, that he will be able to enter the Path.

Now let us look at how Tung-shan expounded the Dharma after his enlightenment. This passage is in *The Record of Pointing at the Moon*, Volume 16. "Tung-shan went up to the teaching hall and asked the assembly: 'How is it when you are going toward it? How is it when you are upholding it? How is it when you are working on it? How is it when you are working on it together? How is it when you are working on your work?'"

Passages like this are called recorded sayings: they are records of what he said at the time, in vernacular language. "When you are going toward it," means when you are going toward this Path, and your meditation work is about to get there. "Upholding" is the same as lifting something up; it means getting a grasp on something, taking a firm hold. What is "going toward it"? When you are about to be enlightened, but you are not yet enlightened, if we take a comparison from *The Surangama Sutra's* "realm of the skandha of form," it is like when you are about to break through the realm of the skandha of form. The sky is about to brighten: it seems light but it is not yet light. It seems you understand but you do not yet understand. "Upholding it" means you have properly reached it. But when you have awakened, you still have to make efforts. Thus Tung-shan asks, how is it when you are working on it? "Working together" and "working on your work" are both stages in the process of cultivating realization.

Altogether, there are five stages in the process. Thus in the Ts'ao-Tung school they speak of the five positions of lord and minister. They differentiate five steps from making efforts in meditation work, to awakening, on to complete success.

"A monk asked: 'What is going towards?' Tung-shan said: 'How is it when you eat food?'" This monk understood this statement, and did not ask a second question. Next he asked: "'What is upholding?' Tung-shan said: 'How is it when you turn your back?' The meaning of this was: how is it when you turn around?'"

"The monk asked: 'What is working?' Tung-shan said: 'How is it when you put down your hoe?'" In other words, when you have been doing something and working at it until you are tired, how is it once you relax? This really means abandoning everything.

"The monk asked: 'What is working together?' Tung-shan said: 'Not finding form.'" The physical body made up of the four elements is in the category of form, and so are things like the meditative realm of purity of the single expanse of light.

"The monk asked: 'What is working on work?' Tung-shan said: 'Not common.'" This refers to the qualities unique to the enlightened ones, which they do not have in common with the unenlightened.

Tung-shan was afraid not everyone would understand, so he composed some verses. In these verses the Ts'ao-Tung school tells us a step-by-step progression of meditation work in the Dharma Gate of the mind-ground. These verses describe methods of meditative effort. You are wrong if you read them as mere literary creations.

Tung-shan's verse on "going toward":

> The sage lord always models himself on the sage
>     emperor Yao
> He manages people with proper norms of conduct,
>     sinuous dragons at his waist
> Sometimes he passes through the noisy city markets
> Everywhere he goes the cultured people hail his
>     sagely court.

This is "going toward." When you reach this stage, and you have awakened to the Path, you are correct whether you are moving or still. You are always in this realm, and you never change. This is almost enlightenment. This is "going toward."

Tung-shan's verse on "upholding":

> The wash water and the rich make-up:
>     who are they for?
> The cuckoo's cry warns people to return
> The hundred flowers have all fallen,
>     but the bird's cry is endless
> It is still calling in the depths of the chaotic
>     mountain peaks.

Tung-shan's verse on "working":

> On the withered tree flowers bloom,
>     a spring beyond the ages
> Mounting the jade elephant, riding the unicorn

Now hidden on high beyond the thousand peaks,
The moon is bright, the wind is pure,
    it's a fine day.

Tung-shan's verse on "working together":

Sentient beings and buddhas do not infringe on
    each other
The mountains are high by themselves, the waters
    are deep by themselves
The business of understanding clearly the myriad
    differences and distinctions
Where the partridge calls, the hundred flowers
    are renewed.

Tung-shan's verse on "working on work":

The horn on the head has just sprouted—
    it is not yet worthy
Intentionally seeking buddha is very embarrassing
Far away, the empty eon—no one knows
Sudhana went south to visit fifty-three teachers.

What these poems describe is all step-by-step meditation work, all a process of cultivating practice.

After the Five Dynasties period, the Zen of the Ts'ao-Tung school influenced Sung dynasty Taoism and Neo-Confucianism, and especially *I Ching* studies. What the Taoists call joining *k'an* and *li* [the hexagrams which represent water and fire, and by extension, primordial awareness and conditioned awareness], and the like, all come from the Ts'ao-Tung school.

"When Ts'ao-shan was bidding farewell to Tung-shan, Tung-shan told him: 'When I was at my late teacher Yun-yen's place, he personally sealed me with the Diamond Mirror *samadhi*, the essential point for fully fathoming everything. Now I entrust it to you.'"

Tung-shan's poem on the Jewel Mirror *Samadhi* said:

The Dharma of Thusness
Was intimately entrusted
    by the buddhas and patriarchs

Now you have gotten it:
You must preserve it well
The silver bowl is filled with snow,
The bright moon conceals the egret:
When we compare them, they are not equal.

This is what Tung-shan said to Ts'ao-shan, the disciple with whom he was most satisfied. This is a very important statement made on the occasion of transmitting the Dharma. When the silver bowl is filled with snow, both are white. The egret in the bright moonlight is also white. When we look at them, they are both white, but they are not the same. People who study Zen must have another eye on their forehead to see this clearly! The poem continues:

Mix them together and you will know
    where they are
The meaning is not in the words,
But it goes to meet incoming potentials
Make any move, and it becomes a cliche
Miss it and you fall into looking back
Turning away or making contact are both wrong.

Take the things that are not the same and mix them together so they are the same: only then will you know a bit of the method for entering the gate. Written and spoken words are not sufficient to express this thing. When you are lucky enough to bump into it, then you will awaken. As soon as you move or act, and try to express it—for instance, if you say "Mind itself is Buddha"—despite your intentions it becomes cliche. Deviate by the slightest margin and you end up off by a thousand miles. Thus, the realm of ordinary people is, of course, not it, and going along with this realm is not it, either.

[This Dharma] is like a great mass of fire
If you only engage in literary brilliance,
This belongs in the realm of defilement.

This line, "it's like a great mass of fire," comes from *The Great Prajna Sutra*. The general meaning in the sutra is that a person of great wisdom is like a great mass of fire. A giant fire is burning there: into it you throw your whole mind, the good and the bad. The more heretics and demons throw into it, the larger the fire becomes: the more fuel there is, the more lofty the wisdom. Therefore, great transcendent wisdom is like a great mass of fire.

"If you only engage in literary brilliance / This belongs in the realm of defilement." This means that once you descend into words and language, this already has nothing to do with the fundamental true nature. The poem continues:

Just at midnight it is bright
When the sky brightens it does not show.

This is correct meditation work. In the dark of night, this thing is even brighter. When the sky gets bright at dawn, it cannot be seen anymore. What is the reason for this? In his time, my teacher Mr. Yuan studied this meditation case, and when he had understood this, he had almost mastered the Buddhist Path.

I will reveal a secret. When the six sense faculties do not move at all, and you don't know anything, inherent true nature becomes manifest. As we are sitting here now, with our eyes looking and our ears listening to this secret, how bright our six senses are! We are blocked by ignorance. "Just at midnight it is bright / When the sky brightens it does not show." When there are no dreams and no thoughts, where is the host? You should study this for yourselves and see.

[This Dharma] makes guidelines for beings,
Using them uproots all suffering.

Tung-shan is telling Ts'ao-shan: when you go forth from here, you must save the world's sentient beings, you must save all the people who are in the midst of suffering and difficulties.

Though this is not contrived activity,
It is not wordless either.
It is like facing a jewel mirror:
Shapes and reflections behold each other.
You are not it,
But it is you.
It is like an infant in the world,
Complete with all the characteristics of a buddha.

It neither goes nor comes,
It neither arises nor abides.

> [Babbling like a baby] "baba wawa"—
> Is there anything said or not?
> In the end it does not apprehend anything
> Because its speech is not yet correct.
> [It is like] the six lines of
> the double *li* hexagram.

The Ts'ao-Tung school in its five positions of lord and minister uses the method of the *I Ching* to explain cultivation practice and doing meditation work, and in particular makes use of the two hexagrams *k'an* [water] and *li* [fire], with the hexagram *li* representing the lord.

> The biased and the correct interchange
> Piled up, they make three
> When the transformation is completed,
> they make five.

The *I Ching* speaks of the transformations of the three lines. In the six lines of an *I Ching* hexagram, the third and fifth lines are considered the most important.

> It is like the taste of the five flavored herb,
> Like the diamond scepter.
> Subtly included within the correct,
> Inquiry and response both come up,
> Penetrating the source and penetrating
> the roads there.

When meditation work has arrived, it comprehends both the source and all the scriptural teachings.

> It includes integration and it includes
> the route to it:
> They intersect and it is auspicious.

This passage also uses the principles of the *I Ching*. The Ts'ao-Tung school's five positions of lord and minister apply the theory of the *I Ching* to explicate the work of cultivating practice. The poem continues:

Do not violate it!
It is naturally real and subtly wondrous:
It is not in the province of delusion
        or awakening.
In causal conditions, times and seasons,
Quiescent, it shines bright.
It is so fine it enters the infinitesimal,
It is so large it is beyond location.
If there is the slightest deviation,
You do not accord with the proper attunement.
Now there are [views of enlightenment such as]
        sudden and gradual,
Upon which different approaches are established.
Once different approaches are distinguished,
Then there are guidelines.
When the basis is mastered and the approach is
        followed through to the end,
True Eternity flows on.
Outwardly still, inwardly moving—
[Sentient beings are] like tethered colts
        or trapped rats.
The former sages pitied them,
And created the teaching to bestow on them.
Following their delusions,
[The sages] called black white.
When their deluded thoughts are extinguished,
The willing mind acknowledges itself.
If you want to follow the ancient track,
Please observe the ancients:
When about to accomplish the Buddha Path,
[The ancient buddha Mahabhijnanabhibhu in *The
        Lotus Sutra*] gazed at a tree for ten eons.
Like a tiger leaving part of its prey,
Like a horse with a white hind leg.
Because there are the lower sort,
[The devas provide enticements to enlightenment-
        like] jewel pedestals and precious garments.
Because there are the startlingly different sort,
[The world furnishes mundane examples of inherent
        enlightenment-like] cats and cows.

The master archer with his skill and power
Could hit the bull's eye from a hundred paces.
But when the arrow points meet head on,
What does this have to do with skill and power?
When the wooden man finally sings,
The stone woman rises to dance.
This is not something feelings or knowledge can
    reach:
How could there be room for thought?
The minister serves the lord,
The son obeys the father:
Not to obey would be unfilial,
Not to serve would be unhelpful.
Hidden practice, secret function,
Acting like an idiot or a fool.
But the ability to continue
    [the transmission of the Dharma]
Is called the host within the host.

All of this refers to the sequence of steps in meditation work and the cultivation of practice, and to seeing truth. All of you should pay attention to it and study it carefully.

Tung-shan said: "In the age of the End of the Dharma, many people have dry [sterile] wisdom." In this present age of ours, the Correct Dharma is not there anymore. People do not have real meditative accomplishments. They can expound theoretical principles so that it all seems like the Path, but they themselves have not experienced it. This is dry [sterile] wisdom, and it is useless.

Tung-shan said: "If you want to distinguish the real from the false, there are three kinds of leakages." Do you want to tell if someone is enlightened or not? There are three kinds of problems: once you see them, you will know.

Tung-shan said: "The first is called the leakage of views. Your mental workings do not leave the station you have attained, and you fall into a sea of poison." People who do not have a thorough, penetrating view of truth cannot jump out of the limits of what they have attained. They just stay within those limits, and are poisoned—poisoned with their own bit of learning and knowledge, and poisoned with that little bit of seeing truth.

Tung-shan said: "The second is called the leakage of sentiments. You are stuck in going toward and turning away, and your perception is one-sided and withered." In other words, these are subjective sentiments and feelings. You attain a little bit of an experiential realm, and you have feelings toward that realm. You think: "Ah! How comfortable it is when I begin sitting. Hey! This is it." Some people think: "Our old teacher has probably never gotten to this: he knows nothing about this experience of mine." In fact, you have already fallen into the leakage of sentiments. The "sentiments" referred to here are not what is commonly called emotions. It means getting bogged down in the level that you have attained.

"You are stuck in going toward and turning away." For example, with a person who has fallen into emptiness, once there is a thought there moving, he will not act. If you tell him to come out and do something for people, he will not act. This is the leakage of sentiments. There is a distinction made between going toward and turning away, between good and evil. At the level of seeing truth, this falls into dead-tree Zen: it will become one-sided and withered.

Tung-shan said: "The third is the leakage of words. You delve into the subtleties but lose the guiding principle, the source. Your potential is benighted from beginning to end, and defiled knowledge flows on and on." Here "words" includes all Buddhist studies and learning. If you rely on texts to interpret meanings, if you roll around in learned thinking, and fail to understand the true seeds of the Buddha Dharma, how can this create a basis for the functioning of your potential, for the adaptive use of methods of cultivating practice? How can you realize the fruit of enlightenment? If you fall to the leakage of words, you will never understand the key to success at all.

In the age of the End of the Dharma, in this evil world of the five corruptions, people who cultivate practice are revolving in these three kinds of patterns. Tung-shan told his disciples that they must know about these three kinds of leakage.

When we study the enlightenment and the deeds of each and every one of the ancestral Zen masters, in terms of the ten forms of mindfulness, this is mindfulness of the Sangha. When we read of their actions, and we intensify the efforts we are making in our own cultivation of practice, this is the Dharma Gate of mindfulness of the Sangha.

The story of Tung-shan continues: "Tung-shan was unwell, so he sent a novice monk to inform Yun-chu." When Tung-shan was about to die, he ordered a novice monk to bring word of this to Master Ying of Yun-chu.

"Tung-shan instructed the novice: 'He may ask if your master is happy and well, or not. Just tell him that Yun-yen's road is about to be cut off.'" Yun-yen was the teacher from whom Zen master Tung-shan got the Dharma.

"Tung-shan continued: 'When you say this you should stand some distance away, or else he may hit you.' The novice received these instructions and went to carry them out. Before he had finished giving the message to Yun-chu, Yun-chu had already hit him."

This was a maneuver on the part of Tung-shan toward this novice monk. He wanted to teach this young monk, but being already old himself, and having high hopes for this young monk, he directed him to his brother-teacher Yun-chu, hoping that Yun-chu would instruct him. People who have already reached home on the Buddhist Path, like Tung-shan and Yun-chu, do not have to send messages back and forth to each other to understand how to work together. Tung-shan knew that as soon as the young monk got there, he would certainly get hit, so he told the young monk how to say what he had to say. Of course Yun-chu, too, understood clearly, and as soon as he saw this young monk he knew that he had great potential to become a vessel of the Dharma, even though he seemed slow-witted. When Yun-chu hit the young monk, it was a didactic device, a method of teaching. Otherwise wouldn't all this hitting be a case of not playing with someone else's children as children?

"When Tung-shan was about to reach perfect quiescence by dying, he said to the assembly: 'I have useless fame in the world. Who can get rid of it for me?'" In other words: I have lived many decades, and in the outside world my fame is very great. But this fame has nothing to do with anything. Which one of you will sweep it away for me? At this point, the young monk stood up and spoke.

"At that moment, the novice monk came forth and said: 'May I ask your Dharma-name, Master?' Tung-shan said: 'My useless fame has already vanished.'"

This young monk was not making a casual remark. He said: "Master, may I ask you what your Dharma-name is?" His master's name was Tung-shan: how could he not have known this? Tung-shan was delighted and said: "Good! My useless famous name has already vanished." Tung-shan knew that this young monk had already awakened to the Path, and he now had someone to pass the Dharma on to.

The account continues: "A monk asked Tung-shan: 'You are sick, Master, but is there also one that is not sick or not?'" Their teacher was an enlightened man, but in the end he still had to get sick. Thus his disciple had this question.

"Tung-shan said: 'There is.' The monk said: 'Is the one that is not sick watching over you, Master?' Tung-shan said: 'I have a share in watching over him.'" Tung-shan was in effect saying: I watch over him. He is more or less my partner. Do you understand?

"The monk said: 'I do not understand how you watch over him, Master.'" In other words: Why do you have a share in this? I do not understand this, Master.

"Tung-shan said: 'When I am watching him, I do not see that there is any sickness.'" That is: When I am watching him, there is no sickness. In other words, even when I am crying out in pain, there is another one here who is not sick.

Tung-shan then turned around and asked the monk: "'After we leave behind these leaking sacks, where will you meet me?' The monk had no reply." Leaving behind these skin bags refers to our bodies. Our bodies are also called funnels. These funnels are very large: the classic novel *Journey to the West* calls them bottomless pits. The first day they are loaded with three meals, and then they leak out again; the second day, they are loaded up with three meals again, and again they leak out. They keep on leaking for decades, and can never be loaded full. Tung-shan asked the monk: When we have left behind these leaking funnels, I ask you, where will we meet? This monk had not penetrated through to great enlightenment, and so he could not answer. At that point in the story Tung-shan gave a verse:

> Students countless as the sands,
>     but no one awakens
> They pass by looking for their verbal routes
> If you want to forget forms and
>     obliterate their traces
> Try hard and make diligent efforts
>     to walk in the void.

In other words: If you want to get there, you will be able to do so only if you travel on the road of emptiness. After he had finished writing this poem, Tung-shan ordered his disciples to shave his head and wash him and dress him. He sounded the bell and bade farewell to the assembly. Then he sat there in a dignified manner and passed away.

The account continues: "At that time the whole assembly let out cries of anguish, and this went on for a few minutes. Tung-shan suddenly opened his eyes and told the assembly: 'The minds of people who have left home do not cleave to things—this is real practice. If you struggle through life and regret death, you will be sorrowful and sad and gain nothing.'"

After this Tung-shan stayed with them for seven more days and only then departed. This is very funny. This teaching master taught others that they must not have the leakage of sentiments, that they must not have emotional feelings, but he, himself, could not bear to leave the assembly when they started crying, so he came back and played along with them all for a few more days. Then he told them: This time I will not stay anymore. Don't anyone cry! Then he departed. Such a man was Tung-shan.

Tung-shan's most important thing was the teaching device of the five positions of lord and minister. This is equivalent to Lin-chi's four selections of guest and host.

Now I will talk about Ts'ao-shan. *The Record of Pointing at the Moon*, Volume 18, gives this account:

> "Zen master Pen-chi of Ts'ao-shan in Wu-zhou was a son of the Huang family of P'u-t'ien county in Ch'uan-chou prefecture in Fukien province. When he was young he studied Confucianism. At the age of nineteen, he went to Ling-shih Temple in Fu-chou City and became a monk; at twenty-five he was fully ordained.

> Later he went to visit Tung-shan. Tung-shan asked him his name. Ts'ao-shan said: 'Pen-chi.' [*Pen-chi* means fundamental quiescence.] Tung-shan said: 'What a name to ward off ghosts!' Ts'ao-shan said: 'It is not named Pen-chi.' Tung-shan deeply esteemed him as a potential vessel of the Dharma.

Truly brilliant people are really intelligent if they get it right in two tries. Suppose that I asked one of our young fellow students these days his name. "Pen-chi," he would say. If I said, "What?" He would answer in the usual way a Chinese specifies the characters that make up his name: "Master, my name is Pen-chi, *pen* as in *pen-lai* [meaning fundamentally] and *chi* as in *chi-mieh* [meaning quiescent extinction]." Would anyone these days do it differently? To modern people words are the Path, aren't they? Since his name is Pen-chi, what else would he say? This is a clever and intelligent man.

A Buddhist teacher looks for first-rate disciples. After this interchange, Tung-shan greatly esteemed Ts'ao-shan. So Ts'ao-shan stayed there at Tung-shan's place. From this time on, he was permitted to enter Tung-shan's room for private instruction, and he was running in and out of the abbot's room.

The account continues: "From then on, Ts'ao-shan entered Tung-shan's room. He stayed around for several years. Finally he came to Tung-shan to say goodbye. Thereupon Tung-shan bestowed upon him the teaching of his school. Tung-shan asked Ts'ao-shan: 'Where will you go?' Ts'ao-shan said: 'I'm going to the place where it does not change.' Tung-shan said: 'Where it does not change, how could there be going?' Ts'ao-shan said: 'The going too is without change.'"

This is Zen. This is equivalent to what Zen master Yung-chia said to the Sixth Patriarch: "At this stage telling things apart is not conceptual thought." That is, for the enlightened, differentiating among things is itself empty, and there is nothing wrong with it.

"Then Ts'ao-shan paid a visit to the Sixth Patriarch's stupa at Ts'ao-ch'i. He returned by way of the Snail River, and stopped at Lin-ch'uan. The scenery there was beautiful, so he made his abode there. With the intent of showing his respect for the Sixth Patriarch, he named the mountain where he lived Ts'ao-shan."

After leaving Tung-shan, Ts'ao-shan went to Kuang-chou to pay his respects at the Sixth Patriarch's stupa. Then he returned to Lin-ch'uan in Kiangsi, where he settled down and built a temple. Because he venerated the Sixth Patriarch, he named the place Ts'ao-shan.

Ts'ao-shan's teaching tradition was entirely passed on to him from Tung-shan. His teaching methods can be seen in *The Record of Pointing at the Moon* and other such books: how he preached the Dharma, saw the truth, cultivated realization, and carried out bodhisattva vows is all recorded there. The marginal notes were added by followers of the Ts'ao-Tung school in later generations, and you should also pay attention to them.

Here is a sample of Ts'ao-shan's way of teaching: "A monk asked: 'My whole body is sick. Please heal me, Master.' Ts'ao-shan said: 'I will not heal you.' The monk said: 'Why won't you heal me?' Ts'ao-shan said: 'So you won't be able to seek life or death.'"

This is a teaching method. Zen teaching methods definitely cannot answer any questions for you. If you understand because of your teacher's explanation, this harms you: this is your teacher's understanding, not your own. Sometimes you have a question, and the teacher adds another question for you. Only when you encounter the answer on your own is it really correct. The Zen school requires you to give your own consent and reach your own awakening. If one bit of compassion helps you, it has harmed you. If you must have the answer explained for you, the Buddhist scriptures have already explained everything. We have read the Buddhist scriptures, but we have still not become buddhas!

The monk in this story did not ask about the scriptures. He had already studied all sorts of things like *The Treatise on the Awakening of Faith in Mahayana*, and the Dharma Gate of the nonduality of the real and the false—he had studied all this and incorporated all this learning. But nevertheless his whole body was sick, and the doctors could not cure him, so he asked his teacher Ts'ao-shan to heal him. Ts'ao-shan said that he wanted him so that he could seek neither life nor death. What was the monk to do? He had to get himself out of it.

Here is another episode: "A monk asked: 'Isn't a Buddhist monk a man equipped with great compassion?' Ts'ao-shan said: 'That's right.' The monk said: 'If he suddenly encounters six robbers, how will he act?' Ts'ao-shan said: 'He still must possess great compassion.' The monk asked: 'How can he exercise great compassion?' Ts'ao-shan said: 'He will cut them all down with a single stroke of his sword.' The monk asked: 'How is it after he has cut them all down?' Ts'ao-shan said: "Only then will there be harmony.'"

The six robbers represent our own six sense faculties. "Only then will there be harmony," means there will be peace in the world.

At the end, when Ts'ao-shan was about to die, he wrote a poem. The poems written by the great Zen masters of the T'ang and Sung periods when they were enlightened and when they were about to die are all precious treasures, like the Buddhist scriptures. By all means pay careful attention to them! With material from after the Sung period, you must be careful, because they include some recorded sayings from later generations that were written on commission by scholars who were opium smokers, and they cannot be relied on. In later generations there were some self-styled Zen masters who hoped that their names would be included in the Buddhist canon after they died, who therefore hired people to write sayings for them. I have seen such things personally. The extremes to which people in the world go in their love of fame rarely exceed this!

Here is the verse Ts'ao-shan gave to his students:

> Comprehend from causal conditions, and accord
> [with reality] will be swift
> If you stop at the essence,
> empowerment will be slow
> Instantaneous, fundamental, without location
> My teacher provisionally called it
> the inconceivable.

After you have done the work and cultivated *samadhi*, it is all right to study meditation sayings. You will only be able to awaken when the proper time and circumstances arrive. For example, when Master Hsu-yun was in the Zen hall sitting in meditation and studying meditation sayings, he observed the outside world very clearly. Later, as he was carrying a cup of tea, he suddenly dropped the cup on the floor: there was a crash, and it broke, and he was enlightened. There were many such examples among the ancients. For example Ling-yun awakened upon seeing a peach blossom. The causal condition arrives: "Comprehend from causal conditions, and accord will be swift." They come fast.

Therefore, when you are cultivating practice, just ask about plowing the field, don't ask about gathering the harvest. You must not say, "I have cultivated practice for a year: how is it I have not yet been enlightened? It seems it is not worth it at all."

What does "stop at the essence" mean? When we do sitting meditation and work at it, some people latch onto *The Surangama Sutra*, or some other scripture. Some people work with the breath; it becomes entirely empty, and after a certain period of time, it changes again; in the morning they are entirely empty, and in the afternoon they abandon it. This sort of thing is what is meant by the line, "If you stop at the essence, empowerment will be slow."

This is especially true of people who try to work on it after they have understood the principles of Buddhism and Zen: for them it is always the case that "If you stop at the essence, empowerment will be slow." Because they understand the truth of emptiness, as soon as thoughts come, they want to empty them out. Sometimes they can empty them out well enough, and sometimes they can't. This is also a case of "The awareness of original illumination gives birth to objects, and when objects are established the true nature of awareness is lost." Sometimes it is true of this method of observing false thoughts that, "If you stop at the essence, empowerment will be slow."

"Comprehend from causal conditions, and accord with reality will be swift," is the vehicle of the *pratyekas*, the solitary illuminates who are enlightened by contemplating interdependent causation.

"If you stop at the essence, empowerment will be slow," is the vehicle of the *shravakas* [the literalist disciples who cling to the elementary forms of the Buddhist teaching], and the vehicle of the arhats, the vehicle of one-sided emptiness.

What then are Tathagata Zen and Patriarch Zen? "Instantaneous, fundamental, without location." This means the same thing as the quote from Lin-chi I mentioned earlier:

If for one moment causal origination is not born
You transcend the provisional learning of the three vehicles.

This is:

Instantaneous, fundamental, without location
My teacher provisionally called it the inconceivable.

Here is Ts'ao-shan's verse on the four prohibitions:

Do not travel the road of mental states
Do not put on the garment of the fundamental
What's the need to be just so?
By all means avoid the time before birth.

To take the mind that is capable of awareness, and focus on observing these false thoughts, to use mind to contemplate mind—this is what Ts'ao-shan here calls the road of mental states. This is also the question that was asked earlier. This road is a road of cultivating practice, but it is not the best one.

What is "the garment of the fundamental"? The original face is pure and clean. "The ocean of enlightenment is by nature clear and perfect." If you want to hold onto this pure perfect illumination, you have already put on the garment of the fundamental. Thus, there are some veteran practitioners who always want to hold onto a moment of mindfulness. If the pure perfect illumination is lost for a moment, they frantically search for it. How can they find it again! That moment of mindfulness is already not right. As soon as they put it on, they have already been defiled by it. In the Buddhist scriptures, it says not to abide anywhere or be attached to anything. If you are attached to purity, this is already wrong.

"What's the need to be just so?" At this point, how should you act? "By all means avoid the time before birth." How should you act toward any experiential realm at all before a thought stirs? Do you let thoughts start moving? Do you not let thoughts start moving? You will have to go investigate for yourself. Ts'ao-shan doesn't say.

If you hold to the experiential realm before thoughts and feelings are born, it is like what the Confucian classic, *The Doctrine of the Mean,* says: "Before joy and anger and sadness and happiness come forth is called the mean." If you want to hold onto this, you have already put on the garment of the fundamental, and you have made a mistake. *The Doctrine of the Mean* continues: "If they all reach the proper measure after they have come forth, this is called harmony." This means you are already traveling the road of mental states.

If you are not attached to any of this, only then can you talk of Patriarch Zen. "What's the need to be just so? By all means avoid the time before birth." Before a single thought is born, what is it? After it is born, what is it? You must understand this clearly: only this will do.

Right now we are discussing the preliminary reference materials for the road of cultivating practice. How should you cultivate practice? You must get a grasp on this for yourself. Later, when you are concentrating on cultivating practice and you encounter problems, what you have studied here will enable you to think of some impressions, and perhaps you will search out these things and refer to them in your studies.

The heyday of the Yun-men school of Zen was also in the century spanning the end of the T'ang and the Five Dynasties. Later, when the famous Sung dynasty literatus Ou-yang Hsiu was ordered by the emperor to revise the official *History of the Five Dynasties*, he felt very strongly that there were no talented people during the Five Dynasties period: his opinion was that in politics and in other areas, the whole era was totally devoid of talented people. But the opinion of people like Wang An-shih, the great Sung dynasty political reformer, was the opposite: he thought that talented people were very numerous in the Five Dynasties period, but unfortunately they all became monks, and were unwilling to enter upon the worldly path.

The great Zen masters Kuei-shan and Yang-shan, Lin-chi, Ts'ao-shan and Tung-shan, and especially Yun-men, had the mettle of kings. Every one of them had the talent to be a monarch, but they looked down on worldly things. Therefore, the period of political chaos from the end of the T'ang through the Five Dynasties was a period when the Zen school flourished greatly.

The time of extreme disorder of the Northern and Southern Dynasties period was the period when the [abstruse Taoist-derived philosophical style known as] "Pure Conversation" *Ch'ing-T'an* flourished, and it was also a period when culture and philosophy developed greatly. Generally in the past people studying the history of Chinese philosophy said that "Pure Conversation" led the nation astray, as if "Pure Conversation" should take the responsibility for the state of learning in that period. In fact, it is rather the history of the period that must take the responsibility for the contemporary state of learning and culture. As I already said before, "Pure Conversation" never led the nation astray: rather, it was the people in power at the time who led culture astray.

Talented people in the Five Dynasties period recognized that it was a period beyond rescuing, so they stood on the sidelines. They were all people who had great compassion to save the world, so why did they shave their heads and enter the Zen school? You can't tell me they were unwilling to improve the age.

So now I put the question before you. You already understand enough of the path of enlightenment to turn toward cultivating practice. What we have discussed is also enough of a guideline for you to begin the effort. The great masters of the Zen school had the mettle of kings precisely because of their practice, and the same potential applies to those who choose to cultivate in the world today. So, the question is, what are you now going to do?

Cultivation doesn't lead people astray, but those who don't cultivate themselves continue to revolve around in the world of form—deceiving themselves and cheating others. It's hard to say whether we really accomplish anything in life except to prolong deception. If you really want to accomplish something big in the world, or if you are satisfied with what you have and only want a quiet life, regardless as to the route you desire, there is no preparation other than the road of cultivation.

So, what we have discussed is already enough to begin down the road of practice. The rest is left up to you. My hope is that you choose this road and that these words help you succeed in your efforts, for when you really throw your efforts into cultivation, all the buddhas and bodhisattvas know it. So do not be dismayed if you feel that you are alone. Devote yourself to the effort of cultivation and build your practice with patience, step-by-step. In time, the fruits will be readily apparent for all to see. No other promise can be given other than the fact that wherever you turn your mind, there the results of your efforts will manifest. If you cultivate with determination and devotion, you will be sure to succeed.

# TO REALIZE ENLIGHTENMENT

This ends the first half of the lecture series presented by Master Nan in Taiwan. Readers can find further details on many of the Taoist and Esoteric Buddhist terms and concepts presented in these lectures from Master Nan's previous work, *Tao and Longevity* (Samuel Weiser, 1984). Students who wish to continue the study of the final lessons of this lecture series will be interested in the forthcoming volume titled *To Realize Enlightenment: Practice of the Cultivation Path*.

This second series of lectures places more emphasis on actually cultivating samadhi and describes the various exercises for attaining samadhi used by the different cultivation schools. Master Nan discusses how to properly generate, enter, and leave samadhi, and presents details on the different types of samadhi and other experiential realms one can encounter in cultivation. *To Realize Enlightenment* continues to introduce heretofore untranslated poems and texts, and throws new light on many historical stories of the Zen school and Chinese history. An important issue of self-cultivation is to change body and behavior, as well as enlighten the mind. Master Nan discusses the physical experiences that may arise on the cultivation path and goes into the actualities of the bodhisattva's path of conduct and compassionate activity in the world.

# WORKS CITED

There are many Chinese classics mentioned in this work. Some of them may be available in English; many are not. Textual references to these works are presented here for readers who are interested in further study.

*The Abhidharmakosha Shastra* (Vasubandhu), 148, 151

*The Abhisamaylamkara Shastra*, 15

*The Agama-sutra*, 116, 140, 151

*The Altar Sutra*, 188

*The Amitabha Sutra*, 117

*The Analects* (Tseng-tzu), 243

*The Avatamsaka Sutra*, 8, 99, 100, 111, 208

*The Blue Cliff Record (Pi Yen Lu)*, 27, 197

*The Bodhisattva Vinaya*, 8

*The Book of Changes*, (See *I-Ching*)

*The Book of tranquillity (Ts'ung-Jung Lu)*, 197

*The Buddhabhumistra Shastra*, 208

*Ch'eng Wei-shih Lun*, 47

*Chuang Tzu*, 115

*The Complete Enlightenment Sutra*, 8

*The Comprehensive Mirror for Aid in Governing (Tzu Chih T'ung Chien)*, 223

*The Contemplation of Amitabha Sutra*, 117

*The Continuation of the Record of Pointing at the Moon*, 9

*The Creation of the World Sutra*, 154, 155

*The Diamond Sutra*, 8, 10, 38, 39, 85, 144, 166, 180, 188, 189, 199, 226

*The Doctrine of the Mean* (Zi Si), 89, 273

*Dream of the Red Chamber*, 95, 103

# INDEX